The
Maverick
Effect

Dear Barry,

[handwritten signature]

July 15, 2c

Praise for *The Maverick Effect*

Harish Mehta, in this exceptionally written book, provides his unique insights on the tireless efforts it took to set up NASSCOM. For many readers, it will be a revelation to discover the pivotal role of NASSCOM in enhancing the IT sector's global brand image and in helping create the great Indian middle class. I particularly liked how he quotes 'nothing is possible without men, but nothing lasts without institutions' and uses that as an allegory to talk about NASSCOM. I highly recommend *The Maverick Effect,* particularly for the numerous initiatives that the book talks about.

Deepak S. Parekh, chairman, HDFC Ltd.

The digital revolution now driving India started with Harish and his glorious band of founders of NASSCOM. Harish brings together the incredible contribution of this industry to not only Indian economic growth but also to refurbishing India's global image. [The book] is a must for those who wish to make their industry organizations worthy of policy makers' trust by making individual firm profit maximization subservient to national interests.

Rajiv Kumar, vice-chairman, Niti Aayog

In this engrossing book, Harish Mehta deftly interleaves his personal memoirs with the rise of India's software industry. Most importantly, he gives the hitherto untold tale of the amazing software association NASSCOM, where fierce competitors worked collaboratively together to shape the future of an industry that created millions of jobs, solved the foreign exchange crisis and put Indian enterprise and technology on the world stage.

Nandan Nilekani, chairman and co-founder, Infosys

Engaging, informative and inspiring. As our [start-up] ecosystem transitions from starting up to scaling up, we need to learn from the extraordinary journey of the Indian IT services industry.

This book has many lessons for our current generation of entrepreneurs, the most important of which is the need to always think beyond your own company and collaborate with others to shape an industry.

Rajan Anandan, managing director, Sequoia Capital India

Indian IT is the biggest value migration story, which I call 'from Boston to Bengaluru'. Clients came to India for the lower cost but stayed back for quality, scale and talent. The NASSCOM story is a shining example of what an industry association can do for itself, the country and the whole world. This book is a must-read for analysts, policymakers, regulators and all nation builders interested in the story of NASSCOM and Indian IT straight from a passionate founder, Harish Mehta.

Raamdeo Agrawal, chairman, Motilal Oswal group

Harish has written a bold and insightful account of the making of one of our industry's most successful associations—NASSCOM. It is also a deeply moving memoir of Harish's life—despite its many personal setbacks—Harish retains his equanimity. There's much to learn from him.

Rishad Premji, chairman, Wipro

I am so glad that the story of India's IT revolution and the role of NASSCOM in powering it is being told by the person at the centre of the revolution. Harish Mehta, the conductor who got together the entire industry to create the magic. This is our time, our Techade, and the strong foundation of collaboration we have built is exactly what is needed to achieve our dream of becoming a five trillion dollar economy.

Debjani Ghosh, president, NASSCOM

This book provides a comprehensive account of how an industry can work together towards achieving a collective vision that not only creates a world-leading industry but also plays a critical role in nation-building.

S. Ramadorai, former vice chairman, TCS

The Indian IT industry commands a central place in the global innovation ecosystem. As the founding member of NASSCOM, Harish Bhai played a pivotal role in envisioning the future of the industry and creating a roadmap for growth. *The Maverick Effect* offers an insightful account of this journey that transformed the fortunes of our nation and catalyzed the aspirations of millions.

Rekha Menon, chairperson, NASSCOM; chairperson, Accenture India

This compelling book by the Father of NASSCOM, Harish Mehta, should be a textbook for all those who are interested in learning what went into building an ecosystem that has ensured that India will rule the roost for decades to come in the areas of tech services, start-up creation and digital transformation of global and Indian businesses.

Keshav Murugesh, group MD and CEO, WNS

The Maverick Effect is a fascinating narrative of Harish's personal life and his work intertwined with the genesis of NASSCOM, the evolution of the IT industry, the Indian economy and our nation. He effortlessly moves across these four different tangents constructing a captivating memoir that is such a pleasure to read.

Atul Nishar, founder, Hexaware Technologies Ltd.

This story [of the $200 billion industry] had to be told, and this book brings out all the super qualities of an amazing human endeavour and the processes, simplicity, approachability, innovation and most of all, inclusion and collaboration of the builders of Indian IT and NASSCOM.

Ganesh Natarajan, chairman, 5F World

If we were to try and imagine the Indian IT industry without NASSCOM and the critical role it has played (and continues to play), the scenario would be bleak. Harish has written a highly readable and important book that will become an important historical document as it records the development of the Indian IT industry with fidelity.

Harsh Manglik, former chairman, Accenture India

We wouldn't be seeing the start-up frenzy that we are witnessing today without the strong foundations laid by the IT industry and the visionaries who dared to dream when India was barely awake. This is the story of the ones that enabled us! Harish not just devoted his energy towards NASSCOM, but he also took out time to capture, codify and write this important book about the evolution of NASSCOM.

Anupam Mittal, founder, People Group/Shaadi.com

Harish bhai tells the most exciting story in the Indian economy since independence. And he does it so eloquently that you are left wondering why did he hide the storyteller in him all this while. The book narrates the fascinating untold story of NASSCOM's role in making India a proud leader in the global software and IT services industry [and how it went about] seizing the opportunities and steering deftly through a crisis.

Nirmal Jain, founder and chairman, IIFL

I would recommend reading this book for customers of the Indian IT industry who see a different India in offices of IT firms than that on the roads that take them to the office. To understand what went into the foundation to make this industry happen, what therefore is the ethos, the culture, the passion and ambition of this industry, and more importantly, what to expect going ahead.

Vijay Ratnaparkhe, CIO, Robert Bosch GmbH

I would strongly recommend this book to anyone who is trying to grow one's business through the collective strength of fellow people by creating an effective business body (or more likely, trying to rejuvenate a moribund one) or if you are a government functionary in any country, tasked with making global industry around the comparative advantage which your country possesses, you can script a step-by-step solution by understanding what Harish has written.

Raj Nair, chairman, Avalon Consulting

I found the book unputdownable. It's brilliant that Harish has outlined a history of the Indian IT industry, highlighting the critical role of NASSCOM. He, too, emerges as such a wonderful and inspiring figure.

Sanjay Sharma, founder CEO, Tata Interactive Systems

Harish Mehta has beautifully captured the industry and NASSCOM's journey and outlined his future vision for India as a Smart Nation.

Namita Thapar, executive director, Emcure Pharmaceuticals

Every movement and journey needs an anchor and Harishbhai has been the pivotal anchor for NASSCOM and the industry through this journey. *The Maverick Effect* is a wonderfully written first-hand account of this movement that powerfully communicates the different phases of the industry, how to deal with difficult situations, build audacious goals and yet stay true to purpose in Harishbhai's unique style.

Sangeeta Gupta, senior vice president and chief strategy officer, NASSCOM

NASSCOM started as a collective dream and today has reached global glory. The dream could only be realized by perseverance, optimism and collective action of numerous, what Harish calls, mavericks. *The Maverick Effect* is an engrossing account of the story of these mavericks, told with such a brilliant articulation that you cannot miss Harish's love, commitment, and great contribution to NASSCOM.

Ashank Desai, founder and former chairman, Mastek

Harish has taken the avatar of an IT historian and has delivered a book that captures the definitive account of how the industry came into being! The story of the development of the Indian IT industry through the efforts of several stalwarts has been recorded by Harishbhai in a truthful manner.

K. V. Ramani, founder and chancellor, Sai University

I found it hard to put the book down, and Harish isn't quite done yet. Harish, I have always believed, is a pragmatic dreamer; many milestones still beckon this unusual man with boundless enthusiasm for life.

Saurabh Srivastava, chairman, Indian Angel Network

Interwoven with a personal saga of tremendous bravery amidst adversity and overlaid on the background of India's changing economic policies, this book is a must-read for anyone connected with the industry or with industry associations.

Kiran Karnik, former president, NASSCOM

Harish Mehta, more popularly known as Harishbhai, is the rock around which NASSCOM was born, grew and continues to evolve. Our collective understanding of the history of Indian IT, the role played by NASSCOM and the path we took (to create millions of jobs and contribute billions of dollars to the nation's coffers) all would have been seriously impoverished without this book.

Chandrashekhar Rentala, former president, NASSCOM

Harishbhai has brought out lucidly what makes for success and how [IT] industry has continued to stick together with each new generation of entrepreneurs and companies outclassing the previous. [The story is] A lesson in building an inclusive group with only a common purpose and no individual agenda. A great read.

Lakshmi Narayanan, former vice chairman, Cognizant

This is a fabulous book, unputdownable and a story of a fantastic dream. It is hilarious to know that the progress of the IT industry was stopped in its track by the unwilful ignorance of bureaucrats in various departments who could not visualize the internet and the future.

D Sivanandhan, former DGP, Maharashtra

There could not have been a more appropriate or qualified author for [this] book. Harish, as one of the founders of NASSCOM, built it into a dynamic force and helped to get recognition and respect from Government and together frame policies for the common good. As the voice of the IT community and the champion of NASSCOM, Harish comes across as a motivator for our youth to show what can be achieved with cooperation even among competitors.

Walter Vieira, marketing guru and author

The Maverick Effect

The Inside Story of
INDIA'S IT REVOLUTION

HARISH MEHTA

HARPER
BUSINESS

An Imprint of HarperCollins *Publishers*

First published in India by Harper Business
An imprint of HarperCollins *Publishers* 2022
4th Floor, Tower A, Building No. 10, Phase II, DLF Cyber City,
Gurugram, Haryana – 122002
www.harpercollins.co.in

2 4 6 8 10 9 7 5 3 1

Text copyright © Harish S. Mehta 2022

P-ISBN: 978-93-5489-529-6
E-ISBN: 978-93-5489-571-5

Cover design: Saurav Das
Author photo: Courtesy of the author

Typeset in 11.5/15.4 Baskerville
Manipal Technologies Limited, Manipal

Printed and bound at
Thomson Press (India) Ltd

❶❶◉♥HarperCollinsIn

To Shaila.

For being my constant.
For seeing the invisible.
For inspiring me to go beyond what I thought was possible.

Contents

Author's Note

In his seminal work, *Bhomiya Vina*, iconic Gujarati poet Umashankar Joshi romanticizes the idea of wandering amidst nature without a guide and experiencing the ups and downs of life. I find the poem a strikingly accurate description of the journey of my life. For one, I am inspired by nature and seek lessons from the nature of nature. Second, I believe this wandering has served me well.

Written in part as my biography, this book is essentially the story of how NASSCOM started as a small idea and over time snowballed into creating such wide reaching impact over time. The book is about numerous mavericks that came together, added a multiplier effect to the idea and made it larger than what any of us could have imagined when we started.

To be honest, the idea of the book first struck me three years ago when my daughter-in-law, Natasha asked me about why the Indian IT industry, or the NASSCOM doesn't get the due respect for contributing to changing the fortunes of the country. While numerous, fragmented attempts were made by various stakeholders to shine light on the contribution of NASSCOM and the member companies, I could not find a definitive history. So, we decided to partner up to write a book that we'd like to read ourselves!

In writing this book, I took help of numerous insiders, well-wishers and other mavericks that are closely connected to the ecosystem to highlight the contribution made by NASSCOM and the Indian IT industry.

When I look back at the last 35 years, I am reminded of what my friend and acclaimed poet Sitanshu Yashaschandra once told me. He said that we at NASSCOM are like *Surajmukhi*, the Sunflower. The way the flower is guided by the movement of Sun, we took energy from our vision of building for India. And when it was dark outside, just like the disk florets of the flower retain the saffron colour, we kept our heads high and continued to reach for the sky.

I am mindful that the medium of a printed book is restrictive and thus some of the stories, including those about myself and my company, Onward Technologies may appear incomplete to the ones that know me. Further, numerous stories about NASSCOM and the Indian IT industry had to be dropped. I hope you accept this deliberate act of omission.

Finally, I know that I am no one to write history per se. I can only document what I saw when I was around. Most of the anecdotes in the book come from memory, augmented by the notes I've maintained over the years. I am also aware that human memory tends to fade with time and some errors may have crept in. I thus have relied on public sources, internal memos and numerous live interviews with colleagues and friends. My team and I have gone to great lengths to ensure that what I've written and incidents reported are factual, as far as humanly possible. Wherever I was clouded with doubt, I have relied on my values and beliefs. We commissioned research with respected, independent bodies and did a third-party fact check to ensure veracity and accuracy. Should you still find a discrepancy, please do write to me and I would be most eager to correct myself. My team and I are available at factcheck@themaverickeffectbook.com.

I will not keep you from the book anymore. I hope you enjoy reading about the effects that the mavericks had.

Still wandering without a guide,
Harish S Mehta
Jan 2022, Mumbai

Foreword

by N.R. Narayana Murthy

The Maverick Effect is an absorbing book that brings out the story of NASSCOM, and the life story of Harish Mehta. It is a definitive and authoritative biography of NASSCOM as recounted by one who led the creation of NASSCOM in 1988, and has been nurturing it like his precious child even after thirty-three years to the day. I am told that every event has been verified with data and facts due to Harish's penchant for veracity and accuracy. Future historians will rely on this work when they do research on the role of NASSCOM in removing the bureaucratic hurdles during the initial years of the software services industry in India.

The first time I met Harish was in 1979, when I took Late Sri Ghanashyam Gupta, a friend of mine, to meet him. Ghanashyam wanted to establish a data center in Chennai based on a VAX 11/750 computer from Digital Equipment Corporation. Harish was kind, courteous, generous, and open-minded to share the nuances of running a successful data center. That kindness, that infectious enthusiasm and that courtesy to help entrepreneurs has remained undiminished and shining in Harish even today.

NASSCOM is an organization of mavericks. It is an unlikely alliance. NASSCOM was incubated at a time when it was an uphill battle to even get software recognised as a tangible product or a service, and something different from computer hardware! NASSCOM had to fight deep-seated prejudices in an environment rife with suspicion. The ecosystem did not offer the infrastructure needed to create a software services business. The entrepreneurs had to remain patient and lay the groundwork for the future.

The impact that the software services industry has had on the nation has been phenomenal. The industry brought a new ethos to the country. Member companies of NASSCOM embraced competition and meritocracy. They leveraged innovation and strove hard for laudable performance in global markets. They operated as equal opportunities employers. They benchmarked with the best global standards of governance. They created several next practices in corporate governance in India. They focused on transparency in financial reporting. Such a mindset had simply not existed in India till then. The rapid growth of NASSCOM member companies also created huge employment opportunities for youngsters from the tier-2 and tier 3 towns.

I came into NASSCOM in 1989, thanks to the generosity of my colleague, Nandan Nilekani. He suggested that I should take his position and add value to NASSCOM. Nandan is a deep and strategic thinker. I found it wise to accept his suggestions at Infosys. I stood for the election to the executive council (EC) in 1990 and was elected. My colleagues on the EC were kind to choose me as the vice president (now titled vice-chairperson) when they chose Harish as the president (now titled chairperson) for a two-year term starting in 1990. I succeeded Harish as the president of NASSCOM for a two-year term in 1992.

The book starts with the decision of Harish and his wife, Shaila, to come back to their homeland and serve their country. The book is a riveting narration of his effort to achieve the plausibly impossible, his stoic nature to bear the loss of his first-born child and his beloved wife, his tête-à-tête encounters with the realities of life in India of the last fifty years, his hard work, determination, patience and optimism to found and nurture institutions like NASSCOM and TIE, his conviviality to bring peace between conflicting personalities, and his untiring effort to get the best out of a well-meaning, aspirational, hyperactive, and ultra-ambitious Dewang Mehta. I am not sure if anybody else had a ringside seat that Harish had in witnessing the birth and the growing up of NASSCOM like he has. We should be grateful to him for this detailed and honest account.

Harish paints a realistic picture of Dewang both as a professional and as a human being in detail in the book. He gives Dewang huge credit for making NASSCOM the authentic voice of the industry. I agree with Harish. An honor roll for NASSCOM would have Dewang's name up there. It would also have Harish's name and the names of the other founding members like Nandan Nilekani, Ashank Desai, K.V. Ramani, Vijay Srirangan, and Saurabh Srivastava.

Over the years, I have enjoyed every minute of my time with Harish. I have learnt so much from him. Even now, whenever I am in Mumbai, Harish, Ashank, and I spend 3 to 4 hours over an enjoyable dinner at Copper Chimney. Ramani joins us when his visit dates to Mumbai coincide with my dates.

NASSCOM has been a catalytic coopetition platform that has worked hard to remove bureaucratic bottlenecks for its companies to grow at an impressive rate. NASSCOM has demonstrated that two fiercely competing companies in the marketplace can work together on a coopetition platform in a friendly environment to identify and solve supra-company issues. NASSCOM is also a good example of creating a win-win and hospitable platform for both Indian companies and multinational companies. I hope other industry-associations use these lessons of NASSCOM and work in a coopetition mode to accelerate the growth of our economy.

In my opinion, the biggest challenge over the next few decades for our country is whether we, Indians, can develop a culture of aspiration, national pride, benchmarking with the global best, discipline, meritocracy, hard work, quality, productivity, honesty, open-mindedness, pluralism, humility, openness to learn from people better than us, and other attributes needed for India to join the group of developed countries.

This challenge sounds audacious. My belief and fond desire is that this book, *The Maverick Effect*, will serve as a searchlight in this seminal and arduous task.

N.R. Narayana Murthy,
founder, Infosys Technologies

Foreword

by N. Chandrasekaran

A decade ago, I served as Chairperson of NASSCOM, the pioneering industry body that represents India's tech leaders and entrepreneurs. I had the opportunity to work closely with Harish Mehta, the author of this wonderful book, on a project to restructure the organization for the new challenges of the age.

I saw first hand how ambitious he is for NASSCOM, and the energy and creativity he put into making sure those ambitions are realized. Determined yet friendly, Harish is a unifier. He rallied around India's tech leaders to work together and built a credible relationship with every one of them. As a veteran of the sector, I know that is not an easy task. Through NASSCOM, whose vision and history he brilliantly chronicles in these pages, Harish has been one of the great champions of Indian technology.

Founded in 1988, three years before the liberalisation of the Indian economy, NASSCOM was the product of a country that was changing. India, which for decades had loped behind its local rivals, finally began catching up. Millions were lifted out of poverty. An aspirational middle class grew. Many more women entered the workforce and experienced a new freedom as a result. The technology industry played no small part in this transformation, and NASSCOM was at the heart of it all. I do not hesitate to write, in fact, that NASSCOM was essential.

The story of Harish Mehta, told in these pages, is a parable of our shared homeland. Returning to India from the United States in the 1970s, he was the force that brought together a generation of tech entrepreneurs prepared to challenge old certainties and dream big. At the time, the Indian software industry was virtually non-existent. In the late 1980s, its combined exports amounted to a measly $52 million. By 2017, I am happy to say, that figure is some 3,000 times higher at $154 billion.

The role played by NASSCOM in this achievement is the story of this book. NASSCOM educated the Indian government about technology at a time when, as Harish vividly writes, the entire industry's bandwidth was equal to what an Indian teenager burns through in a weekend today. NASSCOM challenged outdated stereotypes about the Indian tech industry, too, ushering in an age when Indian software engineers are coveted the world over and now lead some of its biggest tech companies. Perhaps most importantly, NASSCOM provided a platform where tech leaders could work together for the common good. Amid India's heady growth in the 1990s and 2000s, and the intense competition of this time, this was no mean feat.

The publication of this book is particularly timely given the disruptions of the past two years. Spurred by the Covid-19 pandemic, India is entering a new phase in its development. Millions of Indians now use technology to work from home and keep in touch with friends and family. Technology has become crucial to our daily lives in a way that would have been unthinkable just a decade ago.

The pandemic also exposed the ways in which India must still change. In this book, Harish describes his vision for India as a 'Smart Nation'. This is an India with cleaner air, more equitable distribution of resources, and greater prosperity for all. It is a country with better access to education and to healthcare, and where government decision-making is powered by evidence and data. It is a country where the life quality of the average citizen is among the top five countries in the world, where the literacy rate is 100%, and where we are among the best places in the world to do business.

We have some way to go. Today, too many Indians lack access to basic services like healthcare and education. We have too few doctors and teachers, and not enough schools and hospitals. At the same time, we have a massive jobs challenge. This decade alone, 90 million young people in India will reach working age, four times the number in the United States, Brazil and Indonesia combined. Our current economy, which lacks formal employment opportunities with regular pay and other benefits, threatens to frustrate and disappoint them.

As I laid out in my own book, *Bridgital Nation,* technology will be critical to the solution, creating new jobs, improving access to public services, and creating new opportunities for the next generation of Indian entrepreneurs. It has the potential to transform India, for everyone: young and old, rich and poor, urban and rural. But ensuring that new technology serves the national interest demands that our industry pulls together as one.

Three decades ago, NASSCOM had a vision for India's fledgling tech industry. In bringing it to fruition, the lives of millions were improved and the destiny of our country was transformed. Today, we need to create a new vision for the coming decades. Should anyone today want to learn how such a feat can be achieved, they will find no shortage of inspiration in the pages of this book.

N. Chandrasekaran,
chairman, Tata Sons

Prologue

Reti Ma Vahaan Chalayva
(Sailing Ships in the Sand)

Tyger Tyger burning bright,
In the forests of the night:
What immortal hand or eye,
Dare frame thy fearful symmetry?

—William Blake

Blake could have asked his question of an Asian tiger called the Indian economy: Who dare imagine you? Who dare frame you? Who dare make you?

This is the story of those who dared.

From the 1950s to the 1980s, India's economy grew at the infamous Hindu rate of 3.5 per cent per annum. In the same period, its neighbours did far better. Pakistan managed 5 per cent, Indonesia and Thailand grew at 9 per cent, the Miracle on the Han River grew South Korea by 10 per cent, and the Taiwan Miracle added 12 per cent annual growth to the country. In China, the Mao era (from 1949 to 1977) paved the path of explosive growth that China went through in the last few decades.

Why couldn't India keep up with the Joneses? The reasons were many. Some were the naïveté of a young nation. Others were as inevitable as the passing of the decades.

The aftermath of the Second World War had left nations polarised between the Soviets and the Americans. To buck the new world order, India co-founded the Non-Aligned Movement. In reality, it was closer to the Soviet bloc. The Planning Commissions of Nehruvian socialism resembled the USSR's linear programming methods. By the end of the 1980s, the Soviet Union was crumbling, and the US remained the only superpower. India was left out in the cold.

In fact, at home, trouble had begun earlier. Prime Minister Indira Gandhi was assassinated in the middle of the 1980s. Her son Mr Rajiv Gandhi stepped into her shoes and tried his best, but separatist violence in Punjab raged on. Kashmir and Assam, too, threatened India's territorial integrity. Between Mr Rajiv Gandhi's last days in office and the turn of the decade, four years saw as many prime ministers.

These agitations were mainly driven by the youth's anxiety, probably induced by their inability to secure jobs. That too, at a time when a government job was the most viable occupation. Clearly, the country needed to offer a broader range of career options.

The extra jobs could have come from improved prospects for businesses. Instead, India's struggles with its own politics kept the focus away from economics, leading to a foreign-exchange situation. To add fuel to the fire, in 1990, war broke out in the Gulf, and crude oil prices shot up. India's oil import bill ballooned, exports slumped, credit dried up, and international investors squeezed their money out.

The situation became so grim that India's forex reserves dwindled to a mere two weeks' worth of imports. The safe limit then was about twenty-six weeks. India was staring down the barrel of bankruptcy. The government was on the brink of defaulting on sovereign debts, which set the stage for a major international credit rating downgrade.

No forex meant India could not buy anything from across its borders. Consider oil. No oil meant no vehicles on the streets, no transportation for even essentials like food and medicine. It meant nationwide starvation and disease. When macroeconomics goes wrong, it wears a human face.

In such times, strong leadership comes in handy. Unfortunately, the lack of a clear political mandate had installed a precarious coalition government.

The World Bank and the International Monetary Fund (IMF) refused to bail out India. The country's options were to mortgage its gold or default on sovereign debts. Mortgaging would further embarrass India, but defaulting would devastate it.

Yet, mortgaging was not a simple answer. There were suspicions about the intent of international lenders. Very few countries had extricated themselves from their contracts. Prime Minister Mr Chandra Shekhar's office courageously bit the forex bullet. They airlifted the national gold reserves as a pledge to secure a bailout from the World Bank and the IMF. While it saved the day, it also reinforced the image of India as a backward, poverty-stricken, failing nation full of dysfunctional laws.

One would read the newspapers and wonder, why didn't the government encourage businesses to bring in forex and create jobs? Wouldn't that keep us from pledging our gold reserves? Wouldn't that solve everything?

The answers to such questions are complex. India was a nation born overnight, and it had to quickly set up the rules of its economy. It led to the creation of the notorious 'license raj', a system where you had to acquire a licence from the government to start a business. These licences found their way into the hands of the few businesses that were close to the political establishment. Bribes and favours were commonplace. Political palms were greased and government benefits were sought, even if these large businesses were healthy and did not need them.

If you wanted a phone, you had to wait around four years for it to come home. And you waited some more for the dial tone. If you applied for a scooter as a young man to roam around with your friends, you would have two children by the time you got one. If you wanted to have fresh fruits, people would say, go to Kashmir.

And while a large part of the country was engaged in debates and armchair activism, a tiny group of young technology and software entrepreneurs was busy, meanwhile writing the answers to these very questions.

The Maverick Effect is my attempt at immortalising the story of this group, the individual members, each a maverick, and how we evolved over the years to become a significant movement that has since contributed significantly to the country. We had to innovate on various fronts—often by tackling multiple problems at the same time. We had to put together an organization more significant than any of us. We had to put in place a set of values that would guide our decisions and actions. We had to fix the biases through which the world looked at India. Unknown to us at that time, we were carrying an enormous responsibility. This is the story of the mavericks, the organization we created, the effect we had and how we shouldered that responsibility.

Honestly, when we started, we had no vision of the billions of dollars that the IT industry earns for India today, and the millions of Indians who employed directly and indirectly by the industry. We did not know that we were creating an industry based on meritocracy, enabling equal opportunities for deserving women, or that eventually acting as a backbone behind the vision for Digital India.

This is the story of creating this new middle class. We were merely a bunch of young people with similar mindsets, each exasperated by the state of the nation and our inability to bring about a change.

This is the story of changing India's reputation as a land of snake charmers and one with a bullock cart economy to a country that the entire world trusts as their technology partner and enabler.

This is the story of how one-sixth of humanity went from scarcity to abundance, and how the country's fortunes changed.

This is the story of that change, the courage shown by us and the revolution that we brought ushered into the country.

Come, join me for a ride.

1

A Tale of Two Countries

I know the American Dream. I was in it. It set the course for my life and work and never really faded away. So, that is when this book must begin: in the middle of the 1970s. I was a database manager with a reputable company of that time, American Can. My salary had just risen from $22,000 to an upper-middle-class salary of $28,000. I used to drive around in a Cutlass Supreme and had a comfortable house in Stamford, Connecticut, in which I lived with my loving wife, Shaila, and a newborn son, Chirant. There was every reason for me to rise further up on the corporate ladder.

Professionally, Shaila and I couldn't have been happier, but we couldn't blend into American society. As Indians, we were very social and wanted to participate in the cultural milieu. We wanted to be part of a community. We did have Indian friends, but we wanted to belong to the country we had decided to call home; and it's not like we didn't try.

We tried everything. We joined an opera club that entitled us to six shows every year. The city's who's who attended these. But being outsiders, we didn't know anything about the performances, their themes or the actors. As hard as we strive, we didn't feel welcome. We found it difficult to strike up conversations. It might have been our lack of understanding of cultural cues or the colour of our skin. Even the vegetarian food that we so loved and were used to bonding over was tough to find.

We joined a duplicate bridge group, where some forty couples would turn up for the card game. I remember that it was quite fun, but the moment the game was over, everybody packed up their bags and left. We realized we weren't making friends here, either. To meet people, we even joined political support groups. That, too, didn't help. In hindsight, India's backward image must have impacted us in inconceivable ways. We were, truly, misfits.

It was 1976 when Shaila finally suggested that we move back to India. Despite my growing professional success and our comfortable lifestyle, we had discussed this possibility often. Now she had said it with some finality. We were planning a trip to attend my youngest sister Rita's wedding in India, and Shaila thought we could go, and this time, for good. I agreed. Now that we had a child, we felt our roots beckoned.

The subconscious mind is intuitive and often foreshadows the future. We weren't any different, I guess. Already, we had been buying electrical appliances that could run at both 110V for America and 220V for India. Though the Indian store that sold these appliances limited our choices, we had not complained. We even bought a car with a bench seat instead of bucket seats. Because a bench seat is more practical for the larger family in India. Was it a case of physically being in the US, but mentally longing for home? It definitely seemed so, now that I think of it.

Turning down success is not easy, though. The first step towards returning to India had to be taken in my boss's office. Originally from Finland, he, too, was an immigrant like me. Like most immigrants, he was convinced that the United States was paradise. He couldn't fathom my reasons for wanting to return home. That too at a time when I was all of twenty-nine and when great things were lined up for me at work. He had just gone out of his way to give me a nearly

30 per cent raise in an industry where the norm was 2 or 3 per cent. It was tough to convince him, but finally, he accepted my resignation. He told me that if my crazy move did not go well, my job would still be waiting for me.

My company notice period policy was for two weeks, but my boss asked me to work for another month. I didn't mind, as my sister's wedding was still a few months away. In the meantime, we started winding up. In our farewell get-together, the Indian community in Stamford challenged me that I wouldn't last in India. They wagered that I would be back in the US within three months. They asked me about my plans, and I told them that I honestly didn't know. When they pushed, I told them that I would join my father's established business if nothing else worked. To every child, his father is a hero. But my father, Shantilal Mehta, whom I called Kaka, was indeed extraordinary. Apart from being a globetrotting movie distributor, he was a man of many tastes and interests, from music to philosophy to literature to even numismatics. He had a thriving social life and was among the most respectable people in his various cohorts.

Awaiting our return, Shaila's family was thrilled. Ba, my mother, was delighted. Only Kaka was neutral.

In the United States, our friends had warned us that it was the worst of times back in India, as the government had declared a state of emergency. There was turmoil. Insurgencies had sprung up everywhere. But we assured them that these were isolated incidents, and that we had nothing to worry about. Nobody had seen or heard anything alarming in Sion, Mumbai (or Bombay, as it was called back then), where we lived. In hindsight, I think we were naïve.

Our return was probably going against destiny. On the way back, we almost missed our connecting flight in London. Shaila and I were too occupied with our one-year-old son when the British Airways staff came looking for us. The flight was taking off in twenty minutes. We ran with our heavy luggage and an infant. I ran. I ran away from my comfortable life in the US. I ran to conquer the world. But unbeknownst to me, I was running into an uncertain future.

If any person was thinking how accurate the premonitions of the Indian community in Stamford were, then that person was not me. As I landed in Mumbai, I decided that I would make India my karmabhoomi.[1] To kill any speculation within the family, I gathered them around and, very dramatically, cut up my Green Card with a pair of scissors. My resolve to stay back and set everything right was now clear to all. Even if they realized that I could still get my Green Card back, the sheer audacity of the act removed all doubts in everyone's minds.

But soon, I was in for a rude shock. Kaka's movie distribution business was going under, and my family was in debt. Neither Kaka nor I had a plan B. It dawned upon me that I not only had to figure out my career, but also had to pay back what the family owed. For the first time, I knew anxiety.

My initial reaction was anger towards Kaka. I told him I would not have come back if I had known that the situation was this bad. My career in the US could have easily shouldered the family's financial responsibility in Mumbai as well. Kaka reminded me that he had never asked me to return. This was true. But he had never warned me against coming back either. I should have known better because enough hints had been dropped. He had moved his office to a modest neighbourhood, and I couldn't believe how humble it was. I had seen Kaka travel across the world. He was a learned man, and everybody looked to him for advice. How could his business have come to this? Was he imprudent? Was it bad luck? Was it bad timing? That situation has remained an unsolved puzzle for me.

The office he moved into belonged to someone else, in which he had just a chair. There was no place for any of his visitors to sit. It

---

1   A Hindi language construct that has no real equivalent in the English language. The closest explanation is the land where one works. However, the meaning goes beyond just the *land* where one works.

was like a start-up in a co-working space today, but without any of the luxuries. He had told us it was in the Metro area of downtown Mumbai. In fact, it was much further inside.

At this point, I didn't know what I was going to do. I could either remain angry at him or take charge. However, the first thing I did was find a proper office for myself, so that I had somewhere to go to every morning. Shaila believed it was important to leave the house daily at 9.30 a.m.

Kaka soon moved into my office. Now, I had to figure out what business I wanted to get into.

Surprisingly, even though I was an engineer and a techie by training and experience, a business in technology did not occur to me right away. Instead, I tried reviving Kaka's movie distribution enterprise, and I started meeting people to see what I could do with it.

The movie distribution business is a simple one to explain. As a distributor, you acquired the rights to a film from the producer. The producer would then sell prints of the film to you, which you, in turn, could resell. However, as simple as it may sound, it was far more complex on the inside. To begin with, the film prints were the challenge. We could use them for only 200 screenings. After that, we had to order fresh prints from the producer. Each reorder entailed a fresh renegotiation. Although we had acquired the rights of the films for perpetuity, the need to reorder prints was a clever way of bypassing intellectual property rights. Technically, the distributor owned the rights, but it was meaningless. The producers continued to retain all the power.

My first assignment was to meet an old, vulnerable widow, Mrs Kardar, whose husband had left the rights of a movie with her upon his demise. As I negotiated with this septuagenarian, the sheer irony and awkwardness of the exercise overcame me. I realized that my time in the US had conditioned me to a different business culture.

The other problem with Kaka's business was that most of the rights he owned were of black-and-white films, and with the coming of colour films, demands were changing. I saw the impending challenges. While I could very well start acquiring the rights to colour films—we had the understanding and knowledge of the market—I did not see myself working in that business forever.

This intensified my quest to find a business I could do. When I lived in the US, I had been very impressed by a pouch that American Can made. These pouches were used to store vegetables and other perishables. While I was in the US, I thought manufacturing these pouches in India was a good idea. But now, with the family business in trouble, I lacked the financial resources to go for it. Besides, I realized that the government policies at that time enforced strict control via licenses that could only be obtained through long bureaucratic processes. So, I was back at square one.

My brother-in-law, Arun Meghani, was in the two-wheeler components business. He was always in need of zinc-based nipples that were fixed at the end of the spokes in the wheels to secure them, and he bought them regularly. He advised me that if I manufactured these nipples, he would buy whatever I made. All I had to do was buy the machinery. My exploration to set up this factory took me into the innards of Kanjurmarg, a squalid industrial suburb of the megapolis. The *Gala*, or tiny manufacturing units, were decrepit. In these semi-permanent industrial facilities, labourers worked in horrendous conditions, and their unions were in continuous conflict with the manufacturers. It was a clear no go for someone like me.

No matter where I looked, I could not find a business I could do. In India, I would have to compete with businesses that seldom followed the rules. They found ingenious ways to bend the system. Businesses were known to cheat on excise duties, customs, sales tax, and income tax. I could never figure out the real financial dynamics of an industry. Systems had developed in a way that made it unviable to run businesses if you insisted on following the rule book.

Ironically, my stint in the US had put me at a disadvantage. It trained me to follow the rules and norms. I struggled to come to terms with the ground realities of operating in India, let alone compete with the well-entrenched players. Close relatives, too, saw this problem. They advised me to return to the West.

On the upside, I thought of all that this misadventure had taught me about what I could not do. This could narrow down my search for a vocation. The framework for a business was emerging. I needed a business with an India focus. That much was certain. Then, I knew I would prefer something with export potential. I also wanted to avoid businesses that involved manual labour. I didn't need my brother-in-law's union troubles.

Just like that, I had an epiphany. I knew I had to be in the technology business. I now wonder why it took so long for the realization to come. The only reason I can think of is just how unusual it was to be in the technology business back then. Nobody around me had started such a business in India. My college batchmates had either moved abroad or were in stable jobs.

Technology met all my criteria, except one: a business in it would meet no immediate demand. As they would say these days, there was no 'market fitment'. Yet, I was convinced that it would be a massive opportunity in the long run. So, I went ahead because there was so much else that was good about it. The domain needed sophisticated skills and was completely export-oriented. There was little scope for corruption. Instead, merit was the determinant. I decided to start something small, as I didn't have any money to invest. I set up a one-person IT consultancy. I started attending industry events to meet people and tell them about my business.

Glaxo and Nerolac Paints were my first clients. Both were looking to automate processes. I was happy and eager to take on the work. The adoption of computer technology was still new in India back then, but I was aware of its immense scope.

Forbes was another early client I acquired. Its internal study had recommended a method to automate inventory control. Forbes had asked me for my views on this, so I went through their plans and realized they had simply copied the current manual process and laid it out on computers. I told them that by simply replacing typewriters with computers, they would not solve anything. Instead, it would increase expenses for no additional value. The Forbes managing director (MD) was impressed because he had never heard consultants recommend anything against their personal interests. I lost that project, but I was awarded another one with a broader scope of work because of the trust I won. To me, it was an early lesson in customer-centricity and long-term thinking.

Such consulting projects continued, but the situation at home forced me to start looking for a meaningful job. I reluctantly began interviewing with reputed Indian companies. Among these were the venerable Department of Electronics (DoE), Tata Consultancy Services (TCS) and the Electronics Corporation of India Limited (ECIL).

At DoE, I was interviewed by the legendary Dr N. Seshagiri himself. He was the director of information, planning and analysis group of the Electronics Commission since 1971 and had founded National Informatics Centre (NIC) in 1976. He took me out to lunch. He was impressed by my background in databases, which, in those days, was as exotic as quantum computing is today. By the time we were back in his office, he had an offer letter ready for me. He explained that he had cut governmental red tape to get the letter that would have otherwise taken weeks. Landing a government job then was magnitudes more significant than what it may be today.

At TCS, I was interviewed by none other than F.C. Kohli, the first chief executive officer (CEO) of the company and widely known as the Father of the Indian IT industry. He too offered me a job.

Both offers were lucrative, but I just couldn't bring myself to accept these fantastic opportunities. I turned them both down. Each time, I reminded myself that I had returned to India to be an entrepreneur. If a job were what I really wanted, then the US would have been a better place to be in.

Since then, I have been greatly influenced by the work of Sharu Rangnekar, a leading management consultant, writer and thinker. Along with Kohli and Dr Seshagiri, he motivated me to stay back and contribute to building the new India that was just emerging. He once quipped that if I stayed back in India, I would live here as 'a first-class citizen in a second-class country under a third-class administration'. While he said this in jest, this simple comment left a big impression on me, and my decision was made. It was further strengthened by Kohli's belief that people like me owed it to the country to contribute to the betterment of India.

At the time, none of us knew it, but Dr Seshagiri, Kohli[2] and I were destined to work with many others, very soon, on a much bigger opportunity.

---

2   F.C. Kohli passed away on 26 November 2020. I was lucky to have enjoyed his lifelong friendship and patronage. Among the many things that I learned from him, the lesson on compartmentalization stands out.

He could easily switch between working for TCS, the National Association of Software and Service Companies (NASSCOM) and his other volunteer activities. While he was at work with any of those, he would remain equanimous and not let his other positions of responsibility affect his decision-making.

Once, when he was the chairperson of the prestigious College of Engineering Pune (COEP), he was seeking a government grant for a new building at the campus. It was surprising that a luminary like him was investing so much of his time to request for such a meagre sum. When I asked him about it, Kohli got into a playful argument with me. He asked me, 'What is my name?' I replied, 'Mr Kohli.'

He said, 'No, that's the salutation. What is my name?'

I said, 'Kohli Saab.'

'You're still being formal about it. What is my real name?'

I ventured, 'F.C. Kohli?'

He nodded and then asked me what the F and C stood for?

I knew it and said, 'Faqir Chand.'

He beamed and said, 'That is who I am. Faqir. Which literally means a pauper and for the greater good, I am happy to go to anyone with even a begging bowl.'

I remember meeting Col. N. Balasubramanium; at the time, the head of the computer programme of the Defence Research and Development Organization (DRDO). He pointed me to an opportunity when he told me that the government was soon coming up with a policy to allow for imports of computers for commercial application if the importer could guarantee exports worth 200 per cent of what was imported. At the time, I was not financially strong at all. I was, however, confident that I could raise the requisite capital.

Around the same time, I met Mike Shah for dinner. Mike is a friend from the USA and was the country manager for Digital Equipment Corporation (DEC)[3] in India. I talked to him about a business plan for running a data centre business in Mumbai. He came back to me with a recommendation, asking why wasn't I developing my business plan around PDP-11 (or Programmed Data Processor-11), a minicomputer system with RSTS-E[4] operating system, which DEC had recently introduced to the commercial market. The new minicomputer was much cheaper than the equivalent IBM machines at the time. Plus, I could see that a giant like DEC was entering the commercial market globally. That could only mean that there would be an excellent opportunity to meet the export commitments (of 200 per cent over a five-year period) required by the government, and yet build a profitable business. He further connected me to Pravin Gandhi of Hinditron. Hinditron was selling PDP-11s in India as an agent of DEC. Pravin and I met, and realized that both of us were deeply interested in a similar business. He offered that I come on board as a partner.

---

3 Digital Equipment Corporation (DEC) was among the most respected and technologically advanced computing companies between the 1960s and 1990s, before they were acquired by Compaq in 1998. They manufactured the Vax and PDP range of computers.

4 RSTS was a command line, multi-user, time-sharing OS (operating system) for the PDP-11 series of 16-bit minicomputers. The multi-user application allowed for cost-effective commercial applications, a novelty at the time.

So, in 1977, I finally started my journey with Hinditron.[5] We were primarily a hardware and electronics company that imported and sold foreign products in India.

For me, however, the software itself was the big opportunity. In 1979, the *Financial Express* interviewed me about the future of the IT industry in India. Back then, I had the audacity to declare that the country's software exports could fetch as much net forex as the diamond industry's entire turnover at the time. While the diamond was more reputable and visible to the public eye, it made a margin of less than 5 per cent. Our relatively new industry could easily make a 60 per cent margin at the same base. We were an industry for the future. I also predicted that India would buy 500 minicomputers over the next five years. The numbers look measly today when literally everyone is walking around with a fairly advanced computer in their fist. But, at the time, India had 425 computers in total, and more than doubling that number in just a five-year period was unimaginably ambitious. Despite the prospects of hyper-growth, the industry was so unknown at that time that even the *Financial Express* spelt software as 'softwear' in its headline!

The other disappointment that I had back then and I still have is that the software revenues have always been in what I call the invisible category. They've been invisible since the very beginning, and till the time of writing this book, they remain hidden.[6]

---

5   The Hinditron group consisted of three companies—Hinditron Services, Hinditron Computers and Hinditron Consultancy. I initially joined as a partner at Hinditron Consultancy, which was later merged with Hinditron Computers. Any reference to my association with 'Hinditron' is the Hinditron Consultancy Company up to 1986 or Hinditron Computers beyond that.

6   For writing this book, I wanted numbers on software exports sliced and diced in various ways so as to draw actionable inference and recommendations. However, my team and I went from pillar to post, but could not get this data. Apart from the macro-data available with NASSCOM, the only body that could have plausibly have some visibility on this data is the Reserve Bank of India (RBI). Even there, the numbers were invisible as revenue from software

Even with these missing numbers, with my background in software and buoyed by the optimism of the hyper-growth that would come soon, we knew we were doing the right thing at the right time.

I joined hands with the four other partners at Hinditron, and we rented prime real estate—an entire floor in downtown Mumbai's Eros Cinema building at Churchgate. Business was mostly good. Until it wasn't. Nevertheless, Hinditron was the beginning of a partnership that lasted over twelve years. It set up my reputation as an exporter of software services.

I had finally found a befitting vocation in India. Little did I realize at that time that the modest building in south Mumbai, from where my journey in software began, was to become the epicentre of a revolutionary incubation and an unlikely alliance would emerge that was going to change the way the world perceives the country we call home.

---

was clubbed with other services. How do you go about making policy or strategy for such a large industry if you don't have access to real data?

2

The Real-World Pathshala

A life mirrors the time it is lived in and the people it is lived with.
When India gained independence in August 1947, it was
the defining moment of a long freedom struggle. However, the
liberation came with unprecedented violence and chaos. The country
was partitioned along religious lines. The princely states were asked
to choose between India and Pakistan. This sparked the infamous
disputes in Kashmir and the Hyderabad State. In Kashmir, a Hindu
king ruled a mostly Muslim population. In Hyderabad State, a Muslim
nizam ruled a mostly Hindu population.

Something similar was unfolding in the principality of Junagadh
State. It was ruled by a Muslim Nawab, who chose to go with Pakistan.
This was problematic as Junagadh was not physically connected to
Pakistan and had a majority Hindu population. Because of these
constraints, it was going to be a turbulent transition.

Ba's name was Revaben, and her family came from the small
township of Una in Junagadh State. Even though my family lived in

Mumbai at the time, Revaben wanted to go back to Una for the birth of her second child—me, that is. However, Una turned volatile and sectarian riots threatened to erupt at any moment. Hence, I ended up being born not in a nursing home, but in Kaka's house in Amreli, in central Saurashtra, a part of Gujarat.

I was a breech baby, born legs first. In India, it is considered lucky; and lucky I was to have Ba and Kaka as my parents. While Ba was mostly at home, my father, Shantilal Mehta, was an erudite man of the highest integrity who travelled widely across the world. Wherever there was a significant Indian diaspora, he would sell the exhibition rights of Indian movies that he had bought from producers. His film distribution business took him to the markets of London, Fiji, Beirut and Nairobi. Having had modest beginnings, he grew through a chain of successes from films like *Taj Mahal* and *Faulad*. I remember his business took a leap when the superhit *Mother India* was released.

I grew up in Sion, a modest suburb in Mumbai. I was the second born in a family of five children. My sister Ranjan is the eldest, then me, then my brother, Hiten, followed by my sisters Nila and Rita. My parents were intriguingly contrasting personalities, yet strangely compatible. Kaka was an atheist for all practical purposes, but Ba was highly religious. Born in to a Jain Gujarati family, she enrolled Ranjan and me into a pathshala for religious training when I was barely five. The pathshala was a gathering of young boys and girls of the community. We would sit in the veranda of the neighbourhood's only derasar, Jain temple.

At the pathshala, we were made to recite from the *Be Pratikaman*, an extensive set of difficult mantras, not very different from the shlokas of Hinduism. Panditji, the instructor, sat facing us at his wooden writing desk—the kind that accountants in India use. In every session, Panditji would tell us a story with a lesson in it. Then he would start with a randomly picked out mantra, deliver the first few words, and ask the child sitting in the front to recite the rest from memory. If the recitation test was not to the satisfaction of Panditji, the child was demoted to the back. No matter where we sat at the start, Ranjan and I would invariably end up promoted to the front by the time the pathshala session was over.

Attending the pathshala during my formative years exposed me to the illuminating tenets of Jainism, such as ahimsa, aparigraha, sweekar and anekaantvaad.

Ahimsa is non-violence, widely known and practised in India, thanks to Gandhiji's pervading influence. Aparigraha espouses selflessness and detachment from results and material life. Sweekar, the acceptance of adverse outcomes and uncontrollable events in life, is critical to a mind that seeks to endure and progress with equanimity. Sweekar views hurdles as building blocks in the path to the future. I think I owe many of my successes to sweekar because it gave me the grit and the acceptance that is so essential in business.

And lastly, anekaantvaad is special to me. Anekaantvaad embraces multiple truths instead of just one. There can be varied reasons behind the existence of multiple truths. It could be the limitations of words, language, thinking, logic, emotions or the senses. It is special because it became the kernel of my life, and helped me resolve personal and professional dilemmas.

After we came back from the pathshala, my siblings and I would play with each other. I have fond memories of growing up with my siblings. We played outdoor games such as cricket, lagori, and atta-patta. We would compete over throwing an iron rod the farthest, like a javelin. I also revelled in playing board games and card games, such as rummy, teen-patti and a variant of Bridge, called satiyo. We used to play 'Business', the Mumbai version of the board game Monopoly, which featured familiar neighbourhoods like Walkeshwar, Charni Road, Mahim and Matunga. To ensure that the paper currency lasted longer, we cut up the cardboard covers of old notebooks and pasted the currency bills on them. The entire building's children poured into our house, making for a raucous menagerie, playing together for hours.

I had convinced my youngest sister, Rita, that I was Gandhiji's reincarnation because I had big ears like him. She bought into my story for years. Then, one day, she realized that I was born months before Gandhiji's assassination. While I was known to pull such pranks, I could also stay aloof. Sometimes, my siblings would fight over the radio, whether to keep it on or turn it off, with their fingers on the power button. I would be a happy spectator, enjoying them from a distance.

Kaka was a man of many stories and perspectives. He was my personal walking encyclopaedia. He was a freedom fighter and was imprisoned for several months during the freedom struggle. When he was in jail, the British had beaten him up so severely that he had developed a permanent limp. He had a keen interest in numismatics, the study of coins. He had a cupboard full of old ones. For each coin he owned, he had several anecdotes and historical facts to share. When other collectors came to Kaka, wanting more information about their coins, Kaka would need a mere glance to shed light on the origin and history of those coins. He could go on, seemingly forever, talking about the coins these collectors had brought to him. They couldn't believe how much there was to know about their coins and were often left amazed at the depth of Kaka's knowledge. Everyone was curious about Kaka's coins, including the acclaimed Gujarati writer and Jnanpith Award recipient Umashankar Joshi. However, during the 1970s, the government issued a diktat, demanding the surrender of unique and rare coins, both Indian and international. We were anxious, as it meant giving away his priceless collection, painstakingly curated over decades. However, Kaka gave it away without so much as batting an eyelid.

Kaka would always get us a suitcase packed with gifts from his travels abroad. He would mostly land by midnight, so all of us would stay up. His bag was Santa Claus's sack for us. Out came things like schoolbags, erasers, pencils, dresses for my sisters, and shirts for my brother and me.

Kaka was also fond of collecting books and LP records (long-playing gramophone records). He had amassed over 500 books on varied subjects from across the world. Instrumental music was his way of unwinding. Despite being surrounded by actors, directors and producers, Kaka's major influences came from writers. A love for books was something that he passed on to his children. He was great friends with Pradeepji, popularly known as Kavi Pradeep, who wrote the famous song '*Ae mere watan ke logon*'. It was a privilege to hear him sing for us in our house. For all of us children, this was an early exposure to poetry and the classics, as Kavi Pradeep was a passionate man who shared his talent freely.

Kaka had a group of friends who met for coffee every day at 2.30 p.m. at the iconic Gaylord restaurant in Churchgate. These were not just meetings among friends wanting to hang out. These were deep, philosophical debates among artists, writers, thinkers, and businessmen.

Noted philosopher J. Krishnamurti also held a special place in Kaka's life. Whenever Krishnamurti, or Jiddu, as he was fondly called, visited Mumbai, he would stay in the house of Kaka's best friend. As a young teenager, I would often accompany Kaka to the philosophical get-togethers with Jiddu. In one such interaction, he bombarded me with questions around the theme 'who are we?' He asked me if we are the physical atoms and molecules which constitute us? Or are we our inner thoughts? Combined with my learnings at the pathshala at a younger age, it led me to deep introspection. I give him credit for sowing in me the seeds of a questioning mind that I used in everything I did in my life.

Kaka enjoyed evenings like these, which were laced with intellectual debate and ruminations. His scientific temperament influenced me too. I learnt to not take things at face value and to question everything. Truth has multiple facets which are constantly changing by itself. I started questioning religious gurus, and they would often not have satisfactory answers. I would ask them about vascape, the pinch of saffron-based yellow powder they applied on the foreheads of devotees while chanting mantras. They would tell me just to have faith in the ritual and not look for reasons. I, like Kaka, began tilting towards atheism.

Over time, Ba and Kaka drifted apart intellectually and became opposing influences in my life. Ba wanted me to be a good student of Jainism, while Kaka liked to question its gurus. But it was not just differences on religion. While they remained steadfastly with one another, they were growing in different directions. Barring the children, family and the culture, they preferred to spend time on different things. Ba's health did not permit her to travel with him, even though Kaka boarded an international flight every other month. Kaka liked to dress up, wearing shirts he had bought abroad. If he got them stitched in India, he wanted to get it done by the best tailors. He often quipped, 'I came to Bombay with three rupees in my pocket. Till the time I have just three rupees in my pocket, I'm going to spend, and there is no stopping me.' While Kaka's clothes were getting finer, Ba, in contrast, lived an increasingly simple life. While they differed in how they lived, both shared lofty ambitions for themselves and the family.

My first venture before my first venture

My first venture unfolded while I was still in college. It was entirely accidental, but the experience whetted my appetite for entrepreneurship.

After having spent two years at St. Xavier's College in Mumbai, I secured admission to the College of Engineering Pune (COEP), one of the few engineering colleges in those days. During the second year, my friend and classmate Vikram Desai introduced me to Dr Shantilal Desai, the head of Central Water and Power Research Station, a prominent research institute in Pune. Around that time, the engineering curriculum was being overhauled and was changed from three years to four. Because of this, many books were added to the syllabus, and many were rendered redundant. Most books those days were by foreign authors and publishers, and thus too expensive for most students. As a result, there was a culture of passing down old books from seniors to juniors. But because the curriculum had changed, this chain had been broken.

The worst affected were students who came from families with limited means. It was a shame because they were also the brightest in their hometowns. Dr Desai was keen to help them by starting a free library.

The funds were a challenge, though. Dr Desai encouraged some of us to brainstorm ideas for raising the money. Maybe we could do a charity entertainment event with Gujarati performers, one person wondered. Someone else suggested publishing a book that could be launched at one such event and then collecting the money for it from sponsors.

During the discussion, I mentioned that my father was a film distributor, and we zeroed in on the plan of organizing a Gujarati movie show in Pune. Back then, there were hardly any Gujarati movies shown in Pune. Apart from the ticket sales, we could raise money through sponsorship at the event. The idea was greeted with cautious optimism.

On my next visit to Mumbai, I hesitantly shared the plan with Kaka, and surprisingly, he consented. The producer of the hit Gujarati film *Kalapi* was Kaka's friend. I knew that *Kalapi* was the biography of a famous Gujarati poet, Sursinhji Gohil, known better by his pen name Kalapi. In fact, he was the prince of Lathi State in Gujarat, and had influenced a generation of poets with his works. Even though people might not have heard about the film, everybody knew about the poet. Hence, it would be easier to sell tickets. Also, it helped that the film featured superstars like Sanjeev Kumar and Aruna Irani.

Kaka and I went to meet the producer. When he heard about our intention, he said, 'Young man, I'll give you this film at no charge.' I was elated. Kaka left it to me to take it further.

When I returned to Pune with the news, Dr Desai and Vikram were overjoyed. We started working on organizing the screening. We got tickets printed and started meeting people to raise sponsorship money.

We booked a theatre at the Deccan Gymkhana for a Sunday morning slot from 11 a.m. to 2 p.m. at their prevailing rate. The sponsors were given a certain number of tickets. We sold the remaining tickets in the local market. We further attended several Gujarati events to promote the show.

Finally, the day of reckoning was upon us. I was nervous. Noted industrialist S.L. Kirloskar graced the event as the chief guest. Vikram made the opening remarks, followed by Dr Desai's and S.L. Kirloskar's speeches. I gave the vote of thanks, my first public speaking assignment. At the screening, we distributed booklets that contained information on the movie and about the Gujarati Engineers' Library and the sponsors' ads.

We must have collected around ₹1,00,000 that day—a large sum at the time. The joy that Dr Desai's felt was palpable. It was enough to get our library started. We negotiated a bulk deal for buying the books from a local bookstore. We were allotted some space in the existing library to run our own. I took charge of distributing the books.

When students from remote parts of Maharashtra accessed the library, their excitement and elation made the efforts of the past few weeks feel like a walk in the park.

This was my first brush with social entrepreneurship, aimed at the greater good. I felt fulfilled by the event's success. The selfless contributions of volunteers, the film producer and Dr Desai showed me a path for the future.

Encouraged by our achievement in the first year, the following year, we screened the iconic Guru Dutt movie, *Chaudhvin Ka Chand*, to raise more funds for our library.

Starting out in the real world

When my class graduated, we realized that there were only a handful of quality jobs out there. From a batch of 400, about eighty went abroad. Some twenty-five to thirty joined family businesses, and less than five started businesses of their own. The rest simply took up jobs whenever they were available. Most of these jobs were in manufacturing plants, ensuring that machines kept running in factories, making things like pumps, motors and light bulbs. There were no opportunities to design or innovate, apart from making minor modifications in some materials or reverse-engineering an existing product.

In 1968, I applied to Brooklyn Polytechnic in New York.[1] The college sent me a brochure with attractive pictures of students sitting on a wooden bench and hanging around in a park. I imagined a beautiful green campus around the bench. But when I landed there, I was dismayed to see only a building and no park. When I questioned the registrar about the photograph, he smiled and showed me the bench. Indeed, there was a bench in a corner on the pavement right outside the building. The registrar boasted that the whole of New York City was our campus. I learnt my first thing about the US: its flair for marketing.

I started studying for an MS in electrical engineering. When my roommate, Inder Singh, heard this, he was disappointed. He was a year senior to me and emphatically advised me to switch to computer science, which was the field of the future. Convinced by his argument, I made the switch.

At Brooklyn Polytechnic, I was challenged like I had never been before. My class had Fulbright Scholars[2] and Bell Labs' interns.[3] The class was thus highly competitive. There were so many brilliant people

1   The current name of Brooklyn Polytechnic is New York University Tandon School of Engineering.
2   Fulbright Scholars are part of the Fulbright Program. Founded by the J. William Fulbright in 1946, it is considered one of most prestigious scholarships in the world. Individuals are competitively selected and granted scholarships to study, conduct research, teach or exercise their talents.
3   Bell Labs is widely recognized as a leading industrial research and scientific development organization. Researchers working at Bell Labs are credited with the development of a host of modern inventions. A partial list includes the transistor, the laser, the photovoltaic cell, the Unix operating system, and the programming languages B, C, C++, S, SNOBOL, AWK, AMPL and many others.

there that the benchmark had gone up for me. My batchmates were inadvertently pushing me to work harder.

In comparison of where I was coming from, the US seemed like a much freer country. I was perhaps too young to comprehend the economics of a free market and capitalism at the time. Since I had grown up in India, which was closer to the USSR, I was largely sceptical about the US story and had dismissed most of it as American propaganda. But now, I could see its undeniable technological dominance with my own eyes.

I also experienced conflicting aspects of everyday life in the US. I soon learned that I lived in an area with an extraordinarily high crime rate. On the way to the college, we would have to cross a park where the possibility of being mugged loomed largely. I was told to keep a minimum of $5 with me—not having any money for the mugger was a certain way to get beaten up. I didn't have any insurance, which made the mere thought of being harmed even scarier.

On the other hand, when I went out with friends, I experienced a different New York. We were an eclectic group of five: an Italian, a Swiss, a Spaniard, an Arab and I. We would visit Manhattan or upscale parts of Brooklyn, and enjoy the dazzling lights and the skyscrapers. New Yorkers typically were well dressed and looked confident. Fine dining and jazz were around every corner. Though, for me, the biggest challenge was to find vegetarian food.

I was a big fan of the Beatles. Most places at that time had 45-rpm players. These could play only one disc at a time, and there would be only one song on one side of the disc. I must have heard the song '*Let It Be*' hundreds of times. It indeed was a favourite.

In nearby Woodstock, a music festival had just made history. A future full of peace and love looked imminent.

However, the US–Vietnam conflict raged on. On the other end, the counterculture movement was at its peak.

I was from a completely different world, and even though I couldn't relate to it, Flower Power was omnipresent and fascinating. It was

exhilarating to watch young, long-haired an/
to the streets everywhere. Peaceful demons'
were fearless of powerful authorities. Coming
visualize such open dissent against the government.

The war had also unleashed a dread of the draft. Later,
graduated, my Green Card meant that I could be drafted for the
However, my number was 360 out of 365. I was so low on the list that
it was a running joke that women and children would have to go before
I did. My colleague Anil was not as relaxed as I was. His number was
within the first hundred. He went on a crash diet to bring his weight
down to 110 lbs (almost 50 kg), so that he would be disqualified from
the otherwise mandatory military service. Some others simply went
back to India. And then there were a few who went to Vietnam for the
love of the US of A.

Though the war had diminished the American sheen in my eyes,
I could not ignore the moon landing that had just captured the
imagination of the world. The media everywhere was splashed images
and stories of the astronauts and Apollo 11's historic mission.

Back at college, in 1970, I began working on my PhD. My advisor,
Dr McKellar, was a researcher at IBM and a professor at Brooklyn
Polytechnic. He was convinced that this was the best way forward for
me. But within three months, I decided against it. Perhaps it was my
latent entrepreneurial strain.

My first job was at The Travelers Companies Inc., an insurance
major, in Hartford, Connecticut, where they were headquartered. I
began work as an applications programmer, and my first assignment was
to write code for COBOL programmes for commercial applications.
With my master's degree in computer science, I was among the most
qualified people in the group, and yet, the work was so low skill that
people used to joke that even monkeys with a week's training could
do it.

But I had to take what I could get. The war had slowed down the
economy, and jobs were hard to come by anyway. So, alongside, in the

.gs, I pursued management courses at Rensselaer Polytechnic, ializing in finance and marketing.

I was set for a rewarding career, and the American dream seemed o come true. If not for the trip back home for my sister's wedding.

Finding love

In 1972, I returned to India for my younger sister Nila's wedding.[4] Chatter had begun that I, too, should get married. It was during this trip to India that I met Shaila. Our fathers had been business partners, and our families had known each other for several years. I had seen Shaila at movie previews, but had never spoken to her before.

We were at their residence, an airy third-floor duplex apartment in upscale Matunga. When Shaila entered the room, I was instantly smitten! But my instincts instantly warned me that beauty is skin deep. There's more to a person than just looks, and any union of two people has to have a deeper connection. I found her very sophisticated, intellectual and humorous, yet measured and deep. Now the tables had turned. I concluded that only a strong, self-assured man could impress her. The question lurking in my insecure mind was whether she saw me as that.

Couples in India rarely dated then. We were in courtship, and we were once driving together to attend a function organized by a friend. Shaila was at the wheel of the clunky Fiat, one of the two models of cars that you could buy in India then, and that too after a wait list that could take several years. We were climbing the slope of Kemp's Corner in downtown Mumbai when the car stalled. She couldn't negotiate the gradient. I offered to help, but Shaila was sceptical that I could drive in India. She assumed that because I lived in the US, I must be used to the left-hand-drive cars, and I would not be able to manage the rustic Fiat. But I took the wheel and managed to plough the car out.

---

4   To date, I quip that my life probably has inspired Sooraj Barjatya's films where large weddings are the harbingers of life-changing events!

Later, I learnt that it was at that moment when Shaila finally made her decision.

Soon, we were engaged and married. Though I had come down to India for a short period, the wedding delayed me by forty-five days, and I ended up staying for three months.

Shaila moved to the US with me, and we began building a life together there. She had a master's degree in mathematics. Staying at home was very frustrating for her. She started working at a bank but soon moved to Travelers, alongside me.

On my return to the job, my boss had a $150,000-project waiting for me. I would have to manage three or four programmers and develop a business application over six months. After studying the project for a week, I came up with a better solution. The project would become redundant if we made a minor change to another existing application instead. My value to them was established in that instant. They started calling me 'super-programmer'.

On a different day, someone from the human resources (HR) team called to say that my super boss wanted to see me. I was worried, even though in my humble assessment, I had been an exceptionally good performer. Also, I had worked harder than anyone else in my department, slogging for twice the number of hours, often working into the wee hours.

I dragged myself into his cabin, but I was greeted with a big grin. My super boss told me that he was extremely happy with my work and wanted to show his appreciation by rewarding me with a bonus. At that time, my salary was around $12,000 a year, and I was given a bonus of $3,000. I was truly heartened by this gesture.

A week later, I learnt that the local court had announced a new regulation, making it mandatory for companies to pay overtime to their employees, retrospectively over a year. The way the 'bonus' was given to me had made the mandatory compensation look like a voluntary gesture.

My job profile was upgraded to that of a database software engineer. The data centre was a state-of-the-art building. On one occasion, I was having coffee in the cafeteria during a break. Just then, I heard a very loud and unusual sound. When I moved towards the window, I saw a helicopter land on the campus. I wondered if there was an emergency and if we had to evacuate. But the people who got off the helicopter looked more like engineers instead of emergency responders. They were IBM service providers who unloaded an IBM 370 server to replace a failed one that was running mission-critical applications for Travelers. This commitment and professionalism shown by IBM left me astounded.

At work, I also experienced a shift in cultural ethos. Take coffee, for example. In the US, even the most senior people would have to queue up for their coffee, as if the hierarchy disappeared at the altar of the coffee machine. Coming from a country steeped in caste-based systems, this equality was very inspiring to see.

Even though I was doing well, I felt underutilized and devoid of challenges. Although periodic exceptions to the rules were made to accommodate my growth, it didn't keep me motivated at work. I was restless, and my ambition was growing. It was then that I got a timely call from a search firm that offered me the position of 'database manager' at American Can. This would move me up the value chain. I was eager to make up for the time I had lost doing a job that I was clearly overqualified for. But I almost did not take the offer. It required relocation, and Shaila was well-settled at Travelers. American Can, however, was happy to interview both of us, and that sealed the deal.

In 1974, we moved to American Can. We were in their beautiful 300-acre office in Greenwich, Connecticut. We found a home in neighbouring Stamford. Though the office was idyllic, the 'billionaire town' of Greenwich imposed some unusual community rules that the company had to follow. For example, nobody could park in open areas as parking was restricted to underground lots only. There were no streetlights outside the office. Curtains too had to be kept drawn at night.

It was here that I learnt about the unspoken rule in corporate America. No matter how meritorious, hardworking, or talented you were, if you weren't a WASP, a White Anglo-Saxon Protestant, you could only rise to the level of a vice-president (VP).

In a society largely perceived as driven by meritocracy, I found this debasing. Shaila and I had succeeded on merit alone. We were among the first of our generation in the US, and we had to think hard about whether we wanted to stay on under such circumstances. It started a debate between us, and it eventually strengthened our resolve to return to India.

In 1975, Shaila and I were blessed with our firstborn. We named him Chirantan, meaning a long life. When we felt that the name itself was a bit long for the American tongue, we shortened it to Chirant. His birth triggered more thoughts about returning home.

Chirant is a misnomer

A few months had passed since our return to India. The initial uncertainties, too, were overcome. I had become a partner at Hinditron and was chugging ahead with it. On the personal front, Shaila was more than happy to be with the family. Cherubic Chirant was the centre of our attention; and his cute antics kept all of us amused. The feeling was that we had found our groove. Life was great! Little did we know that it was just a blissful lull before the horrific storm.

It was in January 1979, but the incident is indelibly etched in my mind. I had a Saturday ritual of taking the two-year-old Chirant to our fifth-floor office in the Eros Building. The plan was to conduct a short review meeting, and then I would take him to the Rani Baug zoo or maybe to the horse garden. On this day, one of his cousins was with us as well. As our meeting began, Chirant and his cousin playfully pranced around in my cabin.

The inquisitive Chirant kept asking, 'Hu kya chhu?'[5] I would respond every time I could divert attention away from my meeting. After a few minutes, I realized that Chirant wasn't asking the question anymore. We looked around, and he was nowhere to be found. We finally moved the curtain aside to realize that one of the windows was open. I peered out of the window, and I was aghast at what I saw. The bubbly Chirant lay motionless on the pavement five storeys below. I was devastated. Even as we rushed his lifeless body to Bombay Hospital, I had an ominous feeling. I fought tears and hoped for the best. Alas, he was declared dead on arrival.

The irony in his name fleetingly passed my mind. I dragged myself to make the most difficult call of my life to Shaila, who was initially in disbelief. But as the reality of the tragedy seeped in, she rushed to the hospital and was inconsolable.

Oblivious of the tragedy, Kaka and Ba were vacationing in Udaipur. When they entered their hotel, they were told they had a phone call waiting for them. Sensing something had gone drastically wrong, Kaka told Ba to go to the room and settle down while he attended the call. When he heard about the fatal accident, the resolute Kaka just couldn't control his grief and uncharacteristically broke down. Yet, he gathered himself and withheld the news from Ba. Within a few hours, they were on a flight back to Mumbai with Ba still clueless about what had transpired.

Chirant was cremated the same day. I recall going through the motions of the last rites in a dazed blur. Friends and family attended the funeral. They came up to me, shocked, as I took them through the painstaking details of the fateful fall. I was drifting without comprehending much around me. One of my brothers-in-law had taken charge of the situation and had arranged for the rites. As the flames from the pyre burnt furiously, the smoke reaching out to spread over the skies, I was being tested on how well I had internalized the

---

5   Where am I?

lesson of sweekar and aparigraha. Alas, I just couldn't accept or detach myself from the trauma. The pain would linger with us for a lifetime. I was failing.

We had a prayer meeting on the third day, and we struggled to move on. In retrospect, we were compelled to look beyond the tragedy as our daughter Prachi (born in 1978) was just a few months old then. We had no choice but to nurture her future and leave the past behind. It was easier to be immersed at work, but being alone was dreadful. That's when the tragedy would hit me repeatedly and relentlessly. I know it must have been a lot worse for Shaila. But she braved ahead, wiping her tears, looking for the scant joy that life had to offer. I am reminded of a quote, 'Grief demands an answer, but sometimes there is none.' We had none in our case either. Chirant was no more. Period.

Three months later, Kaka lost one of his closest friends and was left heartbroken once again. I don't know if it was the combined grief of losing his grandson and a close friend in quick succession or just his bad health, but Kaka, too, passed away soon after. He was only fifty-six. I became even more certain that there is no god.

By this time, the incidents of my life, the good and the bad, the happy and the tragic, had all melded to form influences of my past. In the journey of life, Shaila, Prachi and I were joined by my son, Jigar (born in 1979) and daughter, Heral (born in 1982). However, it was sweekar and aparigraha that allowed me to move on to something more purposeful, something much more significant and more impactful: the fledgling industry I was part of. An industry that, in turn, changed the destiny of India.

3

A Caravan Sets Out

I've come up with a set of rules that describe our reactions to technologies:
1. Anything that is in the world when you're born is normal and ordinary
and is just a natural part of the way the world works.
2. Anything that's invented between when you're fifteen and thirty-five is
new and exciting and revolutionary and you can probably get a career in it.
3. Anything invented after you're thirty-five is against the natural order
of things.

—Douglas Adams

If you were born in a world full of computers or started work in it, you know what software is. You belong to one of Adams's first two categories. Imagine explaining software to a person who has never used a laptop or a smartphone. This person is likely to mistake the software on your devices for the hardware it is on. This is the kind of challenge some of us experienced in the early days of the doing business in computers.

In the 1970s, when I started working in India, most decision-makers in the government and business had no idea of what software was. They belonged to Adams's third category. The problem was worsened by the intangible nature of the software. How does one explain the value of something that you cannot see, touch, smell, taste or hear? How do you import or export it? Or tax it?

This reminds me of the story of the six blind men who had never come across an elephant before. They were asked to describe an elephant merely by touching it. The man who held the tail said that an elephant was like a rope. The one who touched a leg thought it was like a trunk. The one who fumbled with the belly said that it was like a huge wall.

Even though they were talking about the same elephant, their understanding differed immensely. Each one ignored the other, who were also true in their own limited experience. As a result, they came to suspect that the others were lying.

The moral of the parable is that humans have a tendency to claim absolute truths based on their limited, subjective experience as they ignore others.

Now, an elephant is a living, breathing thing that you can touch and feel. What do you do when you are trying to explain something intangible, like software? Worse, what do you do when people get the wrong idea about software?

Often, the kind of conversations I had at the time left me flummoxed. A customs officer once asked me what I was exporting. When I told him I was exporting software, he asked me to show him the software. How does one show software? Should I show him the floppy disk I was exporting it in? Or should I show him the printouts of the code? Or should I show him the contracts that were yet to be drafted, forget about being signed? On another occasion, another customs officer told me that I needed to leave samples of what I was exporting with him. I was forced to leave the floppy disk of the software with him. The diligent officer immediately planted a stapler pin through the floppy disk and attached it to the form, thereby destroying the media and rendering it unreadable.

For the longest time, everybody's understanding of software differed immensely. This confusion continued into the 1980s, and it was getting challenging to grow the business. The more I met young software entrepreneurs, the more I realized that my frustration was not unique. Something had to be done.

Then, at a business event, I met a technology teacher. We immediately struck a chord over the problem of always having to explain ourselves and always being misunderstood. It turned out that Vijay Mukhi was not just a teacher but a pioneer. The first thing anyone noticed about him was his compulsive need to learn everything. If he found out about a particular technology, he would lock himself up in a room and emerge from it only after becoming a sort of expert on it. He was filled with a childlike zest for technology. We soon became friends and confidants. Over the years, his inquisitiveness only grew.

In the mid-1980s, many of these conversations were happening at monthly gatherings at Vijay Mukhi's house. Soon, they were brimming with entrepreneurs in the technology business, and these meetings evolved into the Bombay Computer Club,[1] and each month had a different sponsor for the meeting. Even back then, we were sure that the sponsors shouldn't push their personal agendas. All we would offer was to acknowledge their contribution. Such gatherings were probably where the seeds of the National Association of Software and Service Companies (NASSCOM), The Indus Entrepreneurs (TiE), and many such ideas were sown. We would discuss about emerging ideas like the Internet and (Cyber) Security. These gatherings reminded me of Kaka's outings with his friends for those fabled 2.30 p.m. coffee meetings at the Gaylord restaurant.

In one such gathering in 1986, I stood with a large group over drinks. Everyone was venting about the bureaucracy. I had a grievance, too.

---

1   Raj Saraf of Zenith Computers and Chirag Unadkat were early members of the club.

A major joint venture between the venerable DEC and Hinditron had been hanging in limbo since 1985 (eventually, the deal was closed in 1987). Others at the party broke into a tirade about how the bureaucracy had shackled us because it just did not understand software.

In that moment of collective catharsis, I shared an idea that had been brewing in my head for a long time. I suggested that we must, together, form an association to work along with the government on its regulations, and bring a shift in their thinking and approach. We were young software entrepreneurs, who, instead of innovating, were battling paperwork in government offices. Having experienced the well-oiled machine that the US business environment was, I could tell what India was missing out on.

A lot of ideas get slapped on the table under the influence of alcohol. Many get readily accepted, too. But they are as readily forgotten with the hangover the next morning. So, to put things into motion, I quickly called for a meeting to further the germ of the idea. I suggested we meet the very next day at the Sea Lounge at the Taj Mahal Hotel. Though there was no reason to believe then that the others were as serious as I was.

The next day, my fears were confirmed. Of the about thirty people at Vijay Mukhi's party, only three showed up. I consoled myself that it was enough to get the ball rolling. We discussed the next steps and put together a list of the fifteen most influential people from the software services industry in Mumbai.[2] I invited all fifteen to a meeting in the Hinditron office in the Eros Cinema building. They were the decision-makers at the biggest companies. I was doubtful they would come.

My hopes soared when almost all of them showed up. I introduced them to the idea of forming an industry body that could pitch the software industry's interests to the government. The people in the room could not have been more supportive. Each had a personal,

---

2   This included people like Prakash Ahuja, Kanak Pandyan, Shashi Bhagnari (at the time a journalist with Dataquest), Dr Nirmal Jain, Saurabh Srivastava and representatives from Mastek, Datamatics, Patni, Hinditron and more.

grand vision for the potential of the services business. We now had this core group that could start involving everyone else before we officially formed our industry association.

Forming an industry association was, of course, not a new idea. The ancient Romans recognized a collegium or a corpus as a group that had been conferred the status of a legal entity. There were many collegia of sellers who specialized in a craft. For example, the famous corpus naviculariorum was the guild for long-distance shippers in the ancient port of Ostia Antica. In present-day England, there are guilds that are several centuries old. Today, in hindsight, it is hard to endorse the values of most guilds. Many only served the interests of their founders.

In fact, a software industry association in India was not a new idea either. There were already tens of local associations around the country. For instance, the ones in Pune and Chandigarh hosted IT entrepreneurs locally to discuss issues close to them. But because these were sporadic efforts at a local level, they were far from making any impact on a national scale.

The biggest association then was the Manufacturers' Association for Information Technology (MAIT).[3] At that time, very few people had realized the potential of the software. On the other hand, electronics was considered a sunrise industry.

Also, in my opinion, MAIT was a club of Delhi-based industrialists who enjoyed the power accorded to them by their proximity to the politicians and bureaucrats. I remember the CEO of one of

---

3   MAIT was set up in 1982 as an industry body for the information and communication technology industry. Headquartered in Delhi, MAIT primarily has hardware manufacturers and assemblers as members, such as HCL, Wipro, DCM, Zenith, Microland, TCS, IDM, Essen, Computronix and others. Their focus was and remains bolstering India as an electronics manufacturing hub.

At MAIT, if my memory serves me right, the executive committee had some sixteen members representing various types of hardware manufacturers. They had just two members representing the software industry and, of those two, neither was from software services.

the computer hardware companies asked me once, 'Why are you unhappy? What is it that is bothering you? Bataiye, kaun sa officer aapki industry ko pareshan kar raha hai? Hum unko transfer karva denge.'[4] I thus found them a group of businessmen who did things the way they deemed fit, often serving the interests of their companies ahead of the nation.

The first thing that we wanted the government to understand was that there is something called the *software services* business, and it is distinct from the hardware business and the software products business. MAIT's stand was that the software business was a small subset of the larger and more important hardware business. MAIT did have a software division within itself, and to head it, they had the omnipresent F.C. Kohli, the CEO of TCS. At that time, he was arguably the most influential person in the Indian software industry. So, even though MAIT was not the best representative of the software services business, it continued to be the most important industry body.

So, if we had to make the government focus on the software industry's challenges, we would have to lobby for it. It was clear to us that our lobbying would have to eventually go beyond individual companies and the create an ecosystem conducive to the growth of software and software services businesses. Hence, lobbying was not really a goal. It was a means to an end.

Personally, I was convinced that to make a real impact, our association would have to also represent at least 80 per cent of the software industry's top line. In the early days, it was a real struggle to get support, and some of us felt it was all right to go ahead with whatever representation was available. On the other hand, a few of us, including me, refused to start without the critical mass.

I am glad that our small group prevailed, and with the advantage of hindsight, I can say it was the right decision. The 80 per cent representation allowed us to send a powerful message to the entire

---

4   It translates to, 'Tell me, which officer is troubling your industry? We will get him transferred.'

world that we were the voice of the Indian software services industry.[5] We'll never know how things would have unfolded if we hadn't put our foot down about that.

We could not afford to have multiple voices speaking about different agendas to the government, confusing policymakers. When we could not agree on a common agenda and arrive at a common stand, how could we expect policymakers to have the vision for our industry's future? The software industry would have to find its one big voice and represent itself without ambiguity. So, the question haunting us was that if we told people about our plan, would they come on board? We realized we were not doing this for our individual companies alone. If the size of the industry pie grew, our slices would get bigger as well. With enough leftover for many others to join the software ecosystem. If we made this clear to all, there would be no reason for people to be sceptical of us.

We started meeting important stakeholders in the IT industry. Mumbai's IT community had hopped on board quite readily. In Washington, at an earlier meeting of the Indian software delegation, where attendees included the likes of Nandan Nilekani, K.V. Ramani[6], Saurabh Srivastava, and Mr S.S. Oberoi from MeitY[7] (then DoE), another discussion to form a software association took place. Nandan

---

5   In the initial days at NASSCOM, we wanted to become a member of Asian-Oceanian Computing Industry Organization (ASOCIO), a prestigious federation organized by the Information and Communication Technology (ICT) associations from across Asia Pacific region. When NASSCOM requested to join and represent India, we were told that a small association of companies from a tier-2 city was doing so already. We responded by saying that at NASSCOM we were going to represent at least 80 per cent of the Indian IT industry's top line. How was anyone else better positioned to speak for us? We worked hard to get accredited by them and even though we had to eventually wait for two years, we got what was rightfully ours.

6   Ramani is the founder of Future Software and a co-founder of Hughes Software Systems.

7   MeitY is an abbreviation of the Ministry of Electronics and Information Technology. DoE stands for Department of Electronics.

and I further spoke about the association, and he took the initiative to organize a meeting with Bangalore-based entrepreneurs. Similarly, some of us went on a whirlwind tour of Madras, Calcutta and Delhi. I personally met with industry leaders in each of these cities.

We had antagonized the all-powerful MAIT, and, to be an effective lobbying group, we needed as many hands on deck as we could get. Even though personal egos tend to dictate actions at such industry bodies, we had to build consensus from the very first day and take everyone together.

It eventually took us more than two years, from starting the conversation to getting people to sign the dotted line. I think we could come together because we had started working with the right intention. Further, all of us shared the same pain, the same anguish and suffered from the same issues. We even wore the same suits![8]

Thus, even though we represented distinct companies and different business interests, our similarities and shared long-term interests allowed us to develop camaraderie, and work collectively towards a common goal.

Check MAIT

We were not against MAIT. The core group simply wanted to build an industry association dedicated to the needs of the software and software services businesses. But some within MAIT saw us as rebels who wanted to break away. This was not good because we wanted people to take us and our agenda seriously, without being branded as divisive.

Also, some seniors at MAIT saw us as a threat because they were comfortable with the status quo. It suited their individual businesses,

---

8   Even as individuals, we were at same stage in life and were attracted by the same things in life. Once, at a dinner hosted by the US Consulate in Delhi, K.V. Ramani, Dr Nirmal Jain of TCS and I wore the exact same suit! When we spoke to each other, we realized all of us had picked our suits at different times from different outlets of the same American retailer to wear to parties, and everyone picked and wore the same make that day.

and they enjoyed a position of authority when it came to government policy or the lack of it.

Worse, MAIT's president, Dr O.P. Mehra, was also very unhappy with us. Dr Mehra headed the small but influential International Data Management (IDM), a group that inherited the business of maintaining the IBM 1400 series machines when IBM itself exited India.

The core group of our nascent association was keen to clear up the air with MAIT. I decided to meet Dr Mehra at his Mumbai office. His personality was intimidating and authoritative, and he was known for his oratory skills. I sensed that the meeting would end in a showdown of sorts. But I still went ahead with it because I wanted him to know that our intention was not mala fide. I explained to him whom we represented and what we were trying to do. I sought his guidance and implored that his experience in running MAIT could help us.

Dr Mehra himself was polite, but MAIT's displeasure was not hard to miss. He tried his best to discourage me, telling me how difficult it was to work with the government and how futile it was for us to even try. I shared our vision for the software industry and particularly for the software services industry. I further spoke about how it could become a major pillar of the Indian economy by earning net foreign exchange. Despite these solid arguments, Dr Mehra brushed it all aside. He must have seen me as a petulant child asking for the moon.

I reiterated that we didn't have anything against MAIT, and we wanted a separate identity for software services to address its specific needs. He asserted that Kohli was heading the software division for MAIT, and his stature was more than enough to handle the software industry's challenges. After all, TCS and Tata Burroughs represented 60–70 per cent of the industry at that time.

The meeting was over.

When I stepped out of the room, I was shaken, but only for a bit. I began processing what had just transpired. If I was being rational, it was natural for Dr Mehra to discourage me, I reasoned; it shouldn't affect my morale. And I didn't let it.

MAIT's refusal to support our association was a setback. On the other hand, the unstinted support we received from software businesses was uplifting. In spite of umpteen constraints, our businesses were growing. We had to keep going.

The path ahead was clear. We would have to seek the blessings of the government directly. After all, one of the key jobs of the new association was to represent the software industry to policymakers. The DoE was responsible for matters related to us. At that time, it was headed by the erudite Dr N. Seshagiri. He was a scholarly man with big ideas and ambitions for India. But he was also authoritarian and seldom engaged in conversations, preferring to deliver monologues instead. Nevertheless, he was our only hope now.

Dr Seshagiri had immense belief in India's software products' potential. He would assert, 'If India has all the raw material in the shape of the brightest software engineers, then why does it need to import anything?' In my view, academia erroneously believed that making software was simply about writing complex code. Dr Seshagiri would ask, 'Why can't we deploy the required number of bright programmers and invent things in our own country instead of importing products?' To this, I would clarify by asking, 'If someone gave you all the ingredients of a samosa, but not the recipe. Would you still be able to make samosas[9]?' Product development is not just a science, but an art as well. In those days, it took years to make a viable product. Along that journey there would be investments into R&D and a process to learn from failures. Above all, monetization was exceedingly difficult. At Hinditron, we had lost big money in the software products business by then. Again, in my view, a software products industry was not something India was geared for at that time.

---

9   I would often further add that if you did not know how a samosa looked like or tasted like, it would be all the more difficult to make one, even if you had all the ingredients. Reverse engineering a product is easier compared to building it from ground up. In my opinion, at the time, we were not ready for the product business.

But Dr Seshagiri was firm in his convictions. Such was the man I was scheduled to meet.

Eventually, when I went to meet him, I had a single-point agenda: to seek his advice on the formation of our software association. He made it clear at the outset that he did not support it as he did not want the industry to have multiple voices. He pointed out that software was already represented by MAIT. I explained our reasons for creating a separate focus on software, but his mind was made up.

All this was happening in 1987. I was a partner at Hinditron then and was trying to grow the company. We, at Hinditron, were on the verge of entering a joint venture (JV) with the international computer major Digital Equipment Corporation (DEC). The deal with DEC would change the fortunes of Hinditron. At that time, DEC was a force to reckon with. It was the second-largest computer company globally with over 12,000 employees, just on the heels of IBM, and was about to post $11 billion in revenue. Clinching this joint venture meant everything to us. Compared to DEC, we were a young company, and our global footprint was tiny. This JV would be the first major partnership in the private sector in India. We had already become favourites of the press. We were on the front pages of newspapers for months no end.

This JV required the approval from the Government of India, which was represented by DoE, headed by Dr Seshagiri himself. On our side, the JV delegation had several people from both Hinditron and DEC.

The situation got tricky because if I pushed for our association, I stood to antagonize Dr Seshagiri and risk Hinditron's all-important JV approval. Until now, my partners had been supportive of me in starting an industry association. But if it affected our business in a detrimental way, I didn't know how they would react.

Soon, I started getting calls from several industry veterans, asking me to back off. I suspect these were prompted by the people at MAIT. The message was clear. If I kept pursuing the matter of an industry body, the Hinditron–DEC joint venture might not get the government's approval and could get delayed. I briefed my partners at Hinditron–DEC about the situation, and an emergency meeting was called. Anxiety ran high. But I was adamant about giving it another shot.

Even as I steered clear of antagonizing the government, my Hinditron partners and I realized that MAIT had thrown a spanner into the JV works. We noticed that every three months, MAIT would send a letter to DoE complaining about some alleged special treatment given to this JV. The government would then write to us. We would research the issue and file a response with the government. By this time, three months would go by, and we'd face yet another letter that originated from MAIT. The loop went on, seemingly forever. When I asked a DoE officer about why they paid heed to such irrelevant demands, he replied, 'We are a democracy, and we have to respond to requests coming from industry associations.' To me, it seemed that to some policymakers, completing the files was more important than accelerating the economy. They were lakeer ke faqir.[10]

I still believe that government officials did not have any malice per se towards us. They were merely naïve and unaware of the demands of the computer industry. Thus, they played into the hands of some opportunistic businessmen from MAIT. Let me give an example.

At that time, the Government of India had signed an agreement with Norway's Norsk Data to manufacture computers at the indigenous Electronics Corporation of India Limited (ECIL) factory in Hyderabad. It was mandated that all commercial applications must use Norsk Data computers manufactured by ECIL. At the time, DEC's MicroVAX was running the enterprise resource planning (ERP) for manufacturing processes. MAIT made the absurd demand that DEC rewrite their ERP for Norsk Data. To be able to meet the demand, the rewriting of the software would run into millions of dollars, way above the project size in India, let alone the time required to rewrite the software. Not just me, but our colleagues from the industry were also baffled at the absurdity of such demands!

---

10 Someone who follows the 'written word' blindly.

In yet another case of micromanagement by the government, as part of their localization programme, the Government of India felt that computer cabinets should be manufactured locally. However, for the MicroVAX that DEC–Hinditron was planning to manufacture in India, we needed specific cabinets with electromagnetic protection. These were made by one particular plant in the US. When we requested the government to allow the imports of these cabinets, MAIT wrote to them and asked that we be charged an exorbitant 250 per cent import duty.

One could have thought of starting a new cabinet manufacturing plant, but the cost of a new plant was going to be twice that of our entire business. So, while the bureaucrats were well-intentioned, they did not understand the realities of the computer business.

Some people from MAIT had openly declared that this venture would not see the light of day for at least another couple of years. Unfortunately, they succeeded in ensuring their prophecy came true.

Disappointed, we went to Kohli and vented our frustration. How could DEC, the world's second-largest computer company, sincerely interested in building a manufacturing base in India, be stopped by mere assemblers masquerading as hardware manufacturers?[11] These companies would import completely knocked-down kits (CKDs), buy locally manufactured cabinets, do simple soldering work on printed circuit boards (PCBs)[12] and then sell the assembled product.

---

11 Even at the time of writing this book, numerous 'computer manufacturers' in India are still merely component assemblers. The classification as a manufacturer allows these companies to enjoy benefits like tax holidays and import incentives that eventually affect the exchequer and thus prevent real innovation. For a long time now, we have heard silent murmurs and rumours that some hardware companies classify their hardware imports as software (hardware import attracts a higher duty compared to software), thereby hurting the tax collection. They even give away software for free, which, in my view, amounts to piracy.

12 The printed circuit board is the 'base layer' on top of which all electronic components are installed to create a computer.

Kohli, who was unaware of what had transpired, was taken aback. He immediately spoke to Dr Mehra, who himself seemed to be in the dark of the proceedings. Kohli promised us that such a thing would not happen again.

Fatefully, this meddling by some people within MAIT became a blessing in disguise for me. It drove home to me just how powerful an industry association can be. I wondered how a handful of people almost got in the way of a giant like DEC and its JV with Hinditron. I was awestruck.

It is ironic; just when all hope for our software association was lost, my resolve to make it happen turned rock solid because of this MAIT incident.

Convincing Kohli

Several months had passed by. I waited patiently for the JV to be signed. As soon as it was done, I immediately revived the association discussions.

I knew I had to get the bigger players like the Tata Group on our side, even though they did not really need our proposed software industry association. Rather, we needed them.

We already had Tata Burroughs's endorsement, provided we got TCS on board. But getting the much larger TCS was not going to be easy. In our earnestness to form the association, the core group had already antagonized Kohli. Our proposal, I realized, might make him look bad. It could indicate that he had not delivered as the head of MAIT's software division. Even though we had managed to convince his second-in-command, it didn't matter until Kohli was himself on board with the idea.

Despite the good intentions and relations, Kohli declined to join us.

An industry organization without TCS would be meaningless. We would be no different from any other city-based association, where ten people met regularly, and nothing ever happened. The problem was that, in Kohli's view, MAIT was already responsible for the lobbying work, and there was no need for yet another association.

Kohli was a reasonable man. In fact, I have a lot of respect for him. I used to call him a freedom fighter in a new avatar. While some people saw him as an autocratic person, he merely wanted people to do their homework before speaking. I remember, in 1977, when I met him for the job interview, instead of interviewing me, he spent his time trying to convince me to stay back in India. If he didn't see our vision, then we were doing a bad job of explaining it. This continued to prey on my mind. As happens so often with me, the solution came to me as an epiphany. This time, on a late-night walk in Sion. The key to convincing Kohli just popped into my head.

The government didn't understand that software was an *intangible* thing. It duplicated the regulations for hardware to govern software. They hadn't even really defined software. As a result, the RBI, the Income Tax Department, the Excise Department and the customs were clueless about which rules to apply to software. They were used to routing everything through existing hardware rules. However, those rules did not work for software. For instance, you can't show the customs department a sample of something that is being exported through data lines.

MAIT was primarily a hardware industry association. If it represented us, the software would never get the differentiation that was critical for its survival. It might seem obvious today, but we were able to change everybody's minds in our favour only after articulating the intangibility of software.

This intangibility was at the heart of all our problems. The only hope was an industry association dedicated to giving this intangible business an identity. I had hit upon the articulation I so needed.

I sought one more meeting with Kohli and explained all this to him. I gave him a few examples where hardware product regulations were applied to invisible software services. He finally bought the rationale and gave us his blessing. That is what is so great about Kohli. Despite being a part of MAIT as TCS, he knew the issues facing the software industry. He understood that MAIT was not the problem; it was the fact that we needed a greater focus on software, an industry based entirely on intangibles.

Kohli, however, suggested that I speak to Dr Mehra once again before going ahead and formalizing our association.

Buoyed by Kohli's endorsement, we organized a round-table meeting in Delhi and invited Dr Mehra. Instead of meeting him alone like the last time, we decided to bolster our argument with the presence of Nandan Nilekani of Infosys, Saurabh Srivastava of Tata Burroughs, Ashank Desai of Mastek, Joe Cleetus of DCM Data Products, Ashok Narsimhan of Wipro and a few others who were strong advocates of the new association.

Dr Mehra arrived. As he spoke, all of us listened with rapt attention. We could see that he was trying hard to hold on to MAIT. He portrayed us as unethical: as a breakaway group from MAIT. He reminded us that software was only a $50 million industry, while hardware was a much bigger industry. He persisted in his discouragement, chastising us as young people who didn't understand what we were getting into. He insisted that we were better off under MAIT.

Once again, we argued that we were not a breakaway group. We were just a different industry that had its own issues and needed an identity separate from what a hardware association could provide. Sensing the impasse, Dr Mehra left the meeting midway. As soon as the door shut behind him, we felt we were off the hook and could move ahead; we broke into laughter, more out of respite than anything else. By this time, there was nothing unexpected in Dr Mehra's reaction.

It was clear that irrespective of who was opposing or supporting us, we were going ahead with the association.

Assembling NASSCOM

As marvels of modern transportation, highways have a peculiar trait. If you miss the turn you need to take to get on or even get off the highway, you can keep going in circles for hours. Assembling NASSCOM was one such highway ride. We were often lost, and we had no reason to believe that what we were starting was going to last more than a few years. Nevertheless, we went about it very formally. The democratic culture of the founders and their goals would have to survive them if the association were to succeed. That could only happen if the association's daily operations were governed by a system of values. We needed our constitution to formalize our values into rules with legal validity.

So, quite ironically, we roped in MAIT's founder–president, Prem Shivdasani, who had the experience we needed because of his work on its constitution. Then we went shopping around Delhi's Connaught Place. There, we visited the offices of the Federation of Indian Chambers of Commerce and Industry (FICCI) and the Confederation of Indian Industry (CII) and asked for copies of their constitutions. Back in Mumbai, we also checked out the constitution of the Computer Society of India (CSI) and the Indian Merchants' Chamber (IMC).

With all this material on the desk, the core team started debating the finer points of our draft constitution. We met several times in my office, at the Bombay Gymkhana and in Adi Cooper's office. Adi was an advisor to Tata Infotech at that time. He was close to Kohli and continued with the Tatas in this capacity, even though he had quit the group after thirteen years of service. He was one of the first believers in our association and was part of the core team from the very start. Among those in this effort were core team pioneers like Ashank Desai and Sonata Software's Kanak Pandyan. As work progressed, many more got involved with varying levels of enthusiasm. We had begun to roll. Majrooh Sultanpuri would have summed it up thus: '*Log saath aate gae aur kārvāñ bantā gayā.*'[13]

We began to formulate the constitution. We defined all the important positions and their tenures. We learnt from other associations' mistakes

---

13 Translates into, 'Folks joined us along the way and the caravan continued to grow.'

and strengths.[14] To ensure that a set of people with a personal agenda did not end up controlling the body, we decided that no chairperson could hold office for more than one tenure without re-election. This rule put me in an odd situation later, when my term as the first elected chairperson of NASSCOM ended and everyone insisted that I take another term.[15] But I stood firm and made way for the next chairperson.

The membership fee was kept in the range of ₹5,000 to ₹20,000, depending on the turnover of the member company. I recall that soon after starting operations, it was a challenge to make people pay even ₹5,000. Undoubtedly, it was a substantial sum back then, especially for smaller companies, but it was also about the stigma attached to us. People continued to look upon us as a rebel group that broke away from MAIT. It was clear to many that associating with us meant antagonizing the powerful hardware people. On several occasions, money was short, and I was forced to choose between shutting us down and writing a cheque from my own business. I chose to fund it from my company every single time.

A twelve-member executive council (EC) was to be formed, and the procedure of electing its members was documented in the constitution. It would have both elected and nominated members, including past chairpersons and presidents. The EC's powers and functions were clearly defined, too.

It was also evident that we would not run like the community model of Rotary International or even like the IMC. We had no role for

---

14 Most people do not realize that it was because of this flexibility in our approach that NASSCOM could swerve and shift with the times and ever-evolving challenges.

15 The chairperson's tenure started out as two years. It was later shortened to one year so that we could attract more diverse inputs right at the top. Even now, when we induct new office-bearers at NASSCOM, we often do not have the need to. However, it is codified in our ethos that NASSCOM has to be larger than any one individual and thus change is not just essential but vital. Further, it helps us inject new blood into the system and keep it invigorated.

trustees. No position within the organization could become a parking spot for anyone. We were representing a technology industry that changed rapidly. It was critical that our offices see a succession of fresh minds and perspectives. Neither could we be like the CII, with a system of respect for past chairpersons or elderly statesmen. Nor could we depend on the laddering system of the Lions Club, where office-bearers moved up the rungs through the years as a process.

We kept things simple. We trusted and passed on all decision-making powers of the body to the elected members of the EC. We didn't codify much, and the system was kept open to modification by the EC. Further, we were also clear that none of us would have sufficient time to work on ever-evolving, complex issues; so, we decided to build a competent and empowered secretariat staffed with hand-picked professionals who were as committed to the body as we were. We were proud of the meritocracy in our industry; our association would be no different. We also cherished consensus. We could not have situations where members spoke differently from the association's public statements. On 16 June 1988, of the forty founders, seven stepped forward, one by one, to sign the constitution. They were, in alphabetical order, Ashank Desai, Kanak Pandyan, Lalit Kanodia of Datamatics, Prem Shivdasani, Saurabh Srivastava, Yash Pal Sahni of TCS and myself.

Another five of us, K.V. Ramani, Joe Cleetus, Saurabh Srivastava, Prem Shivdasani and I, formed the first executive council required to ink the papers.

Thus, despite all odds, the National Association of Software and Service Companies (NASSCOM)[16] was born,[17] with forty co-founders.

---

16 The task of naming our association also took some deliberation. Someone suggested ISSCOM, which stood for the Indian Association of Software and Service Companies. Eventually, NASSCOM sounded better to everyone's ears and we went ahead with it.

17 At the time, we hardly got any coverage in the media. One of the very few journalists to believe in the future of Indian software industry and support us was Madhu Valuri. A young journalist, he started a magazine titled *Software Review* to further lend support to the nascent industry.

Each person and each company that worked in the early days to get us off the ground is identified as the co-founder of NASSCOM.

This reminds me of an amusing incident. A few years ago, at the NASSCOM's annual leadership event, Salil Parekh (he was with Capgemini at the time) introduced the global COO of Capgemini to me. The gentleman introduced himself as one of the co-founders of NASSCOM. I was dumbfounded as I was meeting him for the first time, and, in all the years I had spent at NASSCOM, I had never heard his name. It turned out that Capgemini had acquired iGate in 2015, which in turn had acquired Patni Computer Systems in 2011, and Patni was one of the co-founders of NASSCOM!

More than anything else, to me, this was a heartening moment. This was testimony to the fact that some people who had rejected the idea of NASSCOM when we had started were now wanting to latch on to the pride associated with being a co-founder of NASSCOM.[18]

At the time of writing this book, it has been more than thirty years since that day. With very few amendments, the constitution survives and continues to serve NASSCOM effectively.

Oftentimes, I pause to think how NASSCOM almost did not happen. Repeatedly. And then I stop. I cannot bear to imagine the tragedy of the alternative reality.

NASSCOM went beyond transforming an industry. It transformed India. The millions of young people that the software industry recruited, trained and deputed around the globe created a new middle class in the country. Which, in turn, created a direct economic effect and contributed to stabilizing and strengthening the foreign exchange position. This helped India insulate itself from the risk of default on its debt. NASSCOM created a new work culture; one that is more egalitarian and global. Most importantly, it changed how the world

---

18 A little earlier, I mentioned an incident where one of our delegations to France was snubbed. For me, the COO of a French company wanting to associate himself with NASSCOM is a moment of immense pride!

perceived India. The stereotypes of the faqir[19] and the snake charmer were replaced with laptop-toting programmers and the ever-helpful people in the call centres.

But I am getting ahead of myself. I must allow the following few pages to complete the story of transformation that is still being written.

---

19   Wikipedia: 'In English, faqir or fakir originally meant a mendicant dervish. In mystical usage, the word faqir refers to man's spiritual need for God, who alone is self-sufficient.'

4

Fold the Future In

In the early 1990s, India was reeling under the aftermath of the implementation of the Mandal Commission Report. At the beginning of the book, I talked about the political and economic environment that forced us to create an industry body like the NASSCOM. We, as a country, were staring at bankruptcy, and the policymakers and the government seemed to have no clue about what to do.

An easy solution would have been to encourage entrepreneurship by loosening the policy framework. However, suspicions, rumours and news of corruption were routine. Politicians were, therefore, shy about openly working with big businesses. The government-industry collaboration required for inspired economic strategy stayed elusive.

If not the politicians, the bureaucrats could have helped. But they, too, had a poor opinion of big, family-run businesses. These were seen as greedy, self-centred capitalists who would do anything to grab profits while evading taxes.

It was clear that if India needed to reinvent its economy; it would have to change this dysfunctional relationship between the government and businesses. The system of mutual disrespect, suspicion and maintaining the status quo would have to yield to respect, trust and accelerated change.

It was not a surprise that NASSCOM's initial conversations with the bureaucrats were met with the same scepticism they had for businesses in general. NASSCOM was set up to do the impossible by trying to align the industry and government into a single-minded mission that would change the destiny of the nation. But before that, it needed to win respect and trust. Only with frequent interactions did it dawn upon the bureaucrats that the set of entrepreneurs in the software industry was completely different[1] from the businesspeople they were so loath to deal with.

We once requested a seemingly empathetic bureaucrat to remove the excise duty that had been put on work-in-progress—ongoing projects that were yet to be delivered. On behalf of NASSCOM, I explained to him that he could not charge excise duty on software services, as there is already a service tax for that. This riled him, and he remarked, 'If I want, I can even tax the air you are breathing.' He felt as though we were confronting his authority. He told us that we could 'request him, but not challenge him'.

We remained persistent until, finally, he relented. He agreed to cooperate and cleverly reduced the duty to 'zero'. If he had made it 'nil', he would have to seek his boss's approval in the future to increase it again. By keeping it zero, he had kept the liberty to raise it at a future date in his own hands.

The pioneers of the Indian IT industry were unassuming yet proud visionaries. These technocrats were mostly educated abroad, familiar with the incredible power of innovation and emerging computing technologies that could change India forever.

---

1   The difference is in the background and intent of these entrepreneurs. These software industry entrepreneurs did not come from privileged backgrounds and did not want to cut corners as they built their businesses.

NASSCOM stood in contrast to how other industries were representing themselves to the government. We insisted on meritocracy. We did not seek partisan protectionism and the favouring of a few big businesses. Instead, NASSCOM demanded open policies that rewarded individuals and companies based on their merit alone. To the bureaucrats' surprise, we were asking for the playing field to be levelled so that we could compete across the world on an equal footing. They were thrilled to see an India-first strategy.

Most businesses and industry bodies were closed about their inner workings, hoping to take advantage of the bureaucrats' lack of domain expertise. In contrast, NASSCOM invited the bureaucrats to every meeting it could and had them visit our companies to get a first-hand insight into the software industry's challenges. That is how 'they' became 'us', and the trust started building up.

We further supported bureaucrats by providing all the data they might need. We gave them head-to-head comparisons with the diamond industry, which was perceived to be champion forex grosser. However, in reality, its net forex earnings were a much smaller amount. In terms of job creation as well, the software industry created many more high-end, disposable-income-generating jobs.

Bureaucrats eventually realized that there was nothing to lose by listening to the software people. If the software did well, they would do well and so would India!

NASSCOM sold its software vision passionately, and we armed the bureaucrats with clarity to fight on behalf of our organization. I would ask bureaucrats, 'What will your children do when they grow up?' They thought that through their goodwill and influence they would get their children placed in respectable jobs; maybe have them settle down abroad. I found these answers extremely disheartening. The software industry could provide their children with the future they dreamed of right here in India, on merit, without calling upon political power or influence. My optimism would light up their eyes, and their attitude towards us would soften immediately.

Popular culture tends to paint all bureaucrats as outmoded, bribe-seeking, selfish people. In my personal experience, this was far from the truth. There were plenty of bureaucrats who genuinely wanted to make a difference. If that were not the case, they would not be entertaining our overtures, year after year without a single incident of bribery.

Our work with the government, bureaucrats and departments, ranging from the DoE and home ministry to the customs, revenue and excise departments to even institutions like the RBI and the Securities and Exchange Board of India (SEBI), ended up impacting more than 100 regulations. Some of these took more than five years of advocacy to bring about change. Such was breadth and depth of our engagement.

Boot crash

Impossible events led to the formation of NASSCOM in 1988. The odds against which it eventually came into being makes it nothing short of a miracle. But there was more to come. Wait till you hear about how the association turned the grinding wheel. The first turn was to put the right people in the right seats.

We had agreed upon a two-person leadership team. The first, the president, would be a full-time employee. The second, the chairperson,[2] would be an industry veteran who understood business challenges.

The chairperson was to be the public face of NASSCOM. This person's stature would become NASSCOM's stature. If we wished to equal MAIT's credibility, we would need someone as revered as F.C. Kohli or Dr O.P. Mehra. Qualities like credibility and assertiveness were functionally crucial for this position.

Ideally, we would have Kohli himself take up office. But he had made it clear that he would continue at MAIT because he wanted to see both hardware and software industries grow in India.

---

2   When we started, there were different titles for these posts, but to avoid confusion, I will go with the current designations.

I could not have held that role because I was just not senior enough. Hinditron also had a JV going on with DEC. Besides, I had suffered a heart attack the previous year.

Eventually, we approached the much-respected Prem Shivdasani, who had just retired from International Computers Indian Manufacture Ltd (ICIM) and started his own software business. ICIM was then one of the top IT companies in the country. Shivdasani had also been the founder president of MAIT. He just fit the bill.

After an initial reluctance lasting six months, Shivdasani promised to come on board, but only until formal elections were held. Once he consented, we started getting other people to join us as well. I took up the positions of vice-chairperson[3] and treasurer. From then on, there was no looking back.

We got Anil Srivastava on board as president. Anil was an advisor to the government, and had held positions in the private sector in the domains of information and communications technology. He was articulate and wrote well; just the man we thought we needed to liaise with the government. NASSCOM was set for a good start.

Or so we thought.

We took the first stumble when we realized that Anil was not aligned with NASSCOM's vision and mandate. We wanted NASSCOM to primarily build an ecosystem that would help software businesses thrive. That, in part, meant focusing on government policy and lobbying for the industry. The ecosystem would evolve, but in those early days, lobbying was the key to getting there. This involved meeting bureaucrats and politicians, and debating industry issues, convincing them to bring in

---

3   In the initial days at NASSCOM, the honorary positions were accorded the titles of president and vice-president. The head of NASSCOM was called the executive director (ED). Both Anil Srivastava and Dewang Mehta joined with that title. However, after Dewang came in to run NASSCOM on a day-to-day basis, the honorary designations were changed to chairperson and vice-chairperson.

the changes we sought. Besides, we expected Anil to set NASSCOM on the path to economic and organizational sustainability.

Anil instead enjoyed writing academic articles in newspapers and other publications. He was good at making presentations, but he lacked the entrepreneurial spirit that NASSCOM desperately needed to stay afloat. He wanted to be an evangelist, not a lobbyist.

There were other issues as well. Within a few months, the always hands-on Narayana Murthy brought to my notice that NASSCOM's expenses were piling up alarmingly. I had remained focused on long-term issues and trusted the team with day-to-day operations. This had led to an accumulated debt of ₹10,00,000. When I started investigating, I realized that we were running NASSCOM with the lavishness of an established business and not that of a non-profit or a start-up. Anil had even rented the fuel-guzzling Standard 2000 sedan at the association's expense. In exasperation, I reached out to Anil and requested him to draw up a budget. He responded by sending me an article titled 'Start-ups Don't Have a Budget'. Thereon, things just went south, bringing our relationship with Anil to an abrupt end. Our experience with Anil gave us an important lesson in managing people and their expectations. We were probably not clear in defining the role and that probably created this mismatch. NASSCOM's ability to deliver took a beating, and something had to be done urgently to stay afloat.

It took our collective confidence to overcome the situation. We had forty members at the time, and we requested everyone to share the burden. The industry agreed unconditionally. Narayana Murthy chipped in by offering an industry-wide training on AS400 (you will read more about this in Chapter 5). It was this faith in the vision that gave NASSCOM another chance even before it had begun to deliver.

We were still picking up the threads after Anil's exit in 1991 when NASSCOM's first election was called. I felt very honoured when about forty members unanimously voted to make me the first chairperson of NASSCOM in 1989. We are proud that to this day, the tradition of consensus-building continues with every election we hold.

Upon becoming chairperson, I got down to searching in earnest for a suitable president. A committee comprising four to five industry leaders was constituted. We wanted a young person with an entrepreneurial spirit at NASSCOM. We interviewed about fifteen people through a recruitment agency, but, none were found suitable. We also looked at the EC for nominees, but at the time, no one volunteered. We searched among professors, academicians, and retired bureaucrats, but none fit the bill. The appointment was beginning to become a concern now. If we didn't find our ideal president soon, NASSCOM was bound to drift away. The search grew frenetic.

Enter Dewang

I first learnt about Dewang Mehta when I read an article that he wrote for the *Economic Times*. He had reported his takeaways from a technology conference. His ability to grasp and communicate the key highlights from that event impressed me. When I found out that Dewang worked as an electronic data processing (EDP) manager[4] for Orissa Cement, I was even more impressed because he had articulated industry issues as well as an insider would, even though he was not from a software services background.

The next time I visited Delhi, I looked him up. We hit it off immediately. We bonded over a common last name and our love for street food, especially chaat. We started meeting regularly on my Delhi trips and talked over paani puri at Bengal Sweets or South Indian meals at Saravana Bhavan. I was amazed by Dewang's high-energy personality that enjoyed being the centre of attention. He wore this Elvis Presley–inspired hairstyle, complete with a grand quiff. Wherever he went, he would form relationships with people, irrespective of their social standing or importance. His memory was astonishing: on a

---

4   At the time, an EDP manager's responsibility was equivalent to that of a chief information officer (CIO) in today's day and age. However, back then, the technology landscape was still nascent and thus, the scope was fairly limited; it can be compared to the responsibilities handled by a delivery manager.

visit to a government office, he was quite likely to chat with an office assistant about his mother's health, the details of which he could recall from a conversation six months ago.

He was fiercely patriotic. Maybe it was because of his schooling at the Bharatiya Vidya Bhavan in Delhi where he inculcated such strong values. Often, while reading about a sordid affair in the newspapers, his eyes would well up with tears. He was particularly affected by the plight of the marginalized and by the abysmal state of the economy. Many times, on reading news of corruption, he would ask me, 'Aapdo desh kyare sudharse?'[5]

My meetings with Dewang overlapped with my search for a NASSCOM president. I started asking him for recommendations as well. And then, in a eureka moment, I wondered: why not Dewang himself?

He was an unlikely candidate for several reasons: firstly, he was not from the software services business and wasn't an engineer. Then, I was aware that his current salary was way higher than what NASSCOM could afford as a non-profit. Also, Dewang had a very assertive personality, which might not have worked within NASSCOM's culture of consensus. Yet, if I could help Dewang channelize his assertiveness, he could be the best man for the top job.

From the moment the idea to hire Dewang struck me, I could not think of anyone else. If Dewang took up the job, it would be a complete career switch from being an EDP manager. It might be commonplace today, but such a dramatic career move at that time was unheard of. Almost everybody started their career in a domain in their early twenties and retired in an extension of the same job at sixty. India's change-averse culture did not look upon career switches as a good thing. Yet, I had a contrary opinion. I continue to believe that shifts and changes are for dynamic people capable of learning and adapting to the times. I've changed my career five times myself and often say

---

5   Translates to: 'When will our country improve?'

that career switches are made out to be a much bigger deal than they are. Many successful business leaders have done great things in the technology space in spite of not having a technology background.

While Dewang did not have all the qualities we wanted in a president, he would go on to redefine that office with the skills he brought in. He was a chartered accountant, which meant he had the skills to get us out of the financial mess that we were in. He was also an award-winning graphic designer and could help us rebrand ourselves in a very professional manner. The newspaper article he had written had already illustrated that he understood technology as a business to some extent and was very articulate. His people skills were easy to see in every interaction I had with him. But more than anything else, he had the mind of a shopkeeper. A typical Indian shopkeeper understands the importance of ending every single day with a positive cash flow instead of investing in an imaginary future. We had plenty of visionaries with us. What we needed was an executor with an eye on the ball. We needed someone who would make sure that we were financially sustainable.

Dewang was only twenty-nine years old at the time but well set in his career. When he heard my offer, he started laughing loudly. He could not imagine working in a non-profit organization. He was earning ₹15,000 per month, which was several times the industry standard for the post of president at a non-profit. There was no structured career path, and nobody knew the future of NASSCOM at the time. Typically, a prospective employee needs to pitch himself to an employer. In this case, I had to pitch the NASSCOM job to him. So, Dewang interviewed me instead. Since then, such has been the calibre of NASSCOM presidents that it has always been us pitching to them.

For Dewang, the clincher, I think, was the opportunity that NASSCOM offered. As its president, he could finally do the meaningful work of building an entire industry and make a difference to the country. His life's purpose and his passion were getting aligned.

Dewang thought about it for a week and eventually agreed, subject to a reasonable salary. I told the executive council (EC) about Dewang, and everybody who knew him agreed immediately. But the big question about his salary was still hanging in the air. At this point, the EC said that if we wanted the right talent, we would have to pay the price for it. They asked me to negotiate with Dewang and bring him on board.

Even then, the maximum NASSCOM could pay was ₹10,000 per month. So, I proposed to Dewang that he could start working four days a week for us and continue with his graphic designing work on the remaining days to make up for his loss of income. After he joined, to the best of my knowledge, I don't think he took up work outside of NASSCOM, even for a day.

The role of the president was an unusual one. There was no experience that could fully prepare a candidate for the job. Dewang, and the presidents that followed, had to undergo behavioural and management conditioning in order to adapt. I told Dewang that he needed to operate like the CEO of a start-up and treat NASSCOM like his own child. I knew his dream for India would propel our industry forward, and he would set an exceedingly high bar for himself. In any case, I would not have been able to set a bar for him because there was no data or precedent to go by.

Dewang needed acclimatizing on functional as well as managerial fronts. As I was the chairperson and because of the personal equation I had with him, the responsibility fell on me. In the world of the export of IT services, he was a complete outsider. So, I started by educating him about the intangibility of software services. I told him that this industry ran on 'evidence-based marketing'. Software services are invisible and cannot be demonstrated like a software product. A prospective client can experience the software service only after its delivery, not at the time of placing the order.

We had many long conversations about the competitive advantages that Indian software services had and the challenges we faced with the Santacruz Electronic Export Processing Zone (SEEPZ), the RBI and the customs. He would often come to my office and spend time just trying to understand the workings of the business. I would answer his questions patiently. There wasn't any official induction programme, but Dewang was constantly seeking me to learn and improve his grip on industry matters.

The other aspect was about managing people. Dewang understood the strengths and weaknesses of a voluntary peer-to-peer model in a non-profit. There was no compulsion for any software company or CEO to remain a member of NASSCOM. Every EC member was a successful entrepreneur. Getting everyone engaged was part of the job. He always said that he had been impressed with the way I had introduced him at the EC meeting by urging everybody to meet him individually before he joined. This was to secure consensus on the acceptance of his candidacy. He had been set up for success.

Among the first orders of business that Dewang and I took up was to create a corporate-style brand for NASSCOM. I had a good experience in rebranding Hinditron. Good graphic designers were hard to come by in the 1990s, but we were lucky to have Dewang's skills available to us.

So, as soon as he joined, he got down to rebranding NASSCOM. Our events started showing the international finesse that we were hoping for. All of them now had professionally designed backdrops at a time when there were no backdrops at most events.

Over the years, the NASSCOM brand became increasingly chic and dramatic. Even global consultants would toe the line that we drew.[6] Further, from fashion shows to industry gatherings, everything had the air of celebration. This was very unconventional in those days. Once, Dr Prakash Hebalkar of ProfiTech asked me, 'Harish, are you running a serious organization or a social club?' I had to explain that we thought it was important to build camaraderie among members.

---

6   In 1996, we first commissioned McKinsey to do a study on the next big thing. The usual practice would have been to release the report with the consultant's name in the title. We, however, insisted that since the report had our data and insights as the trigger on which they built further, the report should be titled the NASSCOM-McKinsey report. They consented.

If we were representing the software industry with one voice, it was imperative that the industry members also drew together as one.

All these activities built up Dewang's public profile. It was also natural that there were ego clashes between him and the chairpersons who followed me. I often found myself gently intervening to restore harmony. But these clashes were always managed gracefully.

I remember an incident, once, when Dewang did not approve of a chairperson's views on some policy. He, therefore, didn't want him to be present at NASSCOM's press conference; however, he was not in a position to ask the chairperson to skip the event. So, Dewang called the chairperson's secretary, found out on what dates he would not be in the country. He held the press conference then.

Personally and professionally, Dewang pushed himself to his physical limits. He had earned a reputation for his conscientiousness. If we were meeting a government officer to discuss, say, section 56 of some law, Dewang would have thoroughly researched its impact on, say, sections 27, 59 and 67, too. He made sure that he did as much of the bureaucrat's work as he could, leaving the least possible scope for counterarguments or the rejection of our ideas. He would ensure that things got done and nothing was ever left incomplete.

In the coming years, while a few of us worked behind the scenes to propel NASSCOM forward, Dewang became the face of India's software revolution. He was now the go-to man for any IT-related policy for the Union Government of India and almost all state governments. He became a close advisor to several ministers. He had reached a stage where he would get uncomfortable if he didn't get mentioned in the *Economic Times* of the day. Dewang was everywhere. With his unique skills and instincts, he set the IT industry into motion, which by 2020, was employing 4 million people directly and, by some estimates, seven to eight times as many indirectly.[7] The impact becomes a lot more evident when you extrapolate numbers and realize that the IT

---

7   As per estimates, one BPO sector job creates up to three or four indirect jobs, while an IT sector job creates up to twelve indirect jobs in some cases.

industry is the economic contributor to approximately 30–40 million households, and has touched almost 10 per cent of the population in the country.[8]

Although it was tough to rein him in, the task was unofficially mine. As a friend, confidant, and mentor, I commanded his trust like no one did. We spoke every alternate day. In the interest of NASSCOM, I had taken it upon myself to temper his ambition when needed and provide guidance as an industry insider to correct his course if he strayed too much.

If I were to pick Dewang's single most important quality, it would be his complete disregard for the impossible. Some thought this was detrimental to NASSCOM. But those were not the people who had ever sat across the table from a sixty-five-year-old politician, trying to convince him that India was about to become an IT superpower; that too without any data or evidence. To do that, you needed the streak of madness that Dewang had.

Vital Vittal

The Department of Electronics (DoE) in the late 1980s was considered a scientific department along with the Department of Atomic Energy and the Department of Space. It thus had technocrats as its secretaries from 1970 to 1988. However, a difference of opinion between two bureaucrats in 1989 led to the department becoming a 'non-scientific department' and an Indian Administrative Service (IAS) officer, N. Vittal, was appointed as the Secretary of the DoE.

Vittal was a non-technical and generalist bureaucrat. He was much more dynamic and business-savvy than the technocrats previously at the department. He was eager to learn about anything that could

---

8   As per the 2001 census, India has approximately 188 million households and just 54 millions of those are in urban settlements. More details at: https://www.censusindia.gov.in/2011-common/census_data_2001.html and at https://censusindia.gov.in/Data_Products/Data_Highlights/Data_Highlights_link/data_highlights_hh1_2_3.pdf.

get the nation out of the economic mess it was in. He started with focusing on only electronics, as he was not aware of the potential of the software business then. Yet, he ended up as our biggest champion within the government.

One of the first things Vittal did after taking office was to invite all industry associations for a meeting. He wanted to understand their expectations. When we received the invitation, we realized that the list was of associations representing hardware businesses. We were the only exception.

We had spent considerable energy explaining the intangible nature of software and our industry's unique problems. With this invitation, we realized how much more needed to be done. We dreaded that our lone voice for the software industry would be drowned out with so many hardware associations around us.

Given that the invitation had come from somebody so senior, the natural thing to do was to attend. But we chose to skip the event. Some thought it was audacious of us because 'the DoE secretary was no less than a god for the industry'.

Indeed, a few days later, when we sought a meeting with Vittal, his personal assistant was terribly upset with us. Speaking with him made us realize that Vittal, too, was miffed. Even as we were worried about having burnt bridges with the new secretary, an appointment with Vittal came through quickly. We wondered what made him grant us an audience. Perhaps it was his curiosity about our motives to not accept his invitation.

Vittal heard us out and grudgingly accepted our reasons. Gradually, he opened up and began understanding our perspectives. We told him about our ambitious vision for the software services industry, wondering if he would buy into it. He did.

When I told him, though, that the software business's potential was $1 billion, he had a hearty laugh and asked me, 'Young man, do you know how many zeroes are in 1 billion?'

When the conversation shifted to our requests, his guard went up. He was expecting us to demand something outrageous. He asked us for our top three pain points, which he could work towards. We told him that would be an incremental approach when what we needed was a complete overhaul of the ecosystem.

The day before, this realization had dawned on us while we were planning for the meeting. NASSCOM was young and had to first become a part of the government's policymaking process. To make an impact, we would have to be on top of their minds. The only way to do that would be to make the DoE agree to consult us whenever they were dealing with policies that affected software businesses. Because NASSCOM did not promote the agendas of a few powerful companies and always thought in terms of industry ecosystems, we were confident our data and our vision would convince the bureaucrats to make the right decisions. Further, we decided to position ourselves as a 'sunrise industry' to Vittal. NASSCOM was like a start-up with nothing much to lose. We were as hungry as we were foolish.

Vittal's surprise was evident when we merely asked to be consulted before any change was made in processes or procedures where the word 'software' appears. The DoE was a nodal agency for 'software' and every change for our industry needed its approval. All the bureaucrats around him warned him against making this commitment to us. But Vittal thought that our request was innocuous. He reminded the bureaucrats that we were only asking to be consulted. The final decision on the policies would still be theirs. This straightforward meeting flagged off a significant period in the government-industry relations.

This simple mechanism of consulting NASSCOM before making any policy change became a game-changer for the industry.

The year 1991 is historic because it kicked off the liberalization of the Indian economy. For the software business, the year is significant for yet another reason. The World Bank was conducting a study to assess the potential of the Indian software business. The government had paid for this research. Initially, NASSCOM had been missed and was not part of this effort. We approached Vittal and reminded him that they were supposed to consult us before taking any decision and that we should have been consulted for this research as well. Vittal not only agreed, he went ahead and made NASSCOM and other industry bodies a part of this effort. When we read the terms of references, our suspicion was confirmed. The report was expected to be focused heavily on software products and largely ignore the software services business.[9]

We met World Bank's Robert Schware, who was heading the research, and explained how it was not software products but software services that held the biggest potential for India back then. Thus, the report should highlight that. We had several meetings with him before establishing our points of view. We even went to the USA to explain the Indian scenario and the changes required for the industry to flourish. We were continually engaged, and went back and forth over data till Schware had all the relevant information. He and his team did their research, and came back with a report that shocked everyone, including Vittal.

The report declared that Indian software services exports had the potential to be a $1 billion industry. Considering that the industry turnover at the time was a measly $150 million, this was a mind-boggling figure. The report said that software services were

---

9   Often misunderstood, software products and software services are entirely different from each other. A product is a one-size-fits-all, off-the-shelf product that functions exactly the same for everyone. A service by its very nature is customizable and is tweaked as per requirements, and is customized for each deployment.

Here is an analogy from an unrelated industry to give you a simplistic example. When you want to get your home painted, you buy paint of a certain colour from a certain brand. This paint is the product. Then you hire a contractor or a painter to apply this paint to your walls. This act of painting is a service.

The paint remains the same for every buyer. The act of painting, on the other hand, differs from painter to painter and house to house.

one of the fastest-growing Indian exports, behind only raw cotton. It said, 'Software service exports can fuel India's economic growth and development.' It stated that offshoring was the future, that it was a segment set to explode, and that India had all the elements required to capture the opportunity.

Apart from the potential of software services, the report listed thirty to forty recommendations to the government for the services business. From the DoE's perspective, the report validated our claims of a bright future, and they were quick to align forces with us.

Vittal came up with the Software Technology Parks of India (STPI) scheme to provide high-speed data links within a city. Consequently, we worked on details of the STPI alongside him. This crucial change in the attitude of the DoE towards us would not have come about without Vittal's proactive support. He not only put the might of his department behind us, but he also talked about us up across the government, bringing in all-round support.

Vittal loved working with NASSCOM and behaved like one of us. He once remarked, 'In NASSCOM, N stands for nuts, A for ass, S for stupid, S for screwball, C for crazy, O for oddball, M for mad. And I am the leader of this group.'

Spurred on by this new-found potential of the software industry, Vittal put out a press release announcing that export benefits to software services had been extended, subject to the industry meeting a target of $400 million in forex earnings within one year. When we read this, we went to Vittal and told him that it was an impossible target. He was asking us to increase our earnings by two-and-a-half-fold in one year. This was just not workable in a project-driven business. What made it even more difficult was that we did not have the requisite number of project managers in the country. Prakash Hebalkar, a bold thinker, suggested we import these project managers. However, hiring from America and UK had its own challenge.

Vittal told us that MAIT had already promised him that the industry would achieve this target. The Electronics and Software Export

Promotion Council (ESC) of India had agreed, too. We realized that the other associations agreed to the target only because they wanted an extension of tax benefits in the 1991 liberalization package. We told Vittal that the benefits were welcome, but we could not claim those under a false assurance. Vittal was pleasantly surprised by our honesty.

It was then conveyed to us that all we needed to do was not openly challenge the target numbers. Vittal narrated an Akbar–Birbal story for us: Emperor Akbar was upset with the court jester, Birbal[10], and ordered him, 'Make a horse fly, or you will be hanged!' Birbal said that he could do that in six months. When a couple of months passed by and nothing happened, Birbal's worried wife asked him if he could really make the horse fly. Birbal replied that he did not know. He had only bought time. 'Who knows? In six months, the horse may die. Or I may die. Or Emperor Akbar may die. Or the horse may fly.' We understood that our target was, in fact, Birbal's horse.

The only difference was that our horse actually did fly. A few years later, when we achieved the target, we learnt of what had really transpired.

Vittal knew we were keen to continue enjoying the tax benefits beyond one year. So, he had met Bimal Jalan, the then secretary to the Ministry of Finance and convinced him that the export of software services was in for extraordinary growth. Jalan wanted Vittal to put a number to it. Vittal told him $300 million. Jalan thought it could be $500 million. They settled on an average of $400 million.

We had been growing at a healthy 15 per cent per annum since 1988, three years before liberalization.[11] Even then, extrapolating from

---

10 My friend Harsh Manglik holds the character of Birbal in high regard. He often telle me that Birbal was probably the most important of the Nav Ratnas in Akbar's court. He further says that Birbal was often considered Akbar's closest confidant and trusted advisor. Harsh is a former NASSCOM chairperson and a former chairperson of Accenture in India

11 As per a 2004 paper titled 'Indian Software Industry', Prof. Subhash Bhatnagar of IIM Ahmedabad found that the industry clocked $330 million in exports in 1994, $450 million in 1995 and $1.1 billion in 1997.

our numbers would not have met the target set by the government, let alone the more significant numbers that the World Bank foresaw for us.

Though the Jalan–Vittal story may sound very unreasonable, it really was not. When you see a vision, you cannot just extrapolate to it.

As the noted management thinker, C.K. Prahalad said, 'You must fold the future in.' And did we fold it? I'll leave you with some numbers and let you decide.

When we seeded NASSCOM in 1988, the IT services export revenue was all of $52 million. In 2017, this number had touched $154 billion, a 10,000-times growth[12] in less than thirty years. The compounding effect of an early start and consistent growth has been staggering.

The forex issue that I talked about at the beginning of the chapter?

Well, today, the IT industry delivers an estimated $150 billion[13] of net forex earning, *each year*! To add perspective to this number, this is almost 50 per cent of India's total services exports. Further, this number is nearly equal to the forex that Saudi Arabia earns each year[14] by exporting oil. We all know of the impact the IT industry has had on the culture, economy and society. Imagine the change that we've brought about in India.

These numbers, the growth and the resultant impact on the country, may sound surreal, but it was a long, hard road. Allow me to show you how we navigated this journey that even the most ardent of supporters thought was impossible to tread.

These numbers may look small, but were way beyond even the most optimistic estimates.

12 We delivered a compounded annual growth rate of over 30 per cent in the 1990s. This takes into account revenue growth for both exports and domestic markets. This growth also includes the dollar rates prevalent in respective years. Further, while the growth multiple is 10,000-times in terms of rupees, in absolute dollar terms, it is approximately 3,000-times.

13 As of FY 2021.

14 As of FY 2020.

5

Thriving in Chaos

Navigating through crises

I had a lot going on in the late 1980s and early 1990s: I've talked about starting NASSCOM and how turbulent the period was for India. There were numerous regulatory blocks that we faced with work. It wasn't just industry and nation, though. My personal life was in chaos as well. My family was dealing with a health crisis, and my career skidded off the highway.

In the summer of 1985, my partner, Mike Shah, and I planned a month-long holiday, along with our families, at the Hinditron guesthouse in Bangalore. It was Shaila's idea that we go on this holiday. Although she loved being among people, she seldom complained about the little time I had for family. Managing three children who were a handful must have been exhausting, but she made it look easy. For me, despite the challenges at work, this was the most blissful life anyone could have asked for.

The Bangalore trip began with a blast. The children went sightseeing every other day. In the evenings, we played antakshari. Shaila would almost always win. She was a great sport and fun to be with.

Then, in the beginning of the second week, Shaila complained of pain in the chest. It was severe. I was concerned.

Mike helped us find a good doctor, who, upon examination, called for a biopsy. The family was anxious for the report. While I was nervous, Shaila didn't seem too perturbed. She probably hid her emotions, as her first instinct always was to protect the children. After an anxious wait, the reports came in. We were numb with shock. Shaila was diagnosed with breast cancer.

She was not even forty yet, and we just couldn't believe anything might happen to her.

There was no history of cancer in her family, and we believed we had a healthy lifestyle. We were in denial and, on our return to Mumbai, immediately visited the Tata Memorial Hospital for a second opinion. The second biopsy confirmed the diagnosis, too.

Too much had happened already. We had lost Chirant when he was a mere toddler. My father had died relatively young as well. If anything were to happen to Shaila, I would be devastated. I had three young children to worry about as well.

We checked with friends in the US and sought to fly her there for treatment. We assumed the West was the best. To our surprise, we were told the treatment in India was adequate and on the right track. In times like these, it is easy to slip into self-pity and ask, 'Why me?' But the doctors explained that breast cancer occurred randomly and had nothing to do with our lifestyle.

A surgery was required immediately. Preparing for the worst, we even got her will made. Within a matter of a few days, Shaila was operated upon for the removal of a breast. Thankfully, the surgery went as planned. But she was not out of the woods; far from it. Post-surgery began the excruciatingly painful process of chemotherapy. Shaila started losing her hair first, and then her vitality. We maintained a silent calm throughout the whole process. Neither of us shed a single tear, and we tried our best to remain positive. It broke my heart to see her go through this, but she kept up a cheerful mood. She joked about her wig and didn't try to hide it from anyone. Neither of us let our worries show; that would devastate our children.

The sword of Damocles dangled perilously over our heads. After a few agonising months, Shaila finally began responding to the treatment. And then came the day when she defeated cancer successfully. Or so it seemed. The doctors cautioned us that there was a chance of recurrence in the next five years and that she must check for it regularly.

Sometimes, putting on a brave facade takes a toll within. Just when we thought we had recovered from Shaila's ordeal, I suffered a heart attack. Perhaps it was due to the stress that came with her illness, maybe because of my smoking, or perhaps both. All that had seemed to be mending started to fall apart once again. It was 1987. I was forty years old and bang in the middle of doing the DEC–Hinditron JV and struggling to form NASSCOM. Though my business was doing well, I was not wealthy enough to secure my family's future without regular income. I realized I had to make radical changes to my lifestyle and quit smoking. Since that day, I have never had another cigarette.

Minding my business

To go back in time to the late 1970s, I was still a thirty-something 'young man' when I joined Hinditron and put myself up for a rollercoaster ride.

To even get started, we needed to secure the finances required for the import of PDP-11 machines. My partners and I met Lalita Gupte[1] at ICICI Bank to seek a loan. We gave her our business plans and

---

1   She later went on to become a joint managing director at ICICI Bank.

tried to sell the vision of the company. At the time, it was unheard of for banks to extend loans to ideas similar to ours, but she made an exception and got a loan of ₹1.3 million sanctioned for us.

If getting the loan was not challenging enough, due to the policies at the time, we had to take this loan in foreign currencies (the Swiss franc, German mark and Japanese yen). At the time, currency risk hedging was not allowed. With each passing year, these currencies kept appreciating. The cost of capital thus started to rise, and with it, the interest that we owed to the bank. We eventually ended up paying more than double of what we borrowed. Managing this unpredictable foreign exchange fluctuation was a big challenge at that time.

To add to the misery of this uncertain wild ride, the machine that we imported was half-baked. Half-baked may sound harsh, but that's what it was. DEC had force-fitted a commercial application environment on top of a scientific machine, and, as a result, many key features required by the market were missing. For example, the machine did not have a COBOL[2] compiler that was required to write the commercial software that would run on the machine. There was no batch processing capability that was essential to commercial applications. The computing performance was itself three times slower compared to others in the market.

It was a setback right when we started. But after the initial hiccups, it became a relatively smooth ride, and the business grew steadily—the software exports business being the bright spot! We also grew from five partners to six when Arvind Shah joined Hemant Sonawala, Kamlesh Sonawala, Mike Shah, Pravin Gandhi and me.

However, the calm ride was short-lived and we soon hit turbulent times. India's foreign exchange crisis had hit Hinditron especially hard. Just like us at Hinditron, our customers were also required to spend forex to import DEC computers and they started to rethink their decisions.

---

2   A popular programming language back then.

This business was a cash cow for Hinditron, but it was increasingly becoming a struggle to continue running it. The regulations were so restrictive that sometimes it took almost two years for a customer to complete the paperwork and formalities required for the import.

The potential of the business was restricted artificially by the regulators. In the rapidly changing world of technology, this was like a speed breaker on a highway, which was neither desired nor required.

So, in 1986, when India opened up computer manufacturing, it made a lot of sense for a DEC factory in India, with Hinditron as the JV partner.

India was a peculiar choice for DEC to focus on. The local market was small, the tantrums of Indian bureaucracy were well known, and, most importantly, any investment in the country would have needed at least a decade to bear fruit. Yet, DEC agreed to set up a manufacturing facility in India, that too for the latest MicroVAX series of computers.

DEC computers were typically used by research and development (R&D) organizations and defence applications. The MicroVAX was ideal for the Indian commercial environment. After scouting around, we concurred that Bangalore was the ideal location. The city had the talent available in its many R&D institutes and universities. It had an ecosystem of vendors for semiconductors and PCBs. Plus, most of the potential clients were also based in Bangalore.

The JV with DEC was a big break for Hinditron. Dick Paulson was DEC's India head at the time. He had a cowboy-like domineering personality. He drove a Jeep Cherokee in the US and once took me for a drive around Route 121, Boston, the then Silicon Valley of the East Coast. He shared his outlandish dream of replacing all the big IT company logos and hoardings along the route with DEC's signage. The way DEC's stock had risen in the US, Dick's dream seemed to be coming true. Even we at Hinditron dreamed of a big payday when we eventually exited.

Bob Dale, the DEC Asia Pacific chief financial officer (CFO), who was negotiating with us, remarked, 'Have you guys thought about what you will do with so much money on your hands? You are all so young.' Our JV was to be listed on the Bombay Stock Exchange (now called BSE).

However, DEC's financial and legal teams were as strong as its fabled R&D team. The terms of the JV were tilted in their favour.

On one occasion, we went to Dick and requested five changes in our agreement. Dick made it clear that he wasn't going to budge on even one. He said that the contract was derived from the term sheet we had signed earlier, and that he was not going to accommodate any requests. He gave us just an hour to agree to his terms. We found it very discomfiting that we did not have a vote in the JV board while DEC had all the votes. More so, DEC had veto power. We could voice our opinions, but DEC could choose to accept or reject those. It felt unfair, but we were so desperate for this JV to fructify that we agreed to withdraw our request.

We had to endure all kinds of demands from DEC. I remember once we booked a separate room for their executive's dog in Bangalore's finest hotel. I was amused that even their dog enjoyed more privileges than we did.

Later, I realized that this story had played out with many fledgling companies in India back in the time. Today, however, Indian software companies are a force to reckon with. NASSCOM, and the brilliance of the companies it represents, has won this respect and power through decades of hard work.

I may not agree with DEC on a few things, but I cannot deny their integrity in setting up the manufacturing facility. Their code of ethics was unquestionable. There was not even a single conversation about finding a loophole or a way around regulations. At no point did they ever want to mislead any stakeholders, from customers to employees to regulators.

Since with the JV, we did not have a way out, we kept our heads down and continued to work. Once the legal agreements on the JV with DEC were complete, we began setting up the business. Running a manufacturing unit was going to be much more complicated than the business we doing until then. Negotiations started for board seats and the position of the managing director (MD). The MD's position came with a substantial salary, a lavish house, and several other perks. Like most other matters, the MD was going to be decided upon by DEC, not us.

In one of my meetings with DEC in Boston, Dick asked me to take up the position and move to Bangalore. However, I had moved to Mumbai from the US to be close to my family, and there was no way I was moving to Bangalore. DEC did not take my refusal lightly. They were used to people falling at their feet for much less than an MD's job.[3]

Further, DEC had granted us three seats on the board of directors. I knew that Hemant's and Pravin's seats were expected because they were closer to DEC. Given my grasp of the business, I had assumed I would be the third one. But my partners didn't agree that I should represent Hinditron.

When we could not make a headway, we approached DEC, asking it to intervene. They politely refused to get involved in our internal affairs. After protracted discussions, I lost out on the seat as I had only 16 per cent equity in Hinditron's computer business. I was disheartened because I had put all my heart into the organization for so many years. I was eventually appointed as an alternative director of this JV, but, to me, it felt like a consolation prize.

Eventually, in 1988, the JV took off, but hit air pockets right away. At forty-plus, I was no longer 'young'. DEC was competing with Indian manufacturers, who had mastered the art of keeping costs low. A key reason for us to enter a JV with DEC was to compete on a solid footing by reducing manufacturing costs. We expected that we would get the components for lower prices as DEC was producing them at large volumes globally.

What happened instead was that our costs went up.

---

3   Mike Shah took up the MD's position eventually.

There were a couple of reasons for this. One was the sky-high import duty due to India's foreign exchange problems. The second was DEC's purchase process itself. For instance, if we needed memory chips from Nippon Electric Company (NEC), Japan[4], they would buy the chips locally and ship them to DEC, International, in the US. Then DEC, International, would ship to us. Each of these trips across the world padded up the costs for DEC's Indian enterprise. It would be way higher than what local competition paid for the same components. There was no way we could compete on costs with Indian competitors.

Earlier, in 1987, I had looked at the projected balance sheet of the JV and cringed at what I saw. In our next meeting in Boston, I made a presentation along with the Hinditron team to DEC, where I clearly stated that at this rate we wouldn't break even, ever. I stressed that the unit economics were flawed and, unless we brought down input costs, the more we manufactured, the more we'd lose.

DEC told us that the problem was with our selling price and not the costs. My objection was brushed off, and we were told to keep our side of the bargain by selling at a higher price. We knew that except for a few MNCs, no Indian customer would pay 50 per cent higher for just the DEC brand. Some years later, a Dalal Street magazine saw our financials and wrote, 'This JV is a funny business: the more they make, the more they lose.'

The business started to falter, and my stand was vindicated. DEC, too, realized this after a few years. But the competitors had gained considerable ground by then.

It was time I focused my energy elsewhere. With DEC, we were in the commercial enterprise market and far away from the personal computer revolution sweeping across the world. When I saw a COBOL programme running on a PC at a customer's data centre in Andheri, Mumbai, I instantly knew that this would bring about an irrevocable

---

4   At the time, DEC, Japan.

shift in the dynamics of the industry. The market was used to working on MicroVAX and IBM machines, but this was something dramatically different. A programme that used to run on a minicomputer worth about ₹15,00,000 could now run on a single PC worth just ₹1,00,000. The operating costs were far lower as well, as there was no need to create massive data centres for PCs (except servers).

At DEC, probably buoyed by their global success, they failed to see the coming of the PC revolution. They believed that PCs were the toys of hobbyists and these smaller machines were not capable of any serious work. They postulated that the fad would soon fade away.

In fact, Intel had approached DEC, and asked if they could build the robust and proven motherboards of PDP-11s into a chip and create a new market for personal computers. DEC refused, and Intel went ahead and developed their now iconic 286 microprocessor.

Steve Jobs, on the other hand, could see the imminent PC revolution. With his usual flair for the dramatic, he even sent the DEC CEO a coffin with 'DEC Inside' inscribed on it.

Back home in India, I had also spotted the opportunity in PCs, and I decided to sell PCs through Hinditron. For that, we needed to collaborate with a local PC manufacturer.

I knew Apurva Parekh of Essen Computers from my engineering college days. He had started Essen in the early 1980s and had grown it into a dependable company. In his earlier days, he made the SN-23 computer on the PDP-11 motherboards. We sold these computers in the market before we transferred this business to the DEC JV.

He now started making the PC. We signed a contract with Essen and became their resellers. The demand was good, and business grew at a rapid pace.

Soon, there was a demand for maintenance of these PCs, and we started providing that as well. We also tied up with Novell and Autodesk to sell their products as add-ons to strengthen the PC business.

Oh—and DEC did get into the PC market, albeit a bit too late.

End to start

When I joined Hinditron, a company that had five partners, each with a strong voice, the roles had to be clearly defined, and we did just that. Hemant and I were always in the growth mode and willing to take risks. However, Pravin and Kamlesh would play the devil's advocate, and inject reality into our thinking. At the end of our presentations for new projects, invariably, Pravin would voice concerns about raising funds. Or Kamlesh would ask, 'What is in it for us?'

But if we saw an opportunity in the technology space, we went for it without thinking much about how we would acquire the skills.

I read somewhere, 'If somebody offers you an amazing opportunity, but you are not sure you can do it, say yes—then learn how to do it later!' Probably inspired by that, in the early 1980s, for the first time, we decided to dive into exporting software services. We started by exporting software on DEC computers and electronic instruments of companies like Tektronix and Fluke that Hinditron represented.

We had built our company by offering a range of services (including consulting, software, solutions and maintenance) around DEC for several years. There was a non-compete agreement that prevented Hinditron from offering software services on DEC computers after the JV started. To DEC, we were merely a vehicle for entering India. They didn't see that by collaborating with us, they could offer cheaper integrated solutions to newer business verticals, open up new geographies across the globe and eventually grow the market for DEC computers.

With the benefit of hindsight, I can say DEC had as significant an opportunity as Suzuki had. Suzuki had entered India in 1982 when they signed a license and JV with Maruti Udyog Ltd (which, at the time, was owned wholly by the Government of India). The JV was supposed to be mainly an importer of cars. Eventually, to start manufacturing at a greenfield plant in Gurgaon, Suzuki brought in the casting and forging capability, and Maruti, the Indian partner, leveraged the abundant natural resources. The two developed a symbiotic partnership and helped grow each other exponentially. They further upgraded the technology and process know-how of tiny suppliers that had sprung up to service the JV. Some of these have now grown to become global leaders. This trickle-down effect thereon helped India become a major global automobile hub.

DEC with their MicroVAX could have become a similar anchor partner to computer manufacturers in India and helped them grow into world-class organizations. We missed the opportunity to spring a revolution by supporting upcoming entrepreneurs. This would have probably helped DEC retain its leadership position and keep competition at bay.

Surprisingly, DEC had no objection to us offering services and solutions around their competitors' computer systems—primarily IBM, which at the time, was a far more significant direct competitor to them.

So, we decided to spin off a different company for our multisystems software services business. I was fully aware of the harsh, competitive environment. It took time to pitch for a new business and secure it. Scouting for a viable project, working on it, getting the client to evaluate it, and finishing legal and government formalities took several months.

We called the new business River Valley. We decided to focus on consulting and offshoring instead of on-site work.

I had a bias against on-site projects as we had faced our share of issues in the on-site business. We still built it up to a respectable team of 300 software engineers before transferring it to the DEC JV in 1988.

With the on-site business, apart from technical training, we had to deal with cultural issues as well. In colder places, engineers were constantly complaining about the weather. In the US, they had an even tougher time. They missed the assistance of domestic help that they were used to relying on back home in India. There was a frequent struggle to find vegetarian food. Further, whenever they cooked, they'd inadvertently set off smoke alarms.

Meanwhile, the clients could not fathom how culturally diverse India is. They wondered why six Indians spoke six different accents of English. They could not decipher the Great Indian Nod that could mean a yes or a no or any of the million things in between.

Many engineers would quit without informing us. Due to visa issues, they were afraid that they would get deported. It was common to get a call at 3 a.m. from an upset customer in the US. They would complain, 'Your engineer hasn't shown up for three days. Please send the replacement urgently.' Disappearing engineers were a routine phenomenon and it was highly embarrassing. I questioned the business model of the on-site placement I had been promoting. So, at River Valley, we decided as a strategy not to do on-site work unless it was complementing the offshoring business. I often joke with my core team that the product business makes money while you sleep, and the services business does not let you sleep.[5]

When it came to pitching for work, the challenges were many. Both on-site and offshoring ideas were so new back then, there was a natural resistance from clients. This was compounded by India's severely constricting regulations. The sheer number of ministerial approvals, and the trouble involved in getting them, was a mountain to climb. We spent more time and energy resolving these issues than the actual business. The ministerial approvals in Delhi meant days were lost outside government offices, waiting for hearings with babus of assorted temperaments.

Procuring visas was another ordeal. Plus, the RBI had a scarcity mindset with respect to forex and, even if we got the visas, the central

5   It is disheartening that despite being in the business for all these years, Indian companies continue to operate on a time and material business model. From there on, while some have pivoted to an output-based pricing model, we continue to remain far from owning the output.

bank would allocate a meagre forex quota for travel. While travelling, we had to thus depend on friends and relatives abroad, and stay with them as we did not have the forex required to get a hotel room.

For the offshoring business, there was no dedicated link to connect with clients abroad. Without a dedicated 64 Kbps[6] link, how much offshoring could one do? This only underlined the need for industry-level reforms at scale, and became the genesis for NASSCOM.

By then (during the 1980s), the Hinditron Computer Company had done great business around DEC computers. We were one of the biggest players in the market and were growing substantially. Our brand was well known and highly respected. I had invested one-and-a-half decades of my life in the business and was looking forward to reaping the benefits.

But that expectation was about to shatter.

The Hinditron board called for an unscheduled meeting. It was abrupt and irregular, and, even though it felt ominous to me, I couldn't pin the real reason down. The optimist in me had taken over and I thought it must be about some breakthrough we had made.

I entered the room, and the tension was palpable.

The bombshell was then dropped. Dr Arvind Shah and I were asked to resign from Hinditron. The other partners had 68 per cent shareholding, and they wanted to buy out the remainder from Arvind and me.

I felt the ground beneath my feet slip away. I felt betrayed.

What was most hurtful was that it seemed like a meticulously planned operation. The communication was devoid of any compassion or emotion. They seemed to have worked out every step to the point when the separation would be complete. We were in the dark the whole time and did not anticipate what was coming.

---

6   Today, the unit kbps has become obsolete. A normal home broadband connection is at least 25 mbps. For those born after 1995–1996, the Gen Z, 1 mbps = 1,024 kbps.

To me, the pain of separation from Hinditron felt personal as well. It was like getting separated from my kin. After all, they were the first family I had outside of the home I was born and grew up in. At work, we partners spent all our time together and whatever was left after work, we would still be with each other, but this time, along with our families. We celebrated all our festivals together. We socialised together. Our children played together. We even holidayed together. We had each other's back through thick and thin. Just a few years ago, they had helped us immensely during Shaila's and my illness.

It was with this familial confidence that we had built a substantial business in a sunrise industry. At the time, Hinditron was the only company to have two strong JVs with global majors. We had come up with and lived the vision of creating 'better lives through technology'.

I protested vehemently, but was left with no choice. The other partners may have had a multitude of reasons for the split. I will probably never know the real reason. But back then, I knew that you couldn't run an organization with reluctant partners.

After the initial shock and sense of betrayal, I had to settle down quickly and observe where this split was headed.

The first step was that I get compensated for the value of my Hinditron shares. The second was the splitting of various businesses in the company.

I don't know if there is an amicable way to break up a partnership, but ours was certainly not. They looked at valuations very differently from me. According to me, there was a tailwind 'hidden' into the valuation of the business. We had just started and were looking at exponential growth in the years to come. Valuation thus had to account for this impending boom. Further, the DEC shares we owned were held within the Hinditron structure, and the share price did not reflect that.

But they wanted to value only the current business of Hinditron as per prevalent accounting policies.

The valuation of the company became a flashpoint. I took the help of experts and they suggested various mechanisms for a fair measurement of value. The sparring partners, however, weren't willing to budge.[7]

I felt bitter and short-changed. I had a choice to fight it out legally for years and years, or take the crumbs and rebuild my life from scratch. Except for Shaila, everyone suggested I initiate the legal battle. But I decided to move on.

After being nudged out from Hinditron, the big question confronting me was, 'What next?'

Things had become tougher because Hinditron sent out letters to all banks and business partners, including Novell, informing them that Hinditron was '*withdrawing all collaterals and guarantees pertaining to Mr Mehta*', and that they should deal with me at their own risk. It was a standard business practice, but I had not expected this from my partners. It strained my relationship with them further and pushed me into a corner. My severance from Hinditron should have been a slow process, but it happened abruptly.

At NASSCOM, members are companies and not individuals. Even though I was the elected chairperson, I was still a representative of Hinditron. My former partners even sent a letter to NASSCOM stating that they wanted to replace me as Hinditron's representative.[8]

Suddenly, I could not continue in the position! Even before starting to deliver on its promise, NASSCOM faced the exit of one of its founder members. It was too nascent to have survived it. NASSCOM probably needed me as badly as I needed NASSCOM.

Fortunately, Dewang had joined as president by then and he was rooting for me. The NASSCOM constitution offered a solution to this quandary. We could get my new start-up, Onward Technologies, to

---

7   I was right about the hidden tailwind and, in less than four years after the split, the valuation had risen to more than ten times of what it was at the time of my break with Hinditron.

8   They wanted Kalyan Sundaram as Hinditron's representative.

become a member of NASSCOM and then get the EC to appoint me back as the chairperson. Easier said than done. After all, I was almost 44 when I had to bootstrap Onward overnight! Plus, NASSCOM wasn't my personal fiefdom; It was a democratic body that belonged to the industry. And that's the way it is even to this day.

Would the EC agree to my reappointment? I wasn't sure at all. Dewang, however, was confident.

An extraordinary EC meeting was convened. As instructed by Dewang, I sat outside for the first few minutes, awaiting the decision of the EC members. As I waited anxiously, myriad thoughts raced across my mind. If Dewang's proposal were rejected, all my efforts in creating NASSCOM would go to waste.

But it wasn't just about my personal struggle to create NASSCOM; the very existence of the association was at risk. I would be happy if NASSCOM survived in my absence. But I knew very well that the association was too nascent to survive the setback if I didn't come back on the saddle. It was a do or die situation.

In hindsight, if I couldn't get back to NASSCOM, I am sure some other EC member would have picked the baton. Thereon, maybe NASSCOM would have still delivered the impact we've been able to. Or it could have done a lot more. Or it could have become yet another MAIT. I have no way of knowing. But I did know that it was vital that I stayed on because I was confident that I would steer NASSCOM on the road to success.[9]

On Dewang's cue, I entered the meeting. I looked at the board members warily. The apprehension soon gave way to comfort as I was greeted with welcoming smiles. The precious fifteen minutes were utilised skilfully by Dewang to apprise the EC members of the recent developments and how they would affect NASSCOM; he got Onward

---

9   I remain hopeful that in the future NASSCOM will not become a partisan association that is run by a coterie for the benefit of a few, where the nation's interests are sidelined.

Technologies nominated as an EC member, me as the representative and reappointed me as chairperson with consensus.

The EC's swift response reaffirmed my belief that NASSCOM needed me. I was overwhelmed and grateful for the trust that the EC and the founding members had in me.

The dice was rolling once again. It was game on.

6

The Pillars of NASSCOM

Jean Monnet was born in 1888 in Cognac, France. Early on, his father recognised his extraordinary people skills and observed that he would excel in international business. At sixteen, Monnet quit his school and moved to London to start learning business. He eventually travelled extensively across Scandinavia, Russia, the Americas and Egypt for work. When he was twenty-six, France was plunged into First World War as part of the Allied Forces and was cooperating with Britain, Russia, Italy, Japan, the United States and others. Monnet, however, believed in an even greater collaboration of war efforts and the coordination of war resources for a better outcome. He met René Viviani, the then prime minister of France, and managed to convince the French government to see his perspective.

Involved in both the World Wars, Monnet noted in the 1940s that European countries continuously fought each other instead of collaborating on development. To regain and retain peace, he proposed an absurd and whimsical idea of the union of Europe.

After all, European countries had fought each other for centuries. He famously declared, 'There will be no peace in Europe if the states are reconstituted on the basis of national sovereignty... The countries of Europe are too small to guarantee their people the necessary prosperity and social development. The European states must constitute themselves into a federation ....'

Greatly influenced by the German philosopher Immanuel Kant, Monnet saw the importance of competing countries working together. He worked to unite Europe through continental issues that were greater than those of individual nations. He participated in brokering a deal that made France and Germany share resources for coal and steel production. Set up under a High Authority, they were joined by Italy, the Netherlands, Belgium and Luxembourg to form the European Coal and Steel Community. This first step eventually led to the formation of the European Union.

Many things are common between Monnet's union of Europe and NASSCOM.

In both cases, going against their grain, competing entities collaborated for the greater good. NASSCOM's member companies put India ahead of individual interests. And the people involved were passionate about the causes they stood for.

NASSCOM was a similar, unlikely alliance of fiercely competing companies. Over the years, on many occasions, people were convinced that its end was imminent. Yet, here we are. Thirty plus years and counting. At the time of assembling NASSCOM, I guess even the founding team didn't imagine the impact of what we were creating. Nor the longevity of it.

So, what made NASSCOM tackle the seemingly insurmountable obstacles and stay the course for well over thirty years now?

Its success can be attributed to multiple things. There was liberalisation that allowed our dreams to go beyond the country's borders. Numerous, well-meaning bureaucrats had the vision to see beyond the obvious. There were policy decisions,[1] both fiscal and nonfiscal, that allowed us to spread our wings. There was the passion and the shared vision of the founding members and early supporters.

No wonder they say that success has many fathers, but failure is an orphan. While multiple things converged to enable NASSCOM to take flight, I believe there was one special ingredient that allowed NASSCOM to stay together as a cohesive unit.

That cohesion came from the core organizational values that we instituted. These were crafted in the early days and have remained unchanged since. These values are our North Star that shows us the way even in the darkest hours.

While each value is important, for me, the three that stand out are: (a) have 'no personal agenda', (b) 'collaborate and compete', and (c) practise a 'growth mindset'.

No personal agenda

A for-profit organization is bound together by the objectives of turning a profit to the shareholders. On the other hand, a not-for-profit organization has to work hard to keep its people together, let alone stay motivated.

Now consider this: save for the president and a few others, leadership at NASSCOM is voluntary and honorary. Founders, leaders and veterans of some of the largest IT services companies in the country continue to be active in the functioning of this body, even though they do not have any pressing need per se. More than just the leaders, the unsung heroes of the NASSCOM saga include millions of engineers, thousands of officials and hundreds of bureaucrats.

If people are not motivated by any personal agenda, what exactly are they working for? These are times when people, especially business folk, are tuned into the WIII-FM channel. WIII-FM stands for 'What

---

1   You will read more about these in the subsequent chapters.

Is in It for Me?'. So, the challenge is, how do you get them to put in hours and hours of work without any immediate or apparent personal benefit?

The answer is to get them aligned to a vision far grander than what serves their individual pursuits.

The growth of the industry is everyone's growth. Once members understand this, they support NASSCOM wholeheartedly. If one leads by example, and others witness that you are contributing to the greater good without any ulterior or personal agenda, they embrace the bigger vision even more tightly.

If NASSCOM were to succeed, it had to create an environment where all companies felt welcome, large or small. Indian corporations to MNCs to services companies to product companies; each member would have to see value for themself. There was no question of allowing any room for personal agendas. The senior-most members of large companies continue to support NASSCOM to this day because it still is a place where everyone can speak their mind. And where the industry will always be greater than any single company.

Three distinct incidents come to mind that showcase that we, as a group, always stood for agendas larger than an individual. Each incident is from the perspective of a different stakeholder in the ecosystem—an early NASSCOM member, the NASSCOM as an organization itself and Government of India officials.

First, when I was the chairperson of NASSCOM, one of my goals was to stabilise the finances, so that we could focus on long-term initiatives. We requested each member to contribute ₹25,000, a princely sum back then, to cover for the losses carried forward. However, this was not enough. This was when Narayana Murthy and Infosys offered to conduct a paid training programme on IBM AS400, an emerging technology at the time, for the industry. The training sessions were held at the Infosys campus and even competitors could send their software engineers to attend. What made this training unique and noteworthy was that the NASSCOM was the beneficiary of all the fees collected.

Imagine inviting your competitors' talent on your own office campus and training them to compete with you eventually![2]

The other remarkable incident was when we were working with Vittal on the Software Technology Parks of India, or STPIs (you will read more about STPIs in Chapter 8). One of the key decisions was about the location of these parks. For bureaucrats, it would have been simpler to stipulate that these campuses be located on the outskirts and beyond, a move that would greatly benefit companies that were already established.

However, we took a crack at the harder problem. We wanted to be inclusive and level the playing field for all members. We thus worked with Vittal to ensure that even complexes that were bang in the middle of cities could be accorded the status of STPI. This eventually helped smaller companies grow faster and allowed new companies to take birth. Again, we, as a group, looked beyond personal agendas.

When I talk about working without personal agendas, I have to mention how NASSCOM navigated the crisis brought about by the Satyam scandal. The entire industry and the association worked together as one to prevent brand India from getting tarnished forever. You will read more about it later in the book.

Finally, the third, and the most relevant, incident was when we wanted a change in one of the cross-border taxation policies. We submitted our proposal to the DoE, which forwarded it to the RBI. One of the officials at the central bank wanted to make some amendments to it. When he approached the DoE, they told him that the recommended changes had come from NASSCOM, and thus

---

2   Apart from Murthy, many more people made personal contributions to NASSCOM. For example, way back in 1991, it was necessary for NASSCOM to build relationships and credibility around the world. Ashank voluntarily took the responsibility to promote NASSCOM and the IT industry in the Asia Oceanian region (which then consisted of twenty countries like Japan, Australia, and South Korea). He would spend his own money and participate in ASOCIO meetings to represent NASSCOM.

would be fair and inclusive. They added that in case the RBI wanted to make recommendations, they may speak directly to NASSCOM.

Such was the trust we had won with stakeholders.

There are numerous similar incidents where we at NASSCOM worked for a larger objective. Often, I am asked how we managed to do this without any infighting or internal politics. True, it is inconceivable to form a society without politics. Even when a bunch of teenagers come together to play cricket, the political dynamics are evident. It takes courage to look beyond a short-term personal goal. At NASSCOM, the magnitude makes it all the more difficult. So, if NASSCOM somehow worked it out, it was because of another set of values its members had: integrity, trust, and respect for each other. These were further strengthened by like-minded colleagues, each focused on the larger agenda. We eventually articulated these values clearly in various internal communication pieces and consciously encouraged members to live by these values.

The other secret sauce that helped us stay away from internal politics is our emphasis on culture and open communication. I had seen the importance of these two and how they ensure that everyone is aligned to the larger, more meaningful goal.

I must talk about the importance of culture and communication here. In the 1970s, when I was in the US, the work culture there surprised me pleasantly. In India, businesses were hierarchical. There was this 'raja', the king, and the 'praja', his subjects. Juniors addressed seniors with a 'sir' and didn't challenge them. Seniors didn't queue up anywhere. They stayed aloof and maintained their superiority through their demeanour, inaccessibility and high-handedness. In the US, the CEO was treated no different from me, even when I was a rookie engineer.

This work culture also had parallels with my understanding of Jainism and an important value I imbibed as a child. Jainism had emerged partly as a response to the inequalities that were imposed by Hindu privileged castes. It was hailed as the creation of a more egalitarian religion. In the US, I could see this tenet had delivered an evolved society.

This culture is commonplace today. But it was a revelation to me then. And I knew India needed it.

When I came back to India, I worked towards planting this culture in all my organizations. Unlike the norm at that time, I would openly share company matters with my team.

I truly believe that life is not a zero-sum game; I believe in the theory of abundance. Your ability to own a home does not diminish my ability to have one. This belief is shared and practised by many of my colleagues at NASSCOM. Once we understood this, all of us aligned with NASSCOM's larger goal. This is how we managed to successfully project and eventually establish NASSCOM as the industry's single voice, above all personal agendas.

Collaborate and compete

Competition is fundamental to capitalism. It is in an entrepreneur's nature to look at their competitors with envy and scepticism. But whenever a new industry is born, there are systemic and environmental challenges that affect all the players. If then, these competitors do not collaborate, the industry itself could be dead on arrival. In our case, the challenges were so pervasive that all of us were overwhelmed and quickly forged a collaboration.

And how!

Let me talk about an incident that showcases our ability to collaborate and complete. At the request of the Prime Minister's Office (PMO), NASSCOM participated in a business delegation to Russia. The group was top-heavy and included stalwarts like Som Mittal (the then NASSCOM president), Harsh Manglik (the then NASSCOM chairperson and the chairperson of Accenture in India at the time), N. Chandrasekaran (of TCS, fondly referred to as Chandra) and several other prominent people.

At any other gathering, the NASSCOM president would have represented us. However, Som felt that Harsh should speak on behalf of the group. After all, Harsh was the chairperson of not just NASSCOM but also of Accenture India, a multinational IT services company. On the other hand, Harsh recommended that Chandra, the CEO of India's largest IT services company (TCS), was best suited for the occasion. Everyone in the delegation sidelined their egos and unanimously decided that it had to be Chandra.

Ironically, only Chandra could have objected because the NASSCOM presentation contained case studies of four Indian IT companies—TCS and three of its direct competitors.

But Chandra[3] agreed without batting an eyelid. He said that he was representing India, not his company, and he was proud to do so.

Apart from us, a delegation from the pharmaceuticals industry was also invited to make a presentation at the same forum. However, they could not have been more different from us, and, in their presentation, individual company logos and names were prominent.

With NASSCOM, this was unlikely to happen. As a corollary to the 'collaborate and compete' ethic, we spoke in a 'single voice'. The PMO could see these contrasting approaches and complimented us by saying, 'Never give up on your values.'

Another example of this comes from Novell, my JV partner. In 1989 we had signed an agency agreement with Novell to represent them in India. This relationship allowed me to get an insider's view of how they worked.

I saw that they used the 'collaborate and compete' model to dominate the market. Novell had grown globally by partnering with multiple competing companies. It could partner with entity A in

---

3	When Chandra was the NASSCOM chairperson, he and I would meet regularly for coffee at Mumbai's Willingdon Club. At the time, the prevalent norm was to get the executive assistants to plan such meetings. Despite his stature, Chandra remained grounded and humble enough to personally call his friends and his mentors for these meetings.

The other thing that stands out about Chandra is his extreme positivity. Every time I pointed at some of the challenges that he may potentially face at TCS as they started to compete with global IT behemoths, he would politely list each observation, and respond with confident and lucid answers. He was not overwhelmed by the size of his competitors or how deep their pockets were.

country X and compete with the same entity A in country Y. It put business sense and interests above rivalry, and warranted the same trust from its collaborating competitors. This counter-intuitive approach helped Novell become a global leader in personal networking software very soon. At one time, they held almost 63 per cent of the market.

Despite being arch-rivals, Novell and IBM came together to sell NetWare as a white-label solution. Even this led to frequent conflicts. So, the Novell CEO started using the term 'coopetition' to describe co-operation among competitors.

This 'coopetition' model reaffirmed our faith in the way forward for NASSCOM: an IT industry body comprising companies that were rivals, but were collaborating with each other.

'Coopetition' always saved the day for us. I remember in the early 1990s, my good friend, Diwakar Nigam of Newgen, along with some software product leaders, opposed the proposal to remove import duties. Their business plans were hinged on high import duties, and an abrupt change would disrupt everything for them. On the contrary, we, the software services people, desperately needed the proposal to go through. How does an industry reach a consensus in a situation like this?

With coopetition.

At that time, we would often meet in Ramani's hotel room the night before the EC meetings. In these informal meetups, we would bring up such debates (and others like large vs SME, public vs private, export vs domestic, Indian vs foreign, one vote vs proportionate votes and more). Many of these invited heated discussions and yet we could reach a consensus even if that meant continuing till the wee hours of the day.

For this specific proposal as well, we held a series of dialogues and lengthy debates. We realized that more than the change in the duties, their problem was the abruptness of the move and they needed time to adjust. Eventually, we found a solution that worked for all.

We could thus present a uniform, India-first industry voice to the policymakers. This India-first approach did not come from some romantic, utopian patriotism but was in everyone's enlightened self-interest. This self-interest led to committed volunteerism, where everyone was aligned to a common cause and pledged their efforts, time, resources and most importantly, intellectual capital.

Diwakar, to date, may not agree with the decision. However, back then, like any other soldier faithful to the larger cause, he graciously accepted the decision and never complained publicly or privately to the government.

Such was the strength of the people at NASSCOM. We had no fear of retribution from our members. We knew that everyone was looking at the larger picture, and wanted to collaborate to grow the pie and then compete for a share of the same pie.

The opposite of 'collaborate and compete' is 'divide and rule'. The powerful example of East India Company was closer home. We could have followed the lesser lesson and enriched a few at the expense of the many. However, NASSCOM's values prevailed, and a noble and rewarding course was set.

Growth mindset

The IT industry had unleashed growth by leading the way in solving India's biggest problems: forex, jobs, brand India and the GDP. The stakes were high. There was no way that the industry could falter now.

NASSCOM was getting more and more visible every single day. We were relentless about achieving more growth. It was not just about the members anymore. We were incubating an ecosystem that was going to be critical for the country.

Lobbying was our primary tool for making it easier to run software services businesses. But we knew more was needed. We worked with educationists to produce talent. We worked towards building 'brand India Inc.' NASSCOM had to roll up its sleeves and help its members implement global HR practices, world-class quality processes and robust corporate governance structures.[4] It even meant educating financial analysts on the potential of the industry. If the IT industry had created wealth for the promoters of its companies, it had created magnitudes more wealth for its investors, as is evident in how the market capitalisation of IT companies has moved on stock exchanges.

This kind of growth was a struggle to uncork. NASSCOM had to grow secondary and tertiary businesses as well. A new hotel in the area sets off other businesses like taxi companies, bedsheet sellers and food suppliers. In the case of the software services industry, many of its allied services didn't even exist. We had to kickstart those. When economists enumerate the impact of the IT industry on the Indian economy, they must include the turnover of all direct and indirect businesses that were driven by the software services engine. Yet, it would be simplistic just to measure the turnover. The equally big and uncountable challenge to growth was cultural.

To demonstrate the growth mindset of NASSCOM and the member companies, I want to draw attention to how we created the outsourcing business from scratch. We were wading in unchartered waters. Like a professional surfer, we had to balance ourselves on ever-moving, ever-evolving, often uncertain and turbulent waves. We had to spot minor disturbances on the horizon and decide if it had the potential of being a strong wave that we could ride on or if it was merely noise that would distract us.

One such wave that we identified early on was the outsourcing business. Further, baked into its outsourcing pitch, NASSCOM sold a special ingredient: the 'global delivery model'. It's the business model of the IT industry that makes outsourcing purr along. It's an optimum mix of onshore and offshore work. It has three levers of wage arbitrage (compared to counterparts, countries like India have significantly

---

4   Azim Premji and Wipro's contribution towards corporate governance initiatives need to be highlighted. Even though Azim never held office at NASSCOM, he was most active with his support. He was among the first advocates for allowing regulators easier access to offices and books.

lower wages), currency arbitrage (the Indian rupee is significantly weaker against the USD, GBP and euro) and talent arbitrage (we have the critical demographic dividend of a big population of young, English-speaking software engineers) that enable offshoring of IT work.

There are other advantages too. Like the time zones that separate India from its important clients. The gap ensures that work continues twenty-four-seven as it moves between onshore and offshore teams. Better connectivity and immersive collaboration tools have only sharpened this advantage.

While the global delivery model existed in its basic avatar, its viability and benefits were apparent when the IT industry opened up in the early 1990s. Only then did countries like the Philippines attempt to replicate the model.

In the 1960s, Canadian philosopher Marshall McLuhan coined the term 'global village'. He was referring to a world that was increasingly bound together by commerce, migration and culture. India, however, lived on the outskirts of this village. Eventually, when India did enter it, I believe it was with a push from NASSCOM's work on outsourcing. Binding business and society, outsourcing had become a great leveller. It had attracted leadership from across the planet, and taught mutual admiration and respect. In 2007, Delphi CEO Rodney O'Neal said, 'Outsourcing has proved to be the greatest leveller and the greatest binding force for the business community and society at large.'

Apart from the exemplary work on the global delivery model, we caught a few more technology waves well in time: from Y2K to open-source to client-server to mobile to digitalisation. Our ability to catch these waves early came from our sense of collaboration and a growth mindset. While we were working on delivering world-class solutions, we continued to keep an eye out for newer opportunities that were emerging, just like a professional surfer has to.

Once, a delegation from China asked John McCarthy of Forrester Research what would it take for them to replicate India's success with IT. John told them that they'd have to build an institution like NASSCOM to be able to do so! He said he had never seen competing businesses come together and collaborate to solve problems like NASSCOM did. Such was the respect and validation that our work garnered.

I'd say we were (and are) a bunch of good people driven by a unique and powerful combination of shared values. To me, this combination is important. While each of these values is powerful in isolation and can nudge an average business into becoming great, I believe that the giant, tectonic shift we wanted to achieve could only happen if all these values worked in sync with each other.

And did we create that shift?

Well, we were no longer naïve snake charmers. We have built one of the largest pools of high-technology talent that made a difference to the whole world. We were competitive, competent and confident, and even the most powerful forces would think twice before they took us on.

Of institutions and people

When we started NASSCOM, in spite of personal compulsions and a lack of time, many entrepreneurs selflessly prioritized the good of the Indian industry above everything else. Their work propelled NASSCOM into changing the world of software services. NASSCOM is thus not merely an industry body. It is an institution driven by values as much as by people.

The values and people, though, are not independent of each other.

For people to not have a personal agenda, they must fight their entrepreneurial instincts of prioritising growth for their respective businesses. At a deeper level, no personal agenda also means that members must not have any personal biases either. We have to let data and facts guide our decisions and actions. For people to collaborate and compete, they must overcome the bizarre folly of believing that winning is always at the expense of someone else. Even in the seemingly straightforward value of practising a growth mindset, there is a challenge to human frailty. Who does not want growth? But, how many people want to be inconvenienced today for a greater future tomorrow?

Plus, growth has its own challenges. If we don't check the manner in which it is achieved, it could lead us to the point of no return and destroy the very thing we've worked so hard to create. As I reflect on what NASSCOM has achieved, I am proud to say that the growth mindset we inculcated was never at the cost of balance. We did not chase growth for the sake of growth. After all, every action that we take today has a lasting effect that ripples for decades. While we worked, we tried our best to consider the second and even the third-order impact on the societal fabric of the country and the nation itself.

One of the primary purposes of this book is to learn from hindsight. It is not possible to drive a car without looking into the rear-view mirror. But will the values that have served NASSCOM so well in the past continue to drive us into the future?

Jean Monnet said, 'Nothing is possible without men, but nothing lasts without institutions.'

NASSCOM was built by a few entrepreneurs, who were driven by the needs of an industry in its infancy. Today, the institution is indeed bigger than any one person or organization. When we started NASSCOM, we dreamt of making tenfold leaps. We imagined an impossible billion-dollar industry when we were at a mere $120 million. Even when we were at $5 billion, we imagined another unimaginable $50 billion in the next ten years. The actual achievement has far surpassed our wildest imagination.

NASSCOM has continued to be relevant in a rapidly changing world. The question remains, can this juggernaut survive the impending chaos?

7

Roti, Kapda, Makaan, Aur Bandwidth

If money is the measure of wealth, the currency is the measure of money. A rupee is a piece of metal in the pocket or ledger data in the bank. But when it moves from one person to another, it becomes valuable. Money must flow. Money is the currency itself. The coin rocks only when it rolls.

Software and data are no different from money. Information has value only when it moves, only when it is communicated. Indeed, Claude Shannon, the father of information theory, titled his historic paper 'A Mathematical Theory of Communication'. It was this theory of 'communication' that flagged off the information technology revolution.

Look around you: your phone, your computer, the wireless protocols, the radio signals, the optical fibre, the Internet; they all ceaselessly move bits of information around. As though the spinning of the Earth depended on the shunting around of a gazillion bits in the span of every tick of the clock. Bandwidth does make the world go round.

This is the story of how bandwidth changed the destiny of India, first, through the software industry and then through its offspring, the BPO industry. Modern Indian culture and attitudes towards work and play are a product of how bandwidth evolved in the country and the role NASSCOM played in it.

At the time of writing this, India already has over half a billion people plugged into the Internet. Even a minimum wage earner has a smartphone in their pocket. A news report pointed out data in India is the cheapest. The average cost is $0.20 per GB. That's over four times cheaper than nearest contender Russia's $0.90. Malaysia is at $1.1, Pakistan at $1.8, Nigeria at $2.2, Brazil at $3.5, Spain at $3.7, the UK at $6.6, Germany at $6.9, China at $9.8, Canada at $12, the US at $12.3, South Korea at $15, and Switzerland at $20.2. Consequently, sites like YouTube, Facebook and Instagram see significant traffic from India.

Indians today consume data like they breathe in air. But this was not always the case. In the 1980s and 1990s, the IT industry's annual bandwidth diet must be what a teenager today burns through in a weekend. It will be amusing to explain to this teenager what a 9.8 kbps (kilobytes per second) connection feels like. How it was normal to wait several minutes for a few KBs (kilobytes) of GIF (graphics interchange format) to show up. The larger experience went beyond sluggish. It was outright clunky. Getting online was a ritual. You hooked a computer to a modem that would, in turn, be hooked to a phone line. The modem would screech and squawk until you got connected, sometimes after fifteen minutes, often an hour. If you got online, you could only hope nobody called your phone because that would lead to disconnection, forcing you to repeat the mind-numbing ritual. Yet, such was the romance, the modem's torturous sound is today sweet nostalgia to all those who once endured it.

In the 1980s, as a partner at Hinditron, I witnessed genuinely insurmountable challenges in data transfer. Yet, the technology promised to ring in the future. In 1982, for a Computer Society of India (CSI) annual event, we worked with the Department of Telecommunications (DoT) to set up a data link between Mumbai and Pune. The experimental link was used for showcasing remote computing. I wrote the application that would use CSI's dedicated data-link to connect a desktop computer at Pune to a database of CSI members running on a DEC computer stationed 160 kilometres away at the Tata Institute of Fundamental Research (TIFR) in Bombay. Dr Sadanandan of TIFR was my partner on the project and Dr Narsimhan, a director at TIFR, was my mentor.

On the day of the demonstration, everybody was amazed. It felt like magic, and people were fired up by its potential. If this could be scaled, one could service any client sitting anywhere in the world. But our hopes were deflated when we asked DoT to actually scale it. They had no answer.

We already had international clients. But our engineers could not serve them out of India because the cost of transferring data would destroy our financial model. The other route was to mail them floppies and tapes. That was cumbersome, unreliable and uneconomical. So, we continued to deploy our engineers at client locations across the world. Setting up a nearshore centre, closer to the customer, was only a dream. There were umpteen regulations preventing that.

Government policies had us dealing with typical third-world problems, fighting fires all the time. The IT industry was not yet Delhi's favourite, and we were still to be seen as creators of livelihoods and earners of foreign exchange. Nonetheless, we knew all along, the offshoring industry was not going anywhere without connectivity.

In the late 1980s, we approached Sam Pitroda, the then advisor to Prime Minister Rajiv Gandhi. We told him that we needed a fast data link between India and the US. He told us the government couldn't afford leasing one because the balance of payments crisis had left it with little foreign exchange. We persisted. We asked him if he believed the IT industry's exports could grow. He said he did. Then we asked him if he preferred body shopping of Indian engineers or their offshore work. He preferred their offshore work. Once again, we turned it around and asked him how we could do any offshore work without the data link. But Sam Pitroda apologised and reiterated that he did not have the money for it. We had failed to convey the confidence we had in our vision.

VSNL throws us a line

A little earlier, in 1986, the public sector enterprise Videsh Sanchar Nigam Limited (VSNL) was set up to improve international communications. It commissioned the first analog link connecting India to the US. This must not be confused with the Internet, which came a decade later.[1] This link could also send data between a location in India and another in the US. Before this, data in India was very much a physical object that travelled as floppies and hard disks.

The pioneering 9.8 kbps line was not the revolution you may have imagined. In fact, it was useless. The speed on this analog link was impractically slow, even for those days. Besides, the line was faulty and kept disconnecting every few minutes. Each time we lost connection, we had to restart the transfer from scratch. Transferring even a few MBs (megabytes) would require several attempts, leaving us exasperated. To keep our sanity, we innovated. If we had to send a 10 MB file, we broke it into three smaller files. Now, if the transfer failed, we didn't have to resend the entire 10 MB.

---

1   Internet has existed in India since 1987 in the shape of ERNET. ERNET was initiated in 1986 by the Department of Electronics (DoE), with funding support from the Government of India and United Nations Development Program (UNDP), involving eight premier institutions as participating agencies—NCST (National Centre for Software Technology) Bombay, IISc (Indian Institute of Science) Bangalore, five IITs (Indian Institutes of Technology) at Delhi, Bombay, Kanpur, Kharagpur and Madras, and the DoE, New Delhi.

   Internet as we know it was launched by VSNL in India in 1995. Further, the ISP policy came into effect in 1998 and it allowed for private players to offer Internet services in India.

Nevertheless, the data link inspired hope, and in the early 1980s, we at Hinditron pitched for an offshoring project to a new client in the US—Amcor. The only Indian Amcor's CEO knew was his doctor, and he thus regarded Indians highly. But we soon lost the contract as poor connectivity bedevilled us. Amcor was not an isolated case. Our conversion rate for offshoring projects was incredibly low. And the ones we converted, we struggled to retain. Data links were not just bad; they were expensive. Today, project managers do not think about data transfer costs, but in those days, we would keep aside 7–10 per cent of our revenues for it. A 64 kbps link used to cost ₹20,00,000 per year in the 1990s. With such a high upfront cost, many were deterred from starting a software services business.

If there was ever a need for an industry association, this was the time. The signals couldn't have been stronger or clearer.

In 1991, VSNL got a new chairperson, B.K. Syngal. He is yet another bureaucrat who did outstanding work for the industry by providing data links year after year. Immediately after Syngal assumed office, NASSCOM received the call it had least expected. Syngal asked for a meeting with us. We met Syngal at his Fort office in Mumbai. Right away, we asked him for 64 kbps lines. We were asked why we needed those higher speeds when we were not using the 9.8 kbps lines for 90 per cent of the time. The irony was that we couldn't. It just did not meet our requirements. We tried explaining that if a customer needed something important, the data had to be at his desk in an hour. If it took fifteen tries and seven hours to do that, and it wouldn't work for us. It was ridiculous to engage our top engineers, who would then simply wait for data transfers.

Syngal challenged us to lease fifteen 64 kbps links. He was afraid our industry couldn't absorb those. His concern couldn't have been more misplaced, as industry leader TCS coolly said it would take all fifteen links. Syngal was astonished. He enthusiastically assured us that VSNL would work with global telecom providers and start giving us links in six months. He warned they would be expensive, and he would try to provide them to us at a slightly lower rate than the prevailing global prices.

We were elated. The data transfer that took days could now be done in hours. At the time, the speed was state of the art. It felt like the future had suddenly arrived. The amount of work we could service with this speed was massive. We could now pitch to Fortune 500 companies and expand our market tenfold overnight.

We had also shared with Syngal NASSCOM's concerns regarding costs. At that time, there was only one such link in Bangalore via an earth station dedicated to Texas Instruments. It cost ₹45,00,000 for five years and had been paid for in advance by Texas Instruments. Later, Syngal did help by bringing this down to ₹18,00,000 by working with AT&T and others to provide links to TCS, Infosys and Satyam. In fact, Syngal saw this NASSCOM idea as an opportunity for VSNL revenues, and built a few more earth stations in quick succession. Yet, the earth stations did not solve the reliability problem in the links between Indian companies and their clients in the US. The offshoring revolution was still on hold.

Before 1991, connectivity was limited to two small analog cables with limited capacity. Satellite links through the new earth stations too were not what we ordered: a single-hop transmission, where the signal is bounced off a satellite only once, was required. But the ones we got used multiple hops, and that dropped data and caused latency, especially at higher volumes and speeds.

Would India's potential as an offshoring destination collapse just because of poor infrastructure? After Sam Pitroda, Syngal struggled to respond, too. Despair set in as contracts were lost due to a lack of basic delivery systems. The IT industry was at the edge of a precipice.

We needed a physical route to the West. There was one, an undersea cable laid by a consortium of countries. It was called the SEA-ME-WE (SE Asia, Middle East, Western Europe cable). India was not even thinking about data when it was commissioned in 1985. The opportunity had been missed. But fortune knocked a second time. Another undersea cable was being sunk to the ocean floor.

This time, India had to be on the undersea SEA-ME-WE 2 cable. We needed to buy a share of this international pipeline. The question was how much. Typically, you would go by historical capacity, maybe budget for a 15 per cent compound annual growth rate (CAGR). But that would be too low for two reasons: one, demand often doesn't show a linear growth, especially when supply had been an issue earlier; two, India was at the brink of a revolution in software and knowledge industries. The potential of these hadn't been even estimated.

However, someone in the government had proactively proposed for 10 per cent of the cable's capacity. That was massive and would cost $110 million. The file on this matter had been going back and forth between the powers that be, now that India was in an economic and forex crisis.

This time around, it was Syngal who went knocking on the doors of the Telecom Commission. He was also told this $110 million was out of the question, as India had only four weeks' worth of forex reserves on hand. Instead, he was asked to buy indigenous equipment from C-DOT or ITI for gateways that could boost software exports. Syngal countered by saying both C-DOT and ITI were not ready with the products. For software exports, he explained, they could not go on putting up earth stations and commission links. They would still need the SEA-ME-WE 2 undersea cable to avoid latency-generating satellite hops.

Eventually, Syngal was asked to come back with a pitch in four weeks. Syngal and the team put everything they had into a powerful presentation. The last slide argued: 'If we miss the bus now, we would have missed it forever.' But when they landed in Delhi, they found that the chairperson of the Telecom Commission had left for the US the day before, for good. A bureaucrat still went ahead and heard the presentation. It was well appreciated, and permission was granted to go ahead with the cable investment. But there was still no money, let alone forex, to invest in it. Syngal promised he would raise funds somehow, but income from the cable would be given to the government in rupees, not dollars. He then did the rounds of the Planning Commission and the Foreign Currency Affairs Department in the Ministry of Finance, but the money was not to be found anywhere. Syngal finally went back to the cable consortium and asked for their support. The consortium was eager to have India on board. The country's strategic importance, its unmet demand and its software potential were not lost on anyone.

Finally, it was Pandit Sukh Ram, the Minister of Communications and Information Technology at the time, who gave his blessings, and Syngal could go ahead with the project. Credit must go to Syngal for his go-getter attitude. He gave immense confidence to the software industry, not only with his suggestions but his actions. Sukh Ram also played a key role in many more initiatives, as you will read in the coming pages.

The consortium agreed to staggered payments, increased capacity (therefore, increased income for VSNL) and provided forex loans. Finally, the SEA-ME-WE 2 cable deal was signed in October 1991, and connectivity was commissioned in October 1994.

Though we had solved a big problem, we had not solved everything. The prohibitive cost of the 64 kbps leased lines prevented new companies from starting up. Conventional funding was difficult because banks were reluctant to loan money to software service businesses that had no collateral to offer. Without the inclusion of smaller companies, India's software story was incomplete. We had work to do.

Parks in bloom

In 1991, the government had commissioned the World Bank to study the potential of India's software industry. NASSCOM was part of this exercise. The study's report and recommendations were a turning point in the history of Indian IT. Among many things, the report compared the potential of countries competing for a slice of the global software market. One measure was on a scale that quantified a country's ability to communicate with other countries. India scored a -2. The much smaller Ireland scored +8. The government got the message.

Besides connectivity, the IT industry was forever scurrying around in a maze of regulations set by the city, state and central governments.

We used to visit Vittal at the DoE regularly. He made extra efforts to understand our issues holistically and was keen to solve them all.

During my tenure as the chairperson of NASSCOM, in one of the meetings with Vittal, he told us about what he did in an earlier assignment at the Kandla Port at Gujarat.

It was a seaport, addled by regulations of all kinds, including a heap of them from the local government. To make it easy for the businesses there, he began meeting a few ministers. But his masterstroke was by working towards declaring the port as a 'special economic zone', way before that concept had come to India. In many industries, city- and state-level regulations stifle businesses. Laws like the Shops and Establishment Act and the Essential Services Act are minefields for most software entrepreneurs. His creation of the Kandla Special Economic Zone meant that the port was now governed by only one simple set of regulations. This enabled entrepreneurs to now find a way around the Gujarat state regulations and other myriad central government regulations.

At the end of his story, he asked us: 'What if I do something similar for your industry?' We were excited on hearing the concept.

We knew that the discussions with the policymakers and government would span months. Thus, to build trust with bureaucrats (as was our core tenet at NASSCOM), it was clear from day one that the body must have the policy to allow anyone from the government to attend any of our EC meetings without prior intimation. We implemented the same and this led to freewheeling discussions between the industry and the government, where plans evolved continually before coalescing into a final scheme.

Vittal knew the power structure in Delhi and needed to make a compelling case for the scheme. This is where NASSCOM came in, and armed him formidably with numbers and research papers. At the time, the industry turnover was only $150 million. But we had dared to stretch our imagination and extrapolate the value of software exports to $500 million. Of course, we were grossly off the mark. Just a few years later, we were, in fact, magnitudes bigger than imagined.

Finally, Vittal coined the term 'Software Technology Parks of India' (STPI) and got it approved by the ministerial cabinet. Traditionally, Indian manufacturing units have been set up a little away from cities, where land is abundant and environmental regulations can be relaxed. The government had adopted the same approach for the STPIs too. They didn't consider that the talent for the software business was in the cities and that programming caused no pollution. There was no reason for planning an STP facility at Keonics, a distant suburb of Bangalore, or at Talawade, far away from Pune. In the beginning, if we wanted the STPI benefits, we had to work out of those distant buildings. Like I said earlier, we eventually convinced the government to let any building anywhere in a city be allowed to fall under the STPI scheme. Later, state governments, too, were allowed to set up parks under the scheme.

Even though it had teething troubles, the STPI had sent out an important message about the government's support. Any export businesses from these STPI locations wouldn't have to pay taxes. India desperately needed foreign exchange, and the government was determined to help us earn it. IT entrepreneurs needed to spend in dollars on sales, marketing and the setting up of offices abroad. The tax holiday allowed IT entrepreneurs to plough their profits back into their businesses, which further accelerated the industry's growth. It also started up many software services businesses. Just this one government initiative made all this possible.

The STPI idea eventually came through, and all key issues were solved in less than two years. The parks helped us overcome the struggle to clear paperwork with the bureaucracy. It provided a single-window clearance mechanism for several processes, which greatly streamlined IT businesses. An STPI officer was assigned to each office to protect the government's interests and make sure we were not violating the laws. The officer was authorised to clear most documents. So, instead of going to the customs office, we could just pass it through our own office. The officer had the right to question what we were sending out as export data and what was coming in for us. Import duty exemptions were granted as well, and the smoother movement of computers and electronics was made possible. The government began shouldering many expenses. With time, these costs were brought down to a minimum.

The biggest success of STPI was what it did for the small businesses.[2] Hundreds of software start-ups occupied the parks not just because of the tax benefits but because the park put them in the international fray. Every park had a dedicated 64 kbps line that anyone could share. By then, VSNL's earth stations and the SEA-ME-WE 2 deal had the data lines flying too. In fact, the STPIs and VSNL were competing with one another. That brought down the costs and improved quality. After many incremental improvements in infrastructure, data transfer had suddenly stopped challenging us. Syngal made VSNL turn over a new leaf. It could now deliver a 64 kbps line in a snap, as compared to the months of wait earlier. Sometimes, within seventy-two hours. All companies, large or small, were now connected with their clients abroad. We even had multiple lines available and could confidently bid for larger projects without worrying about connectivity! The offshoring revolution was underway.

NASSCOM was early to realize the government was well-intentioned, but needed hand-holding. Luckily, the government was willing to listen. The process of fine-tuning policies and the STPI scheme went on for years as we collaborated and adapted to the ever-changing software business. In four to six years, STPIs had become a force to reckon with and, one of the most impactful government initiatives.

NASSCOM shared the STPI story the world over, telling clients about how the Indian government was a stakeholder. We included STPI in our introductory slides and talked about it at every opportunity.[3]

---

2   Since this was a new scheme at the time, there were scams aplenty as well, where numerous gullible people got cheated under the pretext of 'winning' outsourcing contracts. More details are available on the companion website to this book at www.themaverickeffectbook.com.

3   In 2001, the government withdrew export benefits for all software companies, except at the STPIs. However, I continue to believe that the government

The non-fiscal policy decision of the STPI scheme enabled private and government parks that eventually helped hundreds of small software businesses, employing millions of people. The IT industry was soon flourishing across India, in tier-2 and tier-3 cities, too. Further, the X.25 point-to-point (P2P) communication link allowed the offshore development centre (ODC) market to flourish. Businesses could now move data securely from their offices across the world to their backend centres in India.

Data from India had also begun to flow across continents. This opened up possibilities. Suddenly, the world woke up to the fact that for two people to work together, they needn't be in the same building, city or even country. International companies discovered that complete business verticals could move to cheaper geographies. It led to the creation of the business process outsourcing (BPO) industry. But this offspring of the IT industry is a big story I will reserve for the next few pages.

Nevertheless, my story about bandwidth is not complete without revisiting India's romance with the consumer internet.

Worldwide revolution

During the 1990s several IT companies were established across India, thanks to conducive market environments and the ever-increasing adoption of IT and IT enabled services globally. Many of these companies came out with IPOs that were oversubscribed. We at Onward Technologies were one such start-up. Further, it was in 1993 when Onward-Novell, my 50:50 joint venture with Novell Inc. took off. Let me talk about how it came into being.

The CEO and chairperson of Novell, Ray Noorda, was looking at expanding the business across the world. He wanted to use his

---

must support smaller companies (with less than ₹500 million turnover) with export benefits and more sops. These benefits are required to help the smaller companies grow faster. I understand that the policymakers need to tread the fine line between growth in income (via taxes and forex) and job creation (by giving benefits like tax breaks). These are the areas where the government needs to be sensitive.

now famous coopetition strategy as he scouted for partners. In India as well, they were talking to numerous players, including my recent start-up, Onward. When their team met me, I was sceptical that it would go through. While I had the confidence, I was, after all, a garage operation compared to others in the fray. However, I had two distinct advantages over others.

First, and the more rational, was that I had no affiliations to any particular hardware manufacturer. Everyone else had an existing partnership with a hardware company that they did not want to let go of. Novell products were hardware agnostic, and they wanted a partner who could sell on all hardware platforms. Also, the others did not spot the large opportunity Novell represented and refused to let go of their existing partnerships.

Second, and the more emotional, is that they could see my instinct of taking large, calculated bets. I was, after all, a garage operation and was pitching to sign up a 50–50 JV with the world's second-largest software company!

I think it was the second reason that tipped the scales in my favour. I am told that when they were deciding on the India partner, Noorda bumped into Royden Olsen, the then director of international business development at Novell, in the parking lot of the office at Provo, Utah, and asked about India JV. By then, Olsen was convinced that it had to me. Olsen had seen my garage operation and justified it by saying that even Novell was a garage operation when it started fifteen years ago. He told Ray, 'I've known Harish for the last three years as a representative of Novell in India. I trust him and recommend that Novell go ahead with Onward.'

As I think about this, I think there was a third factor at play as well. The relationships that I was able to forge with Olsen.

Along with the JV came Kanwal Rekhi. He was on the Novell board and came on board of Onward-Novell, too. Just a year before, The Indus Entrepreneurs (TiE) was setup in Silicon Valley and Kanwal was at the helm of it. It was a non-profit for promoting and enabling entrepreneurship with networking, mentoring, funding and education.

In fact, on my frequent visits to Silicon Valley, I was exposed to the power of the internet with the help of Kanwal and his colleagues at Novell. I started believing the internet's impact would be as universal as that of electricity.

The enterprises of Silicon Valley had become my role model for IP-driven businesses. To integrate, we started inviting Valley entrepreneurs to NASSCOM conferences. Among them were legends like venture capitalist and Sun Microsystems co-founder Vinod Khosla; client-server computing pioneer Umang Gupta; former Massachusetts Institute of Technology (MIT) professor, Cirrus Logic founder and TiE co-founder Suhas Patil; and Stanford University economist Rafiq Dossani.

Dewang, too, had grown close to the Valley and was convinced of the Internet's potential. We agreed NASSCOM should take on the task of popularising the Internet in India, though it was not relevant to NASSCOM members in the immediate future. One day, Dewang called me and announced: 'Roti, kapda, makaan aur 3 MB bandwidth per citizen (food, clothes, shelter and 3 MB bandwidth per citizen).' It was a popular Hindi phrase that described the needs of the masses that Dewang had modified into a rallying cry for NASSCOM's campaign. He was prophetic. When questioned, we insisted that the Internet would become an essential utility like water and electricity. It took twenty years for this to become a reality, but we stand validated.

Back then, we had not really gauged our challenge. The size of it dawned upon us when a telecom minister asked, 'Yeh bandwidth kya cheez hai? (What is this thing called bandwidth?)' He had heard our slogan and thought, like bread, clothes and a house, bandwidth, too, was something physical. We quickly realized the importance of our work in demystifying and popularising the Internet.

In 1994, our evangelical plans fell in place when Vijay Mukhi called to say we were going to have tea with veteran Hindi film star Shammi Kapoor. I was thrilled at the prospect of meeting the Bollywood legend. At his home, I saw him connect to Apple's eWorld. This was a year before the actual 'Internet' came to India! He began quickly accessing world news and weather and such. It was impressive. At the time, Shammi Ji was a septuagenarian and a star from decades ago. Yet, he was an Internet enthusiast with an incredibly curious mind. He took to new technologies like fish to water.

I began wondering if Shammi Ji's popularity could further our Internet agenda. Then I saw a film celebrity in a campaign for saving water. My mind was made up: why not have Bollywood film star Shammi Kapoor promote the Internet? We approached Shammiji, who readily agreed, that too pro bono. Vijay and Dewang supported the idea and executed it.

We organized the first event at the Nehru Centre in Mumbai and promoted it significantly. We had a full house. Over 700 people attended the event where Shammi Kapoor spent forty-five minutes on stage, demonstrating how to use the Internet. He passionately told personal stories of his romance with the Internet. He captivated the audience by displaying how he used the Internet to stay in touch with his children who lived abroad. The audience was completely won over. We were overwhelmed with the response.

Shammiji took our campaign several notches up. He started travelling with us all over the country. His personality and presentation skills helped us communicate the potential of the Internet to even bureaucrats. We had many meetings along with him at VSNL, the DoT and DoE. He also helped us immensely to create demand among the general public, who were still largely untouched by the magic of computers.

On a separate thread, Dewang, the storyteller that he was, created a narrative around Manchhaben, a fictional woman who lives in a remote village in Kutch, Gujarat. She is a poor craftswoman who decides to sell her handicraft online. With some hard work and the powerful reach of the Internet, she begins selling across the world and is a successful businesswoman now. The story struck a chord with the masses, who began believing they could improve their lot by using the Internet.

Bringing it together, we helped put together the initial draft of India's first Internet policy in the late 1990s. Eventually, that led to the new telecom policy, which, in turn, led to the privatisation of Internet service providers. Similarly, the National Telecom Policy of 1999 contributed to the growth of ITES (information technology enabled services) and BPOs.[4]

In the middle of all this enthusiasm around the Internet, the telecom industry was stirring up a storm of its own. Telephones had been evolving iteratively every passing decade, but the first new gadget that surprised the nation was the pager. Way back in 1992, I had got one myself to keep an eye on the stock market.

A few years later, I got a cell phone. I remember paying dearly for it, ₹110 per minute for a simple call abroad. This is an industry where costs have fallen with each passing year and have now reached a stage where top data providers allow voice calls for free. Mobile phones have put cheap and fast bandwidth in the grasp of almost every Indian.

When I look back, I am reminded of a Chinese curse: 'May you live in interesting times.' In the days of peace, all is well and rather uninteresting. So, the Chinese wished only 'interesting times' of war and destruction upon those they despised.

How had we lived?

We combated the faulty analog lines of the 1980s and forced them somehow to carry a few MBs of data over 9.8 kbps. We fought out guerrilla strategies to retain customers in spite of the patchy and high-latency 64 kbps lines. We rallied troops of millions of programmers in hundreds of companies by arming them with affordable STPI bandwidth. We threw ourselves into the trenches and wrote a policy that eventually put the promised 3 MB of data into the hands of every Indian citizen. We forced the pricing down to its knees—from millions of rupees for a mere 64 kbps line to measly pocket change. The battle was relentless. Not all wars spill human blood. Some build civilisations without spilling a drop.

Oh, yes. We lived in interesting times.

---

4   The Internet Policy and National Telecom Policy deregulated Internet and telecom in India, respectively. This proliferated national and international private players. The industry could now access Internet and telecom connectivity at scale. This spurred the growth of ITES/BPO sector in India.

8

Proud to be Indian!

The universe is made of stories, not of atoms.
        −Muriel Rukeyser, *The Speed of Darkness*

I believe in the power of stories. The stories we tell may not be accurate or even true. It is what the listeners believe. Bottle the same wine differently and sell it at different prices, people will believe the expensive one tastes better.

To put India on the world map, we had to tell a story that the global businesses could put their faith in. For India Inc., we had to edit out the snake charmers and add the narrative of keyboard tapping programmers, sitting in towers of glass and steel.

Indian software had begun to show promise in the 1980s. It was a time when people in the richer countries knew little about India. At that time, the Western media routinely provided comic relief with pictures of cows obstructing traffic on Indian roads. The country

117

represented poverty and widespread ignorance, a primeval place without infrastructure. Sadly, this was nearly true.

The riches of India lay in its almost mythical heritage, not its present-day culture. It was once a source of great wealth and a centre of knowledge. But civilizations are oceans, and they rise and ebb. Centuries of military conflict, invasions and colonization left the subcontinent impoverished. After India won independence from British rule, it adopted socialism. In the bipolar world of the time, it struggled to stay non-aligned, but grew close to the USSR. By the late 1980s, when the Indian economy fissured to its foundations, the USSR, too, was crumbling. India was left with no friends.

Whenever India broke past its misery, it was ignored by world media. Whenever anything bad happened to it, like floods or a train accident, it was suddenly on the front pages. The news that was fit to print was the news that fit India's sorry image.

It was clearly a branding problem that was staring the country in the face, and yet no one had decided to focus on this.

Through the 1980s and early 1990s, this bad image had become a nightmare for India's first truly global industry: software.

Against the backdrop of a poor nation on the brink, Indians were standing in American boardrooms, making lofty promises to help them conquer their most complex technological challenges. If this were not outright audacious, it would have been quixotic. Indian software entrepreneurs were relentless. Yet, for no fault of theirs, this tenacity did not yield the results they expected. India was not a good country to be associated with. Period.

So, how could India overcome this challenge?

A brand is intangible and complicated. It comprises dozens of attributes. To understand the complexity of this task, let us begin with something as straightforward as trust. How can an American company trust an Indian company with no track record to deliver quality and on time? Unlike consumer goods, where the quality can be ascertained beforehand, a service is experienced after it has been paid for. This is why a list of references from happy clients is essential to a services business. One company here or there may overcome these start-up issues. But how do you help a nationwide scatter of companies that suffer from the West's reluctance to put 'India' and 'computers' in the same sentence?

India was just not ready to do business with the world. Until the 1990s, it had not done much to mint business-friendly laws. A vile nexus of neta (politicians), lala (businessmen) and babu (bureaucrats) would make quick and arbitrary policy changes that helped a few at the expense of a national economic strategy. They would be backed by jhola (media), baba (religious leaders) and judges. The gundas (henchmen) would ensure that there was no dissent. 'Setting ho gaya'[1] was the way of doing business. To make matters worse, the same policies inadvertently led to the image of India being an exporter of poor-quality products. This was yet another branding disaster.

The 'licence raj' had closed the economy to global business. Socialist India hadn't really competed on quality in any category.

In the 1980s, the world was rushing to evolve passenger cars, competing to add innovative features to a new model every year. But India was in a parallel universe, content with the rarely changing, antiquated and ungainly Ambassador car. The joke was that everything in the Ambassador made a sound, except the horn.

Another example from the era is wristwatches. The world produced a range of watches from jewellery-like luxuries to cheaper yet trendy fashion wear. Once again, India betrayed its command-economy mind when it insisted on churning out utilitarian industrial designs from a machine tools manufacturer like HMT, not a fashion company. From cars and watches to just about everything was protected by the government, removing all incentives for innovation and progress.

One of the biggest blows to India's image was delivered by businesses manipulating government rules: struggling with a balance of payments

---

1   'We have made an arrangement.' Often used to describe an arrangement made via coercion or offering bribes.

crisis, India had clamped down on the spending of foreign exchange. Consequently, import licenses were sold at a premium of as high as 700 per cent. But there was a catch. You had to export first to earn the right to use the import license. Just to tick that box, Indian companies exploited this arbitrage opportunity that came as a result of policy and began exporting products of questionable quality. They did not care about reputation, as long as they got the import licenses that they could further sell for a profit. As a result, India earned the notorious and dubious reputation of a nation that peddled poor-quality goods. The stigma prevailed well after the liberalization of the economy and haunted software companies for a long time.

I believe this was as much the doing of policymakers as of the Indian entrepreneurs. The government did not believe in self-regulation and often took decisions that gave them short-term control over situations instead of long-term gains for the ecosystem.

NASSCOM realized early on that brand India Inc. was the real problem. We made it a crusade to change the India story. Slowly and determinedly, industry entrepreneurs and NASSCOM worked on the perceptions of our clients in the West. We kept looking for that big turning point in the narrative when a mention of India would evoke 'technology destination' as a synonym.

Oh, that turning point did arrive, and its place is secure in history. Thanks to the benefit of hindsight, how we did it is now apparent to us. Back then, we merely kept doing our work.

Today, an Indian engineer is respected more than an average engineer from the West. Some of us may take glory for granted. But none of it was accidental.

Ask what you can do

Instead of waiting for the government to overhaul the India Inc. brand, we decided to start our own parallel agenda. This was going to be a long and arduous journey, and there was no time to be lost. Right from the start, it was a concerted effort. We had tasks marked out for everyone: NASSCOM as an organization, its member companies and even individuals.

We began looking for good things to say about ourselves. There were plenty.

Indian engineers were naturals at software development. Largely because of a culture that makes Indians read mathematics as if it were poetry. Mohandas Pai, erstwhile CFO of Infosys, is probably the epitome of this. He can run a large set of simultaneous equations in his head and cut and slice data in many different ways. He can talk about both macro and micro indicators at the drop of a hat. I remember, at a TiE Mumbai conference, a full house of more than 1,000 delegates gave him a standing ovation for his powerful speech. This was the first time I saw the audience cheering for a speaker like that.

Culturally, India is not a homogenous place. As a result, early in life, Indians develop the empathy needed to work with people from different backgrounds. You grow up learning how to decipher, decode and respond to the complex nuances of other Indians around you, who did not speak your mother tongue. This intangible quality was the biggest strength of Indians when it came to executing the 'global delivery model'.

Middle-class values and the accompanying attitude were deeply embedded in Indian engineers. Almost all of them grow up coping with a shortage of almost everything around them. As a response, they develop a solution-oriented mind. Indian engineers also have the inherent advantage of being able to live with ambiguity and shifting goalposts.

We are thus more attuned to the changing management process, one of the cornerstones of the services business[2] and the global delivery model.

---

2   More often than not, in the service business, the business is sealed on a promise. The requirement is not sharply defined and is ever evolving. Thus, it's routine to see changes in quotes, time estimates, resource allocation and even the scope of the service to be delivered.

The other advantage that we offered was that Indians are trained from an early age to speak and think in English. This further added to our ability to service complex global requirements in the language spoken by businesses around the world.

On the upside, India was making stricter anti-piracy laws. The economy was opening up, and Indian talent was getting smarter while continuing to explode in numbers. Indian entrepreneurs had also begun exploring the English-speaking world.

There was plenty of good qualities all around. The challenge now was to corral these, string them into a story and sing it out to the world. And that's what NASSCOM proceeded to do.

It takes colossal effort to change the image of an entire country, even if it's in the minds of a select few.[3] Bereft of resources, every brand-building idea had to be frugal. We worked on the optics first. As I mentioned earlier, we appended five slides to the start of every pitch presentation made by every member company. In those slides, we reinforced that India is the largest democracy in the world. We highlighted India's rich heritage and its knowledge centres; about how an Indian called Aryabhata invented the zero. We also talked about the number of Indian engineering resources and the opportunity we presented as a market of over a billion people. These slides were so important that we offered them to every Indian software company, including those that were not NASSCOM members. All of them readily accepted our suggestion and used the slides in their presentations.

We also asked member companies to train their engineers abroad in the language of the brand messages we had crafted. Suddenly, thousands of engineers started quietly promoting India Inc. in harmony with what we were formally doing.

India's Ministry of External Affairs (MEA) pitched in, too, and sent the NASSCOM slides to every Indian ambassador in the world. With

---

3   We, at NASSCOM, targeted our branding efforts to a set of 5,000–10,000 global companies and their leadership teams. These were the future prospects and potential customers for Indian IT companies.

TiE's help, we also made Indians in the Silicon Valley aware of our branding story, and they retold it for us.

Indians abroad were traditionally called NRIs. Unfortunately, they were also derisively called 'Non-Reliable Indians'. This had to change. So, in the US, we started consciously using the term 'Indian Americans' and reinforcing the right values. These Indian Americans further became our ambassadors—they were making India proud with their conduct, hard work and achievements. They were research scientists, engineers, doctors, NASA scientists, Nobel Prize winners, spelling bee winners and super-successful entrepreneurs (the last in the world's most fiercely competitive market—Silicon Valley). We gave them the extra fodder required to ramp up the reputation of India.

NASSCOM took ownership of amplifying the message with celebrity influencers from the technology and software industry who were visiting India at the time for their respective businesses with Indian IT companies. NASSCOM would keep track of these movements and request them to make positive statements about Indian IT. NASSCOM would then plug these quotes as headlines in the media, both in India and abroad.

These included giants like Eric Schmidt of Novell,[4] Bill Gates of Microsoft, John Chambers of Cisco, and Nicholas Negroponte,[5] the founder and chairman emeritus of MIT's Media Lab.

I remember, once I had invited Eric Schmidt, then the chairperson of Onward-Novell, to India to talk about the partnership. The ballroom I booked at the Oberoi hotel in Mumbai had a capacity of 300. However, more than 1,500 people were waiting, and people had

---

4   Eric was previously at Sun, eventually at Google and, at the time of writing this book, a co-founder of Schmidt Futures.
5   Nicholas is a futurist renowned for predicting, way back in 1984, the now ubiquitous technologies such as e-readers, face-to-face teleconferencing and touchscreen phones. When he came to India, he was so convinced of the India opportunity that he set up an MIT Media Lab in Mumbai.

to queue around the hotel to get a chance to hear him speak. Such was the appeal of these celebrity influencers at NASSCOM forums.

Let me digress for a bit to talk about an incident when Eric was floored by Indian ingenuity. In 1997, Eric was in India. He had little faith in India as a market because the Internet was almost non-existent, and Novell's bread and butter were essentially network solutions. One of the flagship products was Novell Directory, and it required the Internet as the base layer to operate. He had predicted that Onward-Novell would die in a year as India had no Internet at the time. However, when he came down to India, the team at Onward-Novell presented a case study on how India's largest bank, the State Bank of India (SBI), was using Novell Netware as the base operating system for branch automation. We had helped SBI write this software in BASIC. It was not a default choice, but, given the constraints, it was perfect. I am proud that it was written in India by Indian talent. It eventually ran on more than 15,000 branches across India. Compared to this, in the US, to write a complex branch automation software, they would typically use higher-level languages like COBOL or RPG that are closer to English. This opened Eric's eyes to our ingenuity of finding a solution that worked within the constraints of poor connectivity and affordability. He eventually did a volte-face and actually wrote a global company-wide email, saying Onward-Novell was an ideal JV, and all partners must work like it by localizing solutions tailored to the target market.

Coming back, we would use the appeal of these Silicon Valley celebrities to our advantage and further the India Inc. brand.

Missions impossible

In the mid-1980s, for the first time, I went to formally promote Indian software overseas. I was with a delegation led by the Department of Electronics.[6] With great expectations, we landed in the US. Our

---

6   This was before we had started to focus on brand India Inc.

confidence was straining at the leash, ready to break free and win over America. We were confident our event would turn the course of Indian history.

But then, we entered the venue.

The place was filled to near capacity with non-resident Indians. There were no American honchos lining up to meet us. It was a complete failure for the delegation, whose primary goal was to befriend American businesses. Curious about what went wrong, I asked an Indian guest, a former colleague from my days in Hartford, Connecticut. He said he was there to eat authentic Indian food as the event was hosted by the Indian Consulate. We returned, dejected and humbled. We had much to learn about building the India Inc. brand.

At another time, in 1991, when I was the chairperson of NASSCOM, the Ministry of Commerce planned to send a business delegation to France. One of its stated aims was to promote the software business. It was important that the chairperson of the industry body that we were seeding travels with the delegation. However, as the founder of recently launched Onward, I knew my company had no interest in France as a country. At best, I could have furthered Onward's brand. Going with the delegation would have meant an expense of over ₹1,00,000[7] for my fledgling, cash-starved company. I almost didn't go.

Ironically, it was I who had championed NASSCOM's strict policy of not sponsoring anybody's travel expenses even if they were travelling for NASSCOM work. I wanted to reinforce that the organization was not a social club where the office-bearers are showered with free travel, PR opportunities or other perks.

Onward's CEO at the time, Nandu Pradhan, insisted I go and my colleagues supported the decision. So, with reluctance, I mustered the courage, and the cash, to make the trip.

The delegation was led by the Minister of Commerce, Mr P. Chidambaram. We were looking forward to it as France was a

---

7   About ₹800,000 in today's value.

greenfield opportunity. The French treated us warmly to great food and even better conversation. When the meeting ended, we were curious about their discussions among themselves. We hoped they were discussing possible projects and how to make them work. When we asked a French delegate, who I thought was of Indian origin, he reluctantly told us that the general feeling among them was, 'These beggars have landed up. Now what do we do with them?'

Chidambaram's charm and negotiations were a washout. NASSCOM's French counterpart was highly protectionist. France was not ready for any international player. The courtesy was superficial and the event humiliating, to say the least. After a fantastic five-course meal, served with the most exquisite wine, we walked out of that palatial venue demoralized.

There had to be a better way for recasting brand India Inc., earn ourselves respect and recoup our loss of dignity.

Slash of cultures

The Indian software services industry needed to embrace the global culture. India's many diverse cultures meant that not every region in the country was equally well-positioned to participate in our industry.

Consider the irony of Gujarat. Arguably, it is the most entrepreneurial of all places in India. Yet, it completely failed to be a part of the Indian software revolution. I believe that the problem was in the business culture of Gujaratis. A typical Gujarati businessman is a trader by mentality. He likes to run a tight ship. He also keeps as much control with himself as possible. Gujaratis don't employ too many people, either. And even if they must, they would rather employ them from within the family. Though the new generation of Gujarati entrepreneurs was indeed breaking ground, most were focused on asset-driven or capital-driven businesses.

This mindset is the exact opposite of the one needed. A software entrepreneur must trust a large number of people within an organization, build systems and relinquish control. Even as employees, most Gujaratis are not fans of working for big set-ups and would rather strike it on their own, even if in a small way.

What Gujarat largely lacks is structured entrepreneurship. Labour laws have always been a challenge for business owners, and it continues to be so even today—especially in the manufacturing sector. Unions are continually negotiating terms over one thing or another.[8]

Building a services business in the midst of this culture was a challenge. Unlike manufacturing, the business Gujaratis preferred, services companies don't even have guaranteed sales.

Earlier, in the late 1990s, Gujarat Chief Minister Dilip Parikh had called us for an 'urgent meeting'. We rushed to Gandhinagar. He had seen Oracle's campus in the US, and he wanted to replicate the same in Gujarat and make it an IT destination. He almost threw a blank cheque at us and said, 'How much space do you want?' He had assumed replicating the infrastructure would be good enough to help create another Oracle in Gujarat. We tried explaining that constructing a building is not the same as building a successful software business. We gave him a list of recommendations that included finer aspects like working on the English language skills of graduating engineers.

Unlike Gujarat, we had numerous examples from other states and industries where we, as a country, leveraged our diversity to spawn large industries from literally nothing. For example, the automobile industry has thrived in unlikely locations like Gurgaon and Manesar.[9] Even Hyderabad was 'made to happen' by the visionary Chandrababu Naidu.[10]

---

8   The solution was and remains simple. In has three levers. One, Gujarat needs flexible and fair labour laws. Two, it must invite large companies to act as anchors to kick-start the IT business. Three—the most important—is to develop and encourage software entrepreneurs.

9   Geographically, the satellite cities to Delhi are far from an ocean corridor or from any source of raw material—the two things essential for the success of a heavy-industry operation.

10 I read somewhere, 'Bangalore happened; Hyderabad was made to happen.' I couldn't agree more. Hyderabad happened only because of the vision and

The question that remained was: could we take these lessons, navigate the cultural conundrum and establish brand India Inc.?

Casting India

When you think of Germany, you think of engineering. When someone says Italy, we think of styling and design. The French conjure up the fine arts. What did the mention of India evoke? To find out, NASSCOM conducted an informal survey.

It found that there was no single response defining India. We did not really stand for anything in particular.

The optimist in me was certain that India's case was not lost. It was possible. We just had to look harder. My colleagues and I took

---

leadership of Mr N. Chandrababu Naidu, the then chief minister of the erstwhile undivided Andhra Pradesh.

Naidu learnt that one in four software engineers is from Andhra Pradesh. He started wondering why couldn't the state be developed into an IT hub. He was told that it would take more than mere questions; it demanded substantial on-ground actions to make Hyderabad happen.

Naidu could foresee the impact that the IT industry could have on the fortunes of his people. He took steps unheard of at the time.

He identified a team lead by R. Chandrasekhar (Shekhar), who was smart enough to understand what was needed. Shekhar eventually went on to become NASSCOM president from 2014 to 2018.

Naidu allocated land and partnered with the likes of Larsen & Toubro to build sprawling campuses that could house these IT businesses. He knew if he put good infrastructure, a supportive policy framework and strong political willingness together, Hyderabad would happen. Businesses would flock to the city, and they would bring the peripheral things required to let the machinery become a self-sustaining one.

He even gave what most other political leaders typically don't: his personal time and attention. I remember, on one of his trips to Hyderabad, Kanwal Rekhi had a packed schedule and some people wanted him to meet Naidu. Usually, one would expect a long wait before a chief minister would make time for a meeting; Kanwal didn't have that sort of time. However, when Naidu heard about it, he graciously invited Kanwal to meet him as soon as he landed, and even asked him to his house for breakfast at 6.30 in the morning. Politicians like Naidu are a rarity.

encouragement from the story of Japan. How did it overcome the perception of a nation that mass-produced cheap and low-quality products? How did it become synonymous with cutting-edge technology? How did companies like Toyota and Sony come to be?

Then, out of the blue, in 1994, we got lucky. Something happened in a domain none of us could even imagine looking at. Two wonderfully articulate women from India, Aishwarya Rai and Sushmita Sen, won the Miss World and Miss Universe titles, respectively. India's visibility on the global stage shot up. Both women spoke with poise and panache and projected the modern face of India.

At the time, there was no representation or spokesperson for Indian IT's focus on quality. We realized we could use the newfound attention to add a sheen to the reputation Indian engineers had abroad.

To capitalize on this, Dewang proposed that NASSCOM host a fashion show on the theme of Indian heritage. Fashion shows in those days were not as common as they are today. So, ludicrous as it sounded, Dewang further added that in addition to supermodels, the IT CEOs and their spouses would walk the ramp!

At first, I thought he was crazy. NASSCOM was a serious industry body, working with the highest levels in the government and with business leaders around the world. What message would we send out by the frivolity of this fashion show?

After an intense debate, we were eventually able to count enough reasons to go ahead with it. We would not just get the branding in place; we could attract more Indian entrepreneurs from around the world and bigger sponsors to strengthen NASSCOM's war chest.

Dewang contracted the National Institute of Fashion Technology (NIFT), Delhi, to conduct a fashion show with fifteen models walking the ramp.

In the next edition, in 1997, there was a suggestion to take this event all the way to the Elephanta Caves, a UNESCO heritage site on an island off the coast of Bombay. It was a bizarre idea, but we bounced it off Jayant Kawale, CEO of the Maharashtra Industrial Development Corporation (MIDC). To our surprise, he was very enthusiastic.

Organizing a fashion show on the remote site was going to be a logistical nightmare. There was no electricity on the island, and several diesel generators would have to be ferried to it. We would have to build everything from scratch. We would have to ship out chairs and even prepare the food on site. The task looked impossible, but we kept at it. We secured eighteen approvals from institutions such as the forest department, the Coast Guard and even the Indian Navy.

Eventually, over 400 delegates, including many foreigners, were ferried to a mesmerizing event. Speakers had poured in from all over the globe, and the media was in full attendance.

At the peak of the glittering proceedings, I stepped away, took a silent moment and smiled as I recalled our first event where no American client had turned up just a few years ago, even though we were hosting the event in the US itself.

After Dewang passed away, we decided to continue the tradition.

For the next edition, in 2003, we came up with the theme, Vasudhaiva Kutumbakam, Sanskrit for 'the world is a family'. We roped in the actor Nitish Bhardwaj as the master of ceremonies and choreographer. He was extremely popular then as he had played the role of Lord Krishna in the blockbuster TV series *Mahabharata*. The branding subtext was that India is not a predator stealing local jobs in the West. Rather, it is a cultural force unifying the world into one family.

Despite the coverage we were getting for the fashion show, over half of our members believed we had trivialized NASSCOM by turning it into a fancy-dress show. Jerry Rao[11] of Mphasis didn't approve of the religious symbols and words on stage, and he believed it came across as religious propaganda.

---

11 Jerry is a self-made entrepreneur, one of the key figureheads of the BPO industry and a man known to have very strong principles. Everyone I know has the highest regard for Jerry and when he speaks, you take him seriously.

During rehearsals, another leader came up to me and complained, 'Yeh kya tamasha chal raha hai?'[12] I turned it around on him and goaded him to walk the ramp as well, and he almost agreed!

Flexes (banners) had been printed, costumes prepared, yet the disgruntled voices rose to a point where I was uncertain about the event happening at all, let alone the fashion show. I was airdropped into the middle of it to bring the organizers and the sceptics on the same page. I pacified Jerry and told everyone to not take themselves so seriously. We had found a simple solution. We put NASSCOM posters atop the ones that some people had found offensive.

I then dressed up as Swami Vivekananda, the first truly global Indian. Ganesh Natarajan of Zensar dressed as the Maratha icon, Chhatrapati Shivaji Maharaj, and his wife, Uma, wore a nauvari, the nine-yard saree. Atul Nishar, former chairperson of NASSCOM, and his wife, Alka, dressed up as Shankar and Parvati. Many others dressed up as other mythological and religious figures.

Despite the scepticism around the show, the event was a roaring success. The media went to town with it. Many of us who walked the ramp went from nondescript IT bosses to becoming overnight celebrities on Page 3.

The thief of Bangalore

We thought the branding problem was a transient one that, once solved, would not bug us anymore. But creating brand India Inc. was turning out to be riding on a never-ending circle. We realized the severity of the problem when we first heard the American term 'Bangalored'. It was used to describe people losing their jobs to Indians.

From Y2K heroes, we had become job-stealing thieves. I could never have imagined that our branding success was a branding problem in itself. So much so that the phenomenon even made it to popular culture across the globe! In the US, they made sitcoms titled

12 Translated into English, 'What is this circus about?'

Silicon Valley (which ran for six seasons) and *Outsourced* (which ran for one season). In the UK, they made *The IT Crowd* (which ran for five seasons).

Indian engineers had come to love the idea of going abroad for a project. Their reasons varied.

Often, the attraction lay in the promise of a higher salary and cultural exposure. Then there was always the set of pragmatic Indians who wished to put in a few years of hardship to stack up on savings. Unlike them, there were Indians who sought some years of fun before settling down with responsibility. A few planned to settle down in the US for good.

In the initial years of NASSCOM, H-1B US visas were big on the agenda. It took up most of the discussion time in EC meetings. In those days, Indian software services only did on-site projects, which came to be known as body shopping. To serve international businesses, highly educated and qualified Indian engineers had to first be trained by the clients and then placed in their offices. This meant that a company's income was proportional to the number of H-1B visas it acquired. In the beginning, Indian engineers only provided services involving skills like COBOL, Fortran, RPG or data migration. But once they were trained, they were thrice as productive as their American counterparts.

We had started out by using business visas. With these, engineers could go to the US for a short term. However, the arrangement failed us for longer projects. As the business and the impact delivered by Indian engineers grew, both Indian companies and their American clients wanted a practical alternative where talent could stay and work in the US for a longer duration.

This led to the creation of the H-1B visa in 1990 under US immigration laws. About 65,000 H-1B visas were made available for the year. These could be issued to highly skilled professionals who satisfy certain criteria. At that time, giants like Microsoft and IBM were among the largest users of H-1B.

H-1B set the stage for the coming of India's 'global delivery model'. Most Indian software services companies had over 80 per cent of revenues coming from on-site work.

Ironically, in the US, the very same visas had sparked a debate on outsourcing. Politicians thrived by creating fictitious challenges, and India was a target every time an election was around the corner in the US. Till date, India continues to be accused of stealing American jobs and continues to fight loud hate campaigns.

If NASSCOM had to do something about the H-1B controversies, it would have to first address the branding problem. We dropped the term 'outsourcing' and positioned India as a trusted business partner. We recast 'business process outsourcing' (BPO) as 'business process management' (BPM). We explained to the Americans that by bringing efficiency to their industries, we were growing their economy, catalysing growth and improving their business environment. Consequently, we were creating more jobs than we were eating into. A McKinsey global study had found that for every dollar that the US spent on outsourcing, it earned back $1.4.

It took years of effort to change perceptions, but we kept at it. Over the years, in spite of the political backlash in the US, the number of H-1B visas taken up by Indians has kept growing.

Even today, the outsourcing debates persist, but the way Americans interact with Indians has completely transformed.

From back office to boardroom

Some are born great, some achieve greatness, and some have greatness thrust upon 'em.

—William Shakespeare

For a developing nation like India, there are hardly any industries in the third category of greatness. But the IT industry and, most definitely, the BPO industry firmly belong to the second category. In fact, it had to toil significantly to get its due, let alone to find greatness. It was 'a thing' long before it became recognized as a legit industry. The journey from 'we do your mess for less' to a 'strategic business process management partner' has been challenging yet fulfilling.

It started as a business of captive outsourcing centres in the 1990s, where big MNCs would get their non-strategic processes offshored. It soon became a victim of typecast perceptions—night shifts in fancy buildings made of steel and glass, tele callers with fake names with fake accents, cabs that buzzed across the city at all hours of the day and night; and worst of all, displeased US or UK end customers. What started as a back office for global operations continued to expand its canvas with time and eventually became a part of almost every high-level policy discussion in boardrooms across the world.

Even the numbers validate the shift. Consider the Indian BPO industry today—$38 billion in revenue, seventy-eight countries, 1.3 million direct jobs and uncountable indirect jobs. We are easily the global leader by a distance—we have 36 per cent of the global market! Leading with not just quantity but quality, too, we are now providing world-class, deep-domain-expertise-based innovative services across industries.

Is it just about cost? No way.

The Indian BPM industry has gone way beyond cost efficiencies to deliver on process expertise, innovation, cost planning and capacity expansion.

The shift from BPO to BPM was not just a change of name. Neither did it happen by chance.

It was carefully planned and meticulously executed. It was thoroughly enriching for the Indian IT industry and even for the clients' industries. The motivation came from the negative baggage of 'outsourcing' and associated perceptions.

We knew we needed to do a lot more than merely renaming BPO to BPM. The journey went through four distinct stages. The first was when American giants like GE and American Express created captive outsourcing centres in India. The second was brought about by third-party BPOs, often seeded by deep pockets of venture capitalists. These went on to build an impressive portfolio of global clients.

The third stage was when IT services companies started to leverage synergies to create their BPO arms. Finally, in the fourth stage, we saw the emergence of vertical (industry) and horizontal (business) processes focused players.

We, at NASSCOM, had to work in close cohesion with stakeholders, entrepreneurs, regulators, and even the country's legal infrastructure to keep the powerful force marching on.

Just like in the initial days of the services business, the BPM business also had its share of uncalled-for issues. At one time, the DOE wanted to charge a 100 per cent export duty on the salary of each BPM employee. This would have delivered a punch to the guts of not just entrepreneurs but also millions of people who were dependent on BPM jobs. Worse, this would have killed the spirit of entrepreneurship. The second-order effects would have been to miss out on the opportunity to leverage skills inherent to India. The brand India Inc. would have probably felt an irrevocable setback, as well.

Thankfully, the regulation was dismissed.

Today, both IT and BPM services have built capabilities to reimagine and redesign projects that have a far-reaching impact. Case in point? Work from our member companies on governmental processes that have improved the quality of citizen services manifold.

At NASSCOM, we could have dismissed the BPO and BPM business as noise and refused to act on the emerging trend. However, it was the foresight and pre-emptive actions that helped incubate the BPO and BPM business, and encourage the industry to flourish. The strong partnership between NASSCOM, entrepreneurs and leaders at these companies acted as the further catalyst.

The bug that roared

Eventually, irrespective of the region that an Indian engineer came from, the country's software industry did develop a global culture of its own. That came from on-site work in the capitals of the world. The

Y2K bug had drawn young people from the small towns of India and scattered them across the planet.

How real was the Y2K bug? Well, a lot of computer code then had only two digits representing the year. People feared that rolling into the year 2000 would confuse the computers. No computer would be able to tell the difference between the years 2000 and 1000, or even 0000. If that happened, no one could rely on computers. To add to the complexity, the bug could either be at the hardware level, software level or even with both.

By the middle of the 1990s, most industries across the world were already dependent on computers. The media started writing graphic descriptions of the worst-case Y2K scenarios. Mass hysteria set in. People imagined their life's savings getting wiped out in an electronic bank ledger, ships sinking, satellites spinning out of control, aeroplanes dropping from the skies, and, yes, nuclear power stations doing a Chernobyl.

The severity of the problems varied. Though it was mostly harmless, some did need attention against a rapidly approaching deadline.

Even the Fortune 500 giants were alarmed, lost even. They needed solutions that were robust and scalable. And they needed them fast. Hunting down this bug and squishing it meant millions of hours of human effort, which was eventually provided by the armies of Indian programmers. The same problem on processors, or chips, required even more intensive work because it meant going physically to the level of the chip and launching another seek-and-destroy mission.

The software industry had just started out in India, and already it was scrambling to educate, train, orient and deploy young people in this attack on the Y2K bug. Youngsters, who had never stepped out of their dusty, sleepy little towns, were now ranging out in alien worlds. Most were earning a salary in foreign exchange in their first job, and often it was a few times what their parents made.

The biggest dividend of the Y2K bug was not the money that Indian companies made, but it was a positive impact on brand India

Inc. We now had marquee Fortune 500 companies as clients. To an outsider, this may seem like luck. But to us, on the inside, this was a classic case of preparation meets opportunity.

The significance of Indian software services had dawned upon everyone. The brand drove up the capitalization of American and Indian software consulting and services companies listed in the US markets. They rose from 0.7 times the top line to 1.4 times within a matter of a few years. Infosys had become the first IT company from India to get listed on the NASDAQ (in March 1999). Syntel and Mastech Digital too made history on US stock markets.

It helped that Indian engineers were not afraid of learning and making changes to the undocumented programmes written in legacy programming languages. This enabled the re-engineering of customers' systems to respond to newer challenges. The Fortune 500 customers saw tremendous value in using high-quality, low-cost developers from India.

Also, India's ability to quickly gain proficiency in the waves of open-source technologies, the client-server model and the Java language eventually consolidated what the brand had promised.

Many have argued that the Y2K bug was a windfall, like the reforms of 1991. True. Sometimes good fortune achieves more than hard work. But you must be prepared for it. After all, fortune favours the bold and the brave. The Indian software entrepreneurs were both.

Come for the cost, stay for the quality

It was clear to us that brand India Inc. would have to represent more than labour cost arbitrage.[13] The software industry could win respect only by making India a destination for world-class quality.

---

13 However, Indian industry has maintained the labour arbitrage benefit, despite Indian salaries hitting the roof. Simple math reveals that at INR to USD pegged at 50 to 1, an Indian engineer getting an annual salary of ₹7,00,000 with a raise of 15 per cent every year would still be cheaper than an American engineer getting an annual salary of $100,000 with a raise of

Quality has always been a contentious debate. One of the root causes why this plagued software services and clients globally was the lack of a clear project definition or a scope of work. Contracts were often signed without sufficient details. The most relevant pieces of information were never documented, leading to general confusion. Here's an oversimplified example: what does it mean when the client says 'location'? Does it mean the company's headquarters or all locations? Do 'all locations' then include the locations of subsidiaries and contractors? How do you define subsidiaries or contractors?

These problems were neither new nor endemic to India. Even in 1972, when I was working at The Travelers Companies in Hartford, Connecticut, there was this adage on the floor: 95 per cent projects remain 95 per cent done. This is because lack of domain knowledge, compounded by poor communication in English, makes project specifications incomplete. Often, corrections made at later dates lead to major rewrites and renders the systems buggy.

Eventually, the US Department of Defence funded research to find a method to deliver projects on time, within costs and with world-class quality. Later, the Software Engineering Institute (SEI) at Carnegie Mellon University improved upon the initial work and published a paper to define a process where the customer and the developer sign on a well-documented scope of work. The university also began studying companies and graded them for the level of their process maturity. It was called the SEI CMMI (or capability maturity model integration), and its Level 5 was the best grade any company could achieve.

Could this become the currency for brand India Inc.? NASSCOM decided to bring about quality consciousness among software companies, and conducted seminars and workshops all over the country to train software engineers.

NASSCOM also requested every software company employing over 100 software engineers to get the SEI CMMI Level 5 certification.

---

3 per cent per year. In fact, the labour cost arbitrage will continue to offer an advantage to India for a long time to come.

The Motorola Software Design Centre, Bangalore, run by Anand Khandekar, was the first out of the gate. Several Indian companies followed and were among the first few to get the Level 5 certification, and it began a quiet revolution. It marked the beginning of the India Inc. brand being incrementally recognized for the quality of its work.

NASSCOM members saw the importance of these certifications, and one after another, Indian companies started getting SEI certifications. We crossed the highest number of quality certifications in the world. As per research conducted by Prof. V. Rajaraman in 1999, six out of twelve CMMI Level 5 certified companies in the world were in India. It reached a point where, when requests for proposals (RFPs) were floated asking for the CMMI Level 5 certification as a prerequisite, for every RFP, four out of five proposals were by Indian companies. In the same report, Prof. Rajaraman further identified that by 2010, Indian IT companies would be recognized as world-class based on their performance. The major companies had graduated from delivering low-level QA and testing projects to developing end-to-end applications. Instead of costing their projects based on input costs and expenses, Indian companies were now competing for fixed-price contracts to deliver application software of requisite quality in a specified time. The greatest advantage Indian IT companies now had was project planning experience and process maturity, as evidenced by their attaining the SEI CMMI Level 5 certification.

The India Inc. brand strengthened dramatically on this bedrock of solid quality delivery. Clients were assured that India not only offered a lower cost but also delivered on quality.

We, however, had trickier problems to tackle than just solving for processes or quality. The cultural issues confronted us with the biggest challenge. Indians were not seen as good team players. We were considered competitive, but not in a constructive way. A popular joke was that one Indian is greater than one American, but three Indians are lesser than three Americans.

The rebranding effort was far from over.

Yet, the Indian software entrepreneurs did end up solving problems for companies in over a hundred countries. At one point, just TCS operated in more countries than most airlines do. It all came off on the back of extreme effort in strengthening human capital, among other things.

I say extreme effort because companies in India even began initiatives like installing coin-operated laundromats at training centres on their campuses. We were preparing engineers with life skills for the countries they were about to be sent off to. These engineers were also trained to communicate better, including voice and accent neutralization lessons.

Eventually, all kinds of complex projects were executed all over the world. Indian IT was doing it all. Delivery models ranged from outsourcing to right-sourcing; from being a quality destination to a trusted sourcing nation; from on-site to offshore, to nearshore; from data migration to complex projects like the modernization of the London Underground's signalling systems that ensures zero train collisions; and to business transformation projects and more. And everywhere.

We were delivering cost savings for our clients year after year and yet maintaining healthy profit margins. Plus, it was not just about performance it was also about consistency—a sustainable source of competitive advantage. All this was reinforcing the brand India Inc.

Unsafely home

While we struggled to make the world consider India as a technology destination, we realized that this perception was becoming a serious challenge back home as well.

In 2004, Chief Minister Vilasrao Deshmukh was elected a second time to lead the state of Maharashtra. During his first term, he was amongst our strongest advocates and supporters. Now, he seemed unresponsive.

We had guessed the reason for falling out of favour with him. Several recent events had made politicians wary of associating with the software and IT industry. A big one was the failure of the Bharatiya

Janata Party's (BJP) nationwide election campaign in 2004 that had taken 'India Shining' as a key communication plank.[14] The slogan was supposed to rally everyone around economic progress, and the software industry was a big part of that story.

Yet, the campaign failed and the BJP lost the election. The Indian National Congress (Congress) had focused on the 600 million Indians who did not speak English and came out on top. These people were poorer, and economic prosperity had not reached their homes. At least, not directly. Congress positioned themselves as the party on the side of the common man and blamed BJP for serving merely the elite. They had asked questions like 'Aam aadmi ko kya mila? Jinke ghar pehle se shining hai, unke gharon me aur shine aa rahi hai. Aapka kuch nahi ho raha.'[15]

Another direct hit in the same year was when Karnataka's chief minister, Mr S.M. Krishna, failed to get re-elected. He was affiliated with the Congress at the time and had run a campaign that relied heavily on the positive impact that the IT industry had made and had promised to help grow the industry further. His campaign failed. While there were visible advancements that the city of Bangalore had made, people at large in Karnataka refused to buy in to his vision. Yet again, the common man seemed to have ignored the contribution of IT. Mr Krishna was voted out and had to eventually settle for a much lesser office. He was appointed Governor of Maharashtra, a move that political pundits saw as a compromise and an attempt to save face for Mr Krishna.

So clearly, the political environment was not conducive to a leader getting visibly attached to the IT industry.

---

14 More information at https://en.wikipedia.org/wiki/India_Shining.
15 'What did an average Indian, a common man, get? The impact of India Shining is serving merely the ones who are already well-off. You have been left untouched.' The subtext was who the impact of development across the country was merely enjoyed by a select few who could speak English and worked directly or indirectly only for these people.

When we went to meet Mr Deshmukh and asked him about his evasiveness, he told us, 'Mujhe governor banne ki koi jaldi nahi hai.'[16]

We had to fix this because if we lost the patronage and support of the politicians, it would be difficult for us to get things done.

Around 2009, we met the recently elected finance minister of India, Mr Pranab Mukherjee, requesting him to extend software tax benefits for companies located at STPIs. He politely refused, but was of the view that we, as an industry, focused only on India and had failed to work for the bottom 300 million, the non-English-speaking Bharat. I disagreed with his assessment. He neither saw nor accounted for the impact that smaller companies could have as they became larger. He also ignored the cultural transformation being brought about by the IT industry, and the ripple effect created by the direct and indirect beneficiaries. Even a tiny pebble has the potential to create seemingly never-ending ripples in a calm pond. And we held far more potential than the pebble.

If this was not enough, another leading economist further questioned NASSCOM's contribution to the growth of the software industry. He pointed out that it was the British who gave English to us. Pandit Jawaharlal Nehru had built the Indian Institute of Technology, and Rajiv Gandhi popularized computers. According to him, these levers were all that was needed to create India's mammoth IT industry. Though I am non-partisan, the economist had provoked me enough to take a shot at his party. I told him, 'I agree with you because, without the leadership of your party, the average wages in India would not have remained so low that the entire software industry could be built on the base of our cheap labour.'

All's well that ends well

In the end, India did get a synonym: software. The 1990s put India on the global map. Through that decade, the big developments somehow

---

16   Translates to: 'I'm in no hurry to become a governor.'

got pulled together and prepared the country for a role on the world stage. Yet, it needed a script, that one story that would make India arrive. The rise of the IT industry became that story. One of the taglines for NASSCOM was 'Come for the cost, stay for the quality'. I am glad to say that the clients did come for the cost and indeed, they stayed back for quality.

The 2000s and 2010s were about building on the foundation that was laid down in the 1990s. Today, no global business plan is complete without an offshore facility in India.

But there was a time when India was nowhere on the global map and had to scrape for even small technology contracts. None of us could have imagined then that Walmart would spend $16 billion to acquire Flipkart, that Amazon and Netflix would look forward to growth from India, and that Reliance Jio would raise an eye-popping $21 billion.

I now hear stories where Silicon Valley investors are comforted when they spot an Indian name among the founders. The Krishnamurthy who had become Kris is now going back to being Krishnamurthy once again.

So, where were we to go from here?

I did not have to think about it. The way forward was clear: a revolution in entrepreneurship.

During my Onward-Novell JV days in the 1990s, I had first come to experience the Valley's entrepreneurial culture. That ecosystem, even then, was way ahead of any such in the world. In fact, it was unique. Most people were connected with each other. People were willing to mentor upcoming ventures. Everyone freely shared experiences. Deals moved fast because everybody knew what to expect. Trust was a huge factor in the way things worked. Term sheets and contracts were much shorter because the agility of the start-up model drove business. And not paperwork. Deals were signed over drinks, not in boardrooms. Companies were merged easily. Relationships were more personal than official, and people supported and enabled each other.

India needed this spirit if it were to go any further. It came from Kanwal Rekhi. He is a friend, a celebrity entrepreneur, a prolific angel investor and was on the Onward-Novell board. To me, he has been a source of great insight into the Western business environment. Kanwal had sold his company, Excelan, to Novell and was among the first Indians to be on the board of a billion-dollar company. Unlike other wealthy businessmen of his time, Kanwal was keen on investing money in the future and building capability at the very bottom of the pyramid. One of the biggest beneficiaries of his benevolence has been IIT Bombay.[17]

I introduced Kanwal to NASSCOM and explained our India Inc. branding challenges. I told him that we were determined to shrug off the techno-coolies tag. He was initially reluctant to believe us. He had seen India at a time when we were in a shambles, and he had become cynical. I'd even say that he was heartbroken at the state of the country. However, NASSCOM and I persisted.

With time, slowly, he saw the new India emerging at NASSCOM and began warming to this mission. Kanwal[18] further helped us by

---

17 I remember Kanwal once made a profit of approximately ₹3 million in the Indian stock market. Because of RBI restrictions, he could not take this money out of India. He made me the custodian of this corpus, to be used for a charitable cause at a later date. One time, on my recommendation, we had gone to meet Dr Deepak Phatak at IIT Bombay. Kanwal himself had fond memories of IIT as he was an alumnus. When on campus, we saw that the hostel where he had stayed as a student was in a dilapidated condition. Kanwal was moved and he instantly realized that this would be a good place for him to contribute. However, at that point, Dr Phatak could not identify a provision in the bylaws of the IIT to accept external donations. Such was the bureaucratic maze! Dr Phatak had to then spend months working with regulators in Delhi to set up a process to receive external donations. Thanks to the efforts of Dr Phatak, Kanwal's gains could be used appropriately, and students got better facilities. I was an unintended 'beneficiary' as well. Till date, Dr Phatak introduces me as an IITian, even though I am a proud engineering graduate from COEP!

18 Kanwal was probably the first NRI who donated directly to an IIT. This helped open the floodgates of donations from other NRIs to educational

inviting some of the most successful Indian Americans from Silicon Valley at a NASSCOM event, and made them share the stage with Indian IT entrepreneurs. The purpose of this event was to send out the message that Indian entrepreneurs were at par with the biggest names worldwide, and that India had arrived.

Like I had discovered decades ago, Indian Americans realized that if you weren't a WASP, you could only rise to a point and then stop. These capable professionals believed in their potential of becoming CEOs, but had hit a glass ceiling. They then took the brave step of becoming entrepreneurs. Moreover, they succeeded in the cut-throat competitive ecosystem of Silicon Valley.

Kanwal would often tease me and say that by being focused on services, we are getting paid for our sweat and not for our famed grey matter. He would ask me to bring TiE to India to promote the IP-driven businesses in India. I maintained that India was not ready yet, and the services business anyway had a lot of headroom to grow.[19]

However, during the dot-com boom, I spotted interest in the Internet business, and it started to feel that we were missing out on a big opportunity. This was when I told myself that it was now time for TiE to come to India.

---

institutions in India. Another incident that is worth cataloguing for posterity is how the Kanwal Rekhi School of Information Technology at IIT Bombay came into being. One time, Dr Phatak was visiting Silicon Valley and in one of his meetings with Kanwal, he offered to set up a school of information technology in Kanwal's name. Kanwal threw the challenge back to Dr Phatak and offered a grant of $1 million, however with the caveat that Dr Phatak find another million dollars to match Kanwal's contribution. Dr Phatak came back to India and, among others, met Nandan Nilekani. Nandan saw the potential of such a specialized school and told Dr Phatak that he would put in $2 million if Kanwal was willing to match the higher amount. Needless to say, Kanwal issued a grant of $2 million. Thanks to this playful generosity and banter between the two leaders, a world-class institution could get built.

19 Almost a decade later, at one of our more relaxed meetings, Kanwal admitted that back then, NASSCOM was right to have focused on services. The need of the hour was to reach a critical mass.

The need was clear, but I met resistance from the least likely person: Dewang. He felt TiE would cannibalize NASSCOM. He said he, too, wanted to champion entrepreneurship, albeit under the NASSCOM banner. He had no ill intentions and was equally passionate about the agenda. Only his vision and methods differed from mine. In my head, NASSCOM and TiE had complementary roles to play. NASSCOM already was the national umbrella for the software industry; TiE could be the same organization for the start-up ecosystem with city-wise chapters. Plus, TiE had chapters in numerous countries, and could thus provide easy access and connections to the who's who of the Indian diaspora.

Eventually, in 1999, with Kanwal's help, I brought TiE to India by setting up its first chapter in Mumbai. At TiE, we built a catalyst that the new wave of Indian technology entrepreneurs needed. We had to, and we did, build an entire ecosystem of founders, venture capitalists, angel investors, ideation labs, incubators and other service providers. Dewang eventually saw the merit and agreed with the harmonious existence of NASSCOM and TiE.

Today, TiE regularly engages with an active community of entrepreneurs. It has enabled thousands who credit TiE events for the networking and learning opportunities it provided. It has completed an amazing journey of over twenty years in India. At the time of writing this book, TiE comprises sixty-one chapters in fourteen countries, including fourteen chapters in India.

The brand India Inc. story that began with software services exports has now added more chapters to include all kinds of outsourcing stories: ad films for British brands get made in Andheri, Mumbai. The legal industry sends reams of data to be processed to Chandigarh and Mysore now. The BPO industry itself is an offshoot of the IT industry, borrowing heavily on its technologies, processes, and expertise. To me, one of the most exciting developments is that of the 'global capability centre' (GCC). These GCCs are revving up to accelerate engineering services and back-office operations, all set to co-create the future with Fortune 1000 companies.

Some people say India in general and software services in particular lack innovation. To them, I point out that the innovation is in the processes we have built in the software services business. I think former HP CEO Carly Fiorina summed it up at one NASSCOM India Leadership Forum (NILF)[20] session, 'You set out to change India, but you ended up changing the world with the outsourcing business model that you people have innovated.'

Around 2004, I landed in the US and hopped into a cab driven by a middle-aged Indian. Realizing that I, too, was an Indian, he asked me if I worked in the IT industry. When I said yes, he thanked me profusely. He said that because of the IT industry, the way Americans who travelled in his taxi looked at him had changed drastically almost overnight. He laughed and said, 'People who travel in my cab assume I am a PhD student driving a cab to pay for his fees. Aap logon ne humein izzat dilai hai.'[21]

I smiled gently.

His words have stayed with me. I had redeemed my decision to cut my Green Card card a couple of decades ago.

---

20 NILF was NASSCOM's annual flagship conference. The annual conference was a novel idea for India when we started. It was unheard of in the country back then to have an industry forum where competing companies and their employees were in the same room, and they could network with everyone present without any of fear of repercussions. This was our way to continue to evolve by creating a forum for knowledge-sharing. It allowed industry leaders and senior executives to learn from each other.

From the twenty-ninth edition that was held in February 2021, it has been rechristened the NASSCOM Technology and Leadership Forum (NTLF). The event is among the world's largest leadership conferences, attended by the who's who of the business world.

21 Translates to: 'You guys have given us our dignity.'

9

Copyright vs the Right to Copy

'What is your problem with piracy?' a career diplomat once chastised me. 'Let Indians enjoy it. For centuries, the West has looted this country. Now, it is our turn to reap the fruits of their labour.' This high-profile civil servant later entered politics, was elected to the Parliament and became a lawmaker.

You can easily imagine the attitude India has had towards intellectual property (IP) rights—be it copyrights, patents or trademarks.[1] On the other hand, at NASSCOM, we were certain that if India failed to secure copyrights, the world would not recognize it as a business-friendly nation, serious about participating in globalization. This was particularly critical to the nascent IT industry's growth in the late 1980s.

---

1   Even though we have done a lot towards changing the attitude towards IP rights, patents and copyrights, the issue continues to remain relevant even today. Thus, a chapter dedicated to it.

Nevertheless, when we tried to explain this to the government, the response had a simplistic refrain: 'If the Mahabharata and the Ramayana are not copyrighted, why should anything else be?' Even if made in jest, such remarks only revealed the magnitude of our problem. Let alone explaining the benefits of IP protection, we would have to begin by defining it first.

India's intellectual property rights (IPR) mess affected all kinds of industries. In the 1980s and 1990s, it was common to buy a blank cassette and pay the neighbourhood record store for a mixtape. No one realized copyright was being violated, and they were stealing from the musicians they so adored. Movie theatres in smaller towns played pirated prints. These copies were shot off the screen, with a camera smuggled into a ticketed show. Some of these even got redistributed on VHS tapes and CDs. Most college campuses had photocopy shops selling pirated prints of textbooks, often only chapters relevant to the semester's syllabus. Sharing a book's pirated copy was as honoured as the noble act of 'sharing knowledge', instead of the theft that it was. (It'll be ironic if you're reading this on a shared PDF.)

The world over, piracy springs from unavailability or unaffordability. I believe, unlike other places, India has deeper reasons for disrespecting IPR. In my experience, Indians do not like to pay for the intangible. Things like advice from chartered accountants or lawyers are included in this list. Unless they make a brand for themselves, both professions were very poorly paid in India. Another intangible product, literature, suffered, too. Well into the twentieth century, Hindi writers were called munshi (clerk). This is because their creative effort was, in the minds of consumers, reduced to the simple, mechanical act of writing it all down, like a clerk would. Most writers were seen as merely recording existing oral knowledge. For thousands of years, knowledge-sharing in India has been collective, free and altruistic. Further, it has always been passed down to subsequent generations orally. The documentation of knowledge did not start happening till there were printing presses. Even revered teachers and saints like Shankaracharya did not charge any money for their parables. How was it then that we, as Indians, would pay our munshis? Naturally, piracy saw a spurt when this culture encountered computers with the power to replicate and distribute intellectual property (IP) easily.

In the mid-1980s, we had taken a significant write-off on our product development business. We were making software for plugging the gap in the resource-sharing timesharing system extended (RSTS/E) application for commercial users. After three years of investing in it, we shut it down. Disrespect for intellectual property was one of the few reasons for this failure.

Innovation and creativity are traits that are special and unique to the human species, and a strong copyright law to safeguard the new is the bedrock of a strong economy. Human society has gone to extreme lengths to protect this intellectual property. Further, the Western world is testimony to the growth that can be ushered in if individuals and companies are encouraged to create the new. Without IP protection, no scientist's work can be valued, no film producer will be incentivized to pay a premium for special-effects software, no author will put in years to write books, no entrepreneur will be motivated to build a business based on intellectual property. To nurture innovation, India needed, and will continue to need, strong IP legislation, backed by strict enforcement and speedy courts of law.

There were further reasons to work on this.

First was the posturing of the brand India Inc.

Until we could offer confidence to global product giants like Microsoft and Autodesk with a strong message and effective judiciary, they would continue to ignore us as a 'knowledge destination'. Many other companies anyway asked us what were we doing to safeguard intellectual property. If global companies believed that India didn't respect international copyright laws, they wouldn't want to work with us.

Second, if we offered an ecosystem that protected intellectual capital, it would encourage local entrepreneurs to enter the product game and create IP-driven products. If India had to shine in the software products business, overcoming piracy was imperative and stringent copyright laws were a prerequisite.

In business, trust is won as much by good intentions as actions. Before we could actually fight piracy, it was essential to send a message to the world about India's intentions to do so. That would be half the battle won. So, we began with legislation. If the law provided for it, the government and the industry could join hands to stamp out piracy.

One of the reasons China failed to compete against India's software services industry was its lack of respect for IP. To this day, China suffers because of its weak IP protection laws. Their undocumented philosophy, probably unofficially encouraged, has been to copy, replicate and mass-produce. It was important that India, in contrast, developed trust around IP.

NASSCOM members included both software products and software services businesses. When I took over as chairperson in 1990, even though software product revenues were minuscule and we had only a handful of software product companies, one of my big initiatives was to protect intangible software from piracy. In the EC meeting, we decided that a good start would be to seek modifications to copyright laws.

We sought an appointment with Vittal at the DoE. The agenda was to check the rise of software piracy. But when we visited the DoE office, we were shocked to see that their accounting department itself was using a pirated copy of Lotus 1-2-3, the leading spreadsheet application before Microsoft Excel. We appealed to Vittal to start by cleaning up the government.

Vittal was amused. To him, we were young, inconsequential entrepreneurs talking about securing the rights of MNC IT giants. He was surprised by how strongly we felt about something which, according to him, didn't affect us at all.

We eventually convinced him, and once he was on board, he pushed heavily for our fair business practices initiative. Vittal sent out a circular to all central government offices across the country, clearly stating that no government office could use pirated software.

Change in the government can be tedious. Also, Vittal's circular didn't really have any legal authority; it was a suggested guideline. Yet, it sparked a process that changed everything. To heed Vittal's guidelines, the central government offices had to first raise a tender for purchasing software. For that, they would have to allocate a budget. To identify the best fit for the requirement, the government then needed expert advice. Subsequent evaluation of entries and software purchases could take years. But, in the larger scheme of things, a few years is not that long a period. Slowly, all central government offices phased out pirated software and replaced them entirely with licensed versions. The state governments followed suit. Soon everything was legit.

Even as Vittal's circular began hitting government offices, we began our actual work: the effort to improve protection under India's copyright laws. We went through two steps: first, we had to define software as an industry in the books of law; second, we had to get software recognized as something that can be pirated. These two steps were deceptive because they were, in fact, thousands of steps through the corridors of several government offices, like the Income Tax Department, the RBI, customs and excise, the home ministry, the MEA, the Director General of Supplies and Disposals, and the commerce ministry.

NASSCOM lobbied aggressively for these fundamental changes and finally succeeded. In the early 1990s, the Copyright Act, 1957, was amended to include software. At that time, it was estimated that 75 per cent of the systems in India used pirated software. The amendment we had lobbied for was historical in the sense that for more than thirty years, there had been no action to strengthen this law and include software in its ambit.

It sent out a powerful message across the world: India was serious about the software business and protecting IP.

We did not just twiddle our thumbs as we waited for the amendment to come through. Our industry needed to also educate corporates about the importance of using legal software. We were up against a mindset that believed in the 'right to copy' instead of copyrights. We needed a corporate entity to sue pirates. So, in 1992, we formed InFAST, the Indian Federation Against Software Theft, an independent Section 8[2] company for policing piracy.

InFAST and the amendment had encouraged international companies in India to steer the anti-piracy wheel alongside NASSCOM. Later, when the Microsoft-led Business Software Alliance (BSA) came into existence, we retired InFAST.

While NASSCOM continued to work with the government to improve IP protection laws, in parallel, we got busy sending anti-piracy messages to the public as well. Along with BSA, NASSCOM had set up a toll-free hotline for piracy complaints.

Communicating with millions of consumers is always a fiddly job. We needed something dramatic enough to grab the attention of the whole nation in one go. Imagine someone with a million followers sending out a provocative tweet! It was in the middle of all the head-scratching then, in 1992, that Dewang plonked an outrageous plan on the table.

Straightaway, it was clear that this was front-page stuff. He was going to pull a spectacular stunt, right in the middle of Delhi's crowded Nehru Place, the most infamous hub of piracy.

It was like any other morning in Nehru Place. Lazily, the shopkeepers upped their shutters and began arranging pirated merchandise outside their shops. Sales were just about picking up as customers started

---

2   When we started it, it was a Section 25 company. The Companies Act has
     since changed, and it is now classified as a Section 8 company.
     A Section 8 company is a non-profit organization (NPO) and must have a
     defined motive of promoting arts, commerce, education, charity, protection
     of environment, sports, science, research, social welfare, religion. The profits
     (if any) or other income can only be used to promote these objectives. The
     company cannot pay any dividends to the shareholders.

trickling in and browsing through the loot. Suddenly, a big police contingent swooped in and raided the entire market. The pirated merchandise was seized, and arrests were made. The media had been invited in liberal numbers, and journalists were busy covering the commotion. But none suspected the front-page story that was about to come their way.

The seized CDs were piled up in the middle of the plaza. Even as puzzled journalists began asking about the pile, everyone saw a massive, decked-up elephant marching purposefully towards them. On top of it rode our own Dewang. The elephant eventually stopped before the pile. Then, on a single command from the mahout, the elephant raised a gargantuan foot and crushed the pirated CDs to powder.

The media had lapped up the spectacle. The raid made headlines the world over. Journalists had not missed the metaphor. The elephant was India Inc., and it was not going to tolerate anything that caused mistrust or lacked integrity. Brand India Inc. was forever established in the minds of businessmen, planetwide.

At NASSCOM, Dewang's penchant for publicity was satiated, and his sceptics were silenced by the event's impact. One headline read: 'NASSCOM puts its heaviest foot forward'. That summed it up. With almost no expense, a message had been sent ringing across the world.

Institutionalizing a solution

Public perception management aside, the real work on fixing the laws was still going on. In 1994, we had already managed an amendment that imposed a fine on a pirate. But we thought that to really deter people from infringing intellectual property rights, we needed to consider a jail term.

We recommended to the regulators that anyone caught pirating software must be symbolically treated as someone with criminal intent. This, we argued, would scare most wannabe pirates and make a significant impact. They agreed. When the new Copyright Act was unveiled in 1999, it carried a seven-day term. This immediately made

Indian laws stricter than the UK laws. If this didn't send out a strong message to the international community, what could?

The copyright issue was bound to bring several unrelated industries together. One of those was Bollywood—the Hindi film industry—which got in touch with NASSCOM. Bollywood had been menaced by piracy long before the software industry came along. Despite their continued efforts, they had not succeeded in winning the government's support.

I got a call from Amit Khanna, a renowned film director and producer, who had led pioneering efforts to corporatize the film industry. Amit shared his global vision for Bollywood: how Indian films ought to be seen across communities and the diaspora. They wanted to learn how we had earned the government's confidence. Whenever the film industry approached the ministry, they were seen as unscrupulous businessmen. On the other hand, we had become the government's favourites.

On Amit Khanna's request, Vijay Mukhi, Rajiv Vaishnav and I made a presentation to a group of actors and film-makers. It was attended by the who's who of Bollywood, including Yash Chopra, Subhash Ghai, Aamir Khan, Manmohan Shetty and many others. Aamir Khan told us that he held his 35-mm film prints close to his chest before a release. Unlike other businesses, where you reap benefits over time, a filmmaker had a window of just a few weeks, maybe a month, to recover the investment made over months and months of effort.

FICCI, the Silicon Valley-based TiE and NASSCOM, together, formed a virtual association for the film industry. It was called eE@, short for the E Entertainment Alliance. The coming together of IT, software, media and venture capitalists was incredibly significant. But this was missed by the film industry, and it lost interest. Besides, Bollywood was so mired in black money and the mafia influence then that it made no headway in winning the government's trust. The association folded within two years. We learnt that it's not easy to work with multiple-partner organizations.

We, however, continued on our mission to fix piracy of IP.

In the late 1990s and early 2000s, BSA had an index for the copyright situation in every country. Dewang and everybody at NASSCOM was continually monitoring India's rank. From a piracy rate of 73 per cent in 2004,[3] we saw it gradually drop to 68 per cent by 2008.[4] The delta may seem small, but even as the installed base of computers had grown exponentially, we had seen piracy reduce. We were thrilled about getting this validation. Finally, people were not mentioning India and China in the same breath. China continued to languish because of its poor IP protection laws.

Great improvements in Indian laws and some publicity stunts were not enough for brand India Inc., though. We had to keep educating our global customers of our continued efforts and explain why the country was the destination for their software needs. The only challenge was money. Our marketing budgets were too small for this global endeavour. We focused on word of mouth when we couldn't afford advertising, much before today's social media campaigns discovered it. This necessity even mothered an invention. The NASSCOM message for India Inc. would be carried on the first slides of every presentation made anywhere in the world by every member company to the very same audiences NASSCOM wanted to educate.

It is apparent to me why the software products industry never took off in India. When I look back at the early 1980s, there were many issues working against the viability of product businesses and poor copyright laws was definitely one of them.

Culturally, people often pin the blame on centuries of subjugation to alien economies that made Indians risk-averse and intolerant of failure. This nipped the innovation spirit in the bud. In my experience,

---

3   Source: https://www.bsa.org/files/reports/IDC_GlobalPiracyStudy_2004.pdf
4   Source: https://www.bsa.org/files/reports/globalpiracy2008.pdf

very few in the business understood the risks or were prepared for the infamous 'valley of death', a business trajectory all products must trace. Then, early in that decade, there were everyday problems like the absence of a domestic market for alpha and beta tests. There was no product architecture design talent, which resulted in jalebi code or spaghetti code. It made the product obsolete fast because a tangle of code made it impossible to make quick edits and have fast releases, which was critical to a product's competitive response. India's judiciary was also weak and inefficient and did not inspire confidence that the IP would remain protected. If these cultural and ecosystem problems were not enough, the RBI put a cap of a mere 15 per cent commission for distributors and resellers abroad as against an accepted norm of 55–65 per cent.

This is yet another example of how policymakers did not understand our business. At the time, 15 per cent was the commission earmarked for a manufactured product. In contrast, selling a software product required a substantial investment of face-to-face selling, extensive demos and more. Further, the resellers demanded an additional commission, which added to the cost of selling.

In the US, I had seen small companies with less than ten engineers, most with under a year's work experience, bring giants like IBM to their knees. This was the power of the product business. So, when I returned to India in the late 1970s, I wanted to focus on products. However, after burning large sums of money, that, too, when I was in my prime, I quickly learnt that it would be a while before we could build an impactful products business from India.

At the time of writing this book, it is the IT Act, 2000, that reigns. When it came into force, it was very robust, but it has crumbled in a short period. It did not anticipate the power of Web 2.0, the uprising of social media platforms (like Facebook, Twitter and others), streaming services (like Netflix, Amazon Prime Video, Hotstar and more) that are disrupting the entertainment industry, and the power and influence exerted by them. Such is the speed at which technology marches on.

Experts say data is the new oil. Large social networks have been able to exert undue influence over millions of people, as has been evident from the Cambridge Analytica scandal.[5] Dealing with fake news continues to stump lawmakers, who are unable to pin accountability, as every individual becomes the media itself. WhatsApp's P2P security makes policing tough for regulators and lawmakers. In *The Social Dilemma*, the recent Netflix documentary, Renée DiResta, research manager of Stanford Internet Observatory, says, 'The platforms make it possible to spread manipulative narratives with phenomenal ease and without very much money.' Amendments on the lines of Europe's General Data Protection Regulation (GDPR) are on the anvil, and we hope to catch up with the world again. This will be critical if India wishes to produce innovative products. Further, we need an IP framework that enables entrepreneurs to unleash the animal spirit, and conquer the new battlefields and frontiers where data is the key asset everyone wants to corner.[6]

Even though significant progress has been made already, we still have much distance to cover on patent laws. Brand India Inc., by very definition, does not have an expiry date. For perpetuity, each of our actions each day will continue to shape the brand. Thus, it is important to not rest and go easy on practices that challenge our reputation. However, just like brand India Inc. and technology ecosystems, even

---

5   A British consulting company, Cambridge Analytica, obtained the personal data of tens of millions Facebook users. This data was eventually used for political advertising.

6   The importance of data goes beyond it being an asset. A robust and standardized data set allows you to dice and slice it in a manner that makes business sense. A case in point is the extensible business reporting language or XBRL standard that was created for banking transactions. From the time it was mandated that all financial data in India had to conform to the XBRL standard, the regulators have been able to detect frauds that went unnoticed previously. In one instance they found the same financial dataset being used for four different companies.

Data can be leveraged in many more ways. To be able to do that, we need to ensure data is standardized, interoperable and accessible to all stakeholders.

pirates continue to evolve, and often we are left playing catch up with their ingenuity.

There is no time to lose. We must keep forging ahead with conviction and clarity. The good news, though, is that the world is convinced of India's intentions of playing fair.

The country must never forget that the biggest casualty of its earlier disregard for copyrights is the continued lack of original thinking by its entrepreneurs. I have to point out that most Indian unicorns today have only replicated successful business models from the West. Research in Indian universities is nowhere close to international standards, and low wages linger on as our USP. There are two routes that the entrepreneurs could take from here onwards. One is to stay away from greed and not aim at an early exit to make a quick buck. They could leverage the patient VC capital, and get to the IPO and distribute wealth among other employees and shareholders. On the other hand, they could look at product companies from countries like Israel that invest in innovation, sell their IPs at sky-high valuations rather than building global businesses. The decision is theirs to take, but I could strongly urge them to look at the IPO route.

The IT industry's phenomenal growth first rescued the Indian economy. Now it has built a flywheel, set up to power the next wave of innovations. We've built a machine that doesn't just have the acceleration but also the momentum, thanks to the increasing 'mass' made up of the revenue base of billions of dollars, millions of jobs, thousands of entrepreneurs across towns and cities in the country. Much of this would not have happened if NASSCOM had not put its heaviest foot forward.

10

The Maverick Mehta

I won't be a rock star.
I will be a legend.

—Freddie Mercury

A legend. Mythology. A myth. Patriots like Dewang Mehta deserve far more than what rockstars aspire to. They deserve the truth.

Dewang's short and powerful life was pledged to building India's software industry. Every waking minute of his life, every joule of his indefatigable energy was spent furthering the causes of the software industry and helping the country. He literally gave up his life for it. Even his enemies, of which there were a few, cannot dare deny this to him.

Of us all, I was the closest to him. He regarded me as an elder brother. I felt the same. I had spotted his talent for NASSCOM, and I hired him and eventually mentored him till the end. I feel responsible

160

Taken in 1959, this is one of the earliest portraits of my family. My parents, Revaben and Shantilal Mehta, and my siblings (from right to left: Nila, Rita, Ranjan and Hiten) can be seen in it. I am on the far left, next to Hiten. The striking contrast in my parents' personalities is evident. This contrast would go on to shape my thinking and perspective towards the world.

When I worked in the US in the early 1970s, I tried my best to get 'Americanized' and become one of 'them'. However, I was unable to. This photo is from sometime in 1973, at a lunch with my colleagues from Travelers Insurance.

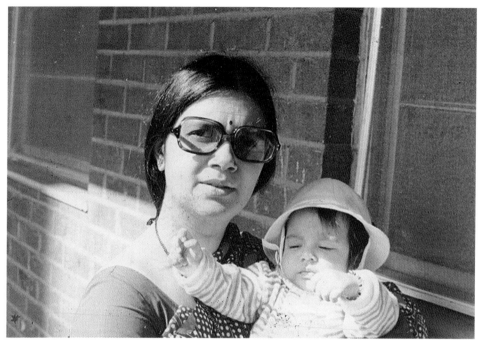

Shaila and Chirant, in 1976.

In 1979, a reputed publication featured me in a story about computer software. The conversation was about how the fledgling industry was poised for growth. Can you spot the irony in the headline?

My office in the Eros Cinema Building, 1989. Jigar had started learning from an early age. Thirty years on, we still sit like this at work. Just that the tables have turned – Jigar is all action, and I am all ears.

Even though Vittal was a government officer, he worked closely with NASSCOM. He considered himself a leader of the pack that would describe NASSCOM as N for nuts, A for ass, S for stupid, S for screwball, C for crazy, O for oddball, M for mad. Here he is, in 1992.

An early recognition of the nascent software industry, a rarity in a hardware-centric environment. This picture is from 1992 when I was the chairperson of NASSCOM.

I had started TPATI, or a Trust to Promote Advanced Technologies, in India in the 1990s. We organized international conferences in visual computing, artificial intelligence, computers and communications, which, as you can imagine, was a very long time before the internet became all pervasive. Here you see Dr Phatak of IIT Bombay (on my left) and Indian database researchers with world's leading VLDB (very large data base) researchers in India in 1996.

In 1997, Eric Schmidt, at the time the chairperson of Onward-Novell, was in India for an event. He told me that when on a short trip, he followed his California bio-rhythm and thus the time he ate and took breaks were still aligned to that of the US. I could only laugh at his strong will, rigour and discipline. No wonder it was an effort to convince him that India could emerge as a key market for Novell.

N. Chandrababu Naidu is one of the rare politicians to have understood that IT could create more jobs. He caught on to the possibilities very early on. In this picture, taken in 1997, Naidu, who was the chief minister of Andhra Pradesh at the time, is standing next to me, with Dewang and K.V. Ramani on the right.

Innovation flourishes under protection. At a time when software piracy was rampant in India, we decided to strengthen our copyright laws. In 1998, Dewang found a brilliant way to showcase the industry stand, to get the copyright laws formalized. This elephant raised a gargantuan foot and crushed pirated CDs to powder. The impact was thunderous. People from across the world applauded us for creating large-scale awareness. It also strengthened the India Inc. brand globally.

Some of the mavericks who contributed to bringing internet to India, in 1998. Like many other initiatives, the seeds were sown at the Bombay Computer Club. From left to right: me, Raj Saraf, Dewang Mehta, A.V. Gokak (then chairman of Telecom Commission), Shammi Kapoor, B.K. Syngal (then chairman of VSNL) and Vijay Mukhi.

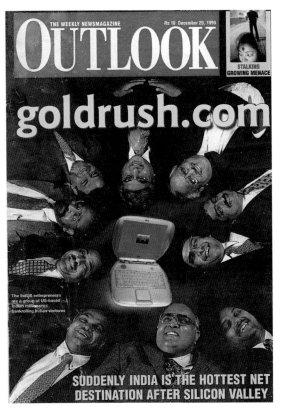

The launch of TiE in India was covered by numerous publications. *Outlook* magazine featured us in its December 1999 cover story. Anticlockwise from the bottom: Kanwal Rekhi, B.V. Jagadeesh, Dewang, Nandan Nilekani, Vijay Mukhi, Rahul Singh, me, Suhas Patil, R.K. Singh and Hemant Kanakia.

At a prayer meeting after the untimely demise of Dewang Mehta in 2001. In attendance are, from left to right, Vijay Mukhi, Shammi Kapoor, me, Pramod Mahajan, Vilasrao Deshmukh, Murli Deora and F.C. Kohli. Even after twenty years, Dewang's life continues to remain an inspiration to all of us.

The Onward Technologies team at its tenth anniversary celebration in 2001.

At a dinner after a NASSCOM executive committee meeting in 2003. Left to right, standing: Narayana Murthy, K.V. Ramani and Ashank Desai. Left to right, sitting: Phiroz Vandrewala, Arun Kumar, Kiran Karnik, Som Mittal, me and Saurabh Srivastava.

At the NASSCOM Indo–UK Conference in 2003, I listened intently as Prince Charles narrated his experience of interacting with software engineers on his visit. He seemed impressed at the capabilities of the talent we had in the country.

At the 2004 NASSCOM Fashion Show that almost did not happen. I am dressed as Swami Vivekananda, the first global Indian. The theme for the event was 'Vasudhaive Kutumbakam' as we wanted to deliver a strong message to businesses around the globe that partnering with Indian IT companies was a win-win for all.

We cherish our friendships out of work. Our families try to meet often, and when we meet we relive old memories and plan for the future. This is from a visit to Mysuru in 2010. From left to right: K.V. Ramani, Shaila, Narayana Murthy, Sudha Murthy, Padma Desai, Ashank Desai and me.

From Shaila's birthday party in 2011.

Behind these amicable smiles are fierce competitors who continue to work together at the industry level. When we meet at NASSCOM, our creative juices start to flow, and we collaborate and co-create for the industry. This was taken in 2012 at the Infosys campus in Bengaluru. From left to right: Kris Gopalakrishnan, Narayana Murthy, N. Chandra and me. You will read more about this meeting in the book.

Cyber Safety is one of the most critical issues that we as an industry need to confront. Since the time we realized that we needed to intervene, we have made numerous advancements. In 2013, Mumbai Police and Bombay Computer Club organized a Cyber Safety month to create awareness about the issue.

At a family function in 2013. This is one of the last photos of all of us together with Shaila.

At F.C. Kohli's ninetieth birthday celebration in 2014. His age was never a hindrance in his enthusiasm or ambition for the country. Even when celebrating, he talked passionately about issues concerning the country and the IT industry. From left to right: Kohli, me and S. Ramadorai.

From the 2017 NASSCOM retreat in Odisha. These retreats are a key part of NASSCOM's culture and help foster camaraderie among competitors. These retreats further help create a trusted environment. At these informal gatherings, we are able to laugh with and at each other. This is also where there are open conversations and thoughts are seeded for possible solutions to seemingly impossible problems. Left to right, standing: Debjani Ghosh, Rishad Premji, Ashutosh Vaidya, Sushma Rajgopalan, Rajesh Nambiar, Chandrashekhar, Keshav Murugesh, Kamal Agarwala, C.P. Gurnani, Raman Roy, Mohit Thakural, Pravin Rao, Samir Yajnik, Nirupam Chaudhry, Jaimin Shah, Arvind Thakur. Left to right, sitting: Kiran Karnik, Harsh Manglik, Krishna Kumar, Rajendra Pawar, Mohan Reddy, me, R. Chandra, Ganesh Natarajan, Ashank Desai, Atul Nishar, Saurabh Srivastava.

In NASSCOM's 25th year, the Prime Minister recognized its contributions and referred to NASSCOM as a 'revolution' beyond its time-tested role as an association. This was at a ceremony recognizing some of the mavericks that made it possible. From left to right: Jayant Sinha, Ravi Shankar Prasad, me, Prime Minister Narendra Modi, R. Chandrashekhar and N. Chandrasekaran.

As a family, all the Mehtas love to travel. This is from one of our recent trips to Rome in 2019.

In 2019, with N. Chandra (centre) and Keshav Murugesh (left) at Chandra's office receiving the first copies of his book, *Bridgital Nation*. In the book, Chandra and his co-author postulate that India is a unique nation with unique challenges (access to citizen services and job creation). This book has been one of the key pillars in my thought process.

From the 2019 NASSCOM retreat at Varanasi, Uttar Pradesh.

When Kanwal visited India in 2019, industry colleagues and friends gathered at my home. Known as Funda Singh for his prowess with numbers and algorithms, it is always a pleasure to debate with him. Left to right: Pradip Udhas, Kanwal Rekhi, Keshav Murugesh, Atul Nishar and me.

Young technopreneurs from India and abroad, in attendance at TiECon 2020. This, to me, is the beginning of India becoming a start-up nation and transforming to become the talent capital of the world.

for all the good, not so good and even the bad that came from Dewang's remarkable life.

Those of us who were deeply committed to the growth of the software industry were willing to brush aside his unconventional, impulsive and often brash actions. This is because we were convinced that Dewang could not knowingly do anything that would harm our industry.

Only a few of us were aware of his fierce patriotism. Most times, the term patriotism is used carelessly. But with Dewang, it was astonishingly accurate. On one side, he had implored the noted filmmaker Bharat Bala to allow us to play his iconic film on the '*Jana Gana Mana*' (India's national anthem) four years before it started playing in cinema halls. And, on the other side, Dewang would have tears in his eyes while reading the bad pieces of news in the papers. Literal tears in a grown man's eyes because of stories of corruption or government apathy, stories that most adults are jaded with.

It pains me that Dewang's memory has not grown larger than the life he lived.

I want to use this chapter to set the record straight.

I also want to explain why so many critical news reports about Dewang were a misreading of his enthusiasm and impatience. His only fault was his haste in his mission to take India and Indian software farther than imaginable.

Jekyll

NASSCOM is in Dewang's debt, not just for his dauntingly tireless work but for his flamboyance.

Many people forget to thank him for what he did with his personality. At the expense of his personal life and health, Dewang snapped up one public event after another, moving unceasingly from one spot of the limelight to another. He knew NASSCOM just did not have the cash for the kind of marketing the industry needed. He also knew what his natural desire for media attention was doing for our cause.

With every passing year, Dewang became increasingly visible in the media. He had become the public face of India's IT revolution. A revolution that had become one of the largest growth stories in the world.

It was natural that Dewang became the go-to guy for all IT-related discussions for most ministers. To sell the Indian IT Act, 2001, he made presentations to fourteen political parties. After mutual consultations and inputs from NASSCOM leaders, he was designated as our lead to help draft the IT policies of at least sixteen state governments. He hung out with the who's who and was chosen as one of the '100 global leaders of tomorrow' by the World Economic Forum. He was speaking at multiple events every week, he was adept at managing the media to NASSCOM's advantage and rose up the social ladder faster than anyone else.

He used two mobile phones at a time when they were extremely rare, and both phones would ring all the time. He was rapidly acquiring a cult following. Wherever he went, the media followed, and even the general public would mob him. For a while, all this worked very well for NASSCOM. For a while...

Hyde

Dewang did not have to read Coase's *Essays on Economics and Economists* to know its truism: 'If you torture the *data long enough*, it *will* confess to *anything*.' Dewang did not want to wait; if he wanted a certain report to project certain numbers, he would find a way to publish those numbers. If one expert didn't agree, he would find another. He was dashing to get the software industry's growth where he wanted it to be. Everyone knew. Nobody objected. When the media started grumbling about the data, Dewang was fending it off alone.

There is always some trouble in paradise. Ours had started to show.

Dewang was moving so fast that he was treading on several toes. He often remarked that if the president of NASSCOM had waited for the chairperson's approval on every trivial matter, the software industry would not have grown at the scorching pace it did. In the end, everyone simply yielded to his well-intentioned energy.

Once, I was at an event in a Mumbai hotel when VSNL director S.K. Gupta approached me. He was fuming: 'Aap log apne aap ko samajhte kya ho?'[1] Responding to my bafflement, he explained he had met Dewang the previous day in Delhi to discuss the bandwidth for communication links we wanted VSNL to provide. Dewang demanded that VSNL go from 50 gbps to 300 gbps, which was just not feasible at the time. VSNL's total budget then was ₹50 billion, but Dewang's requirement itself was going to take at least ₹150 billion. S.K. Gupta was unable to contain his rant: 'Yeh 15,000 crore kya mera baap dega?'[2]

Dewang's demand was so outrageous that I had no response. Besides, it made NASSCOM look immature. It was all very embarrassing. I immediately called Dewang, and asked him what he was thinking and where did he get that 300 gbps number from. He told me it came from a consultant NASSCOM had hired. I had to get to the bottom of it, so I studied the report and found it was for providing 3 mb of bandwidth to every citizen. This was not the need of the IT industry, and NASSCOM had no business asking for it. We were not the Indian government's telecom department. Dewang had not even discussed this with the chairperson at the time, which was basic protocol.

I remonstrated Dewang, pleading with him that he understand the context and the technicalities before putting forth such a demand on behalf of the industry. Before speaking to external agencies, he should have consulted one of our telecom experts, such as Vijay Srirangan, a senior VP at Tata Burroughs. Yet, all through it, I knew what had really happened. Dewang had allowed his patriotism to push for India's agenda through an industry's channel.

On one occasion, he arrived late for an important event, and the front row was already full. But he was not one to sit in the back.

---

1   Translates to: 'What do you guys think of yourselves?'
2   Translates to: 'Do you expect my father to shell out ₹15 billion?'

Dewang knew everyone, and everyone loved him. So quite easily, he got the organizers to create a new front row by dragging in a sofa. And he plonked himself on it.

People were offended when they witnessed such behaviour. Someone asked him why he had become so arrogant. Dewang then explained. He said he was the embodiment of the Indian IT industry. If the president of NASSCOM could not be respected, how could the industry be?

To almost everyone, Dewang's reason might sound presumptuous or even glib. I don't blame them. But those who knew him well will tell you that is exactly how he must have felt. His style was unconventional and over the top. Mostly, it served NASSCOM well. Sometimes it went awry.

The trouble with Dewang usually began where his patriotism did. He swayed everyone around with his feverish optimism for India's growth. Oftentimes, the bigger picture made him ignore the immediate needs and constraints of the software industry. I had to remind him about who was paying his salary: the 1,200 members of NASSCOM. I had to repeatedly ask him to prioritize the organization's goals over his personal vision of India's needs. Reining in Dewang was tough, and unpleasant because he was so genuine. But the NASSCOM EC had washed its hands of him, leaving me with the job.

The chairpersons were understandably upset with Dewang because he was taking away any kind of visibility that came with the stature of being NASSCOM chairperson.

Nevertheless, no chairperson ever publicly spoke out against Dewang, as his intent and energy were unquestionable.

Dewang was indeed becoming larger than NASSCOM. Yet, such was the contradiction that he expected 100 per cent loyalty to NASSCOM. Such expectations were impractical and unfair. Dewang did not appreciate another association commenting on government policy with respect to the IT industry. According to him, it was understandable if someone joined another business association, but they should not be vocal about our industry issues on that platform.

I didn't agree with Dewang. If someone wanted to associate with another industry organization for whatever reason, it did not necessarily mean they were against the larger goals of advancing the IT industry. However, I did agree with him that the views of representatives must remain consistent with NASSCOM's, even if they came from a different forum.

In the crucial 1990s, the president of NASSCOM was a role with enormous responsibility and impact. It involved engaging with influencers from all fields, including ambassadors, world leaders, and foreign delegates. Dewang kept rising through the decade in full alignment with the software industry's growth. But towards the end of the decade, that stopped.

There were murmurs about his political ambitions. He definitely had the clout for it; the skills and the personality, too. The list of dissenters kept growing longer. CEOs of smaller companies felt ignored by NASSCOM and vented their discontent to the media. They felt Dewang and NASSCOM were focused only on the big guys. Many of them also came to me with their insecurities. It was hard to keep them with us. After a point, it seemed as if Dewang only wanted to be seen with the bigwigs in politics, celebrity CEOs and entrepreneurs. His own celebrity and vision had eventually begun to blur his focus on NASSCOM and industry priorities.

TiE breaker

By 2000, Dewang was the public face of NASSCOM for almost a decade and had become synonymous with the organization. In spite of his brilliance and his unmatchable contribution to the creation of India's IT revolution, it was becoming increasingly difficult to keep him in the position. The buzz about a succession plan was growing louder. Meetings were getting increasingly skewed, with Dewang talking down to the EC. His political ambitions were becoming more apparent every passing week. Yet, almost everyone knew that would be impossible to uproot him.

I would constantly challenge Dewang on certain statements where he was clearly out of line. He would give his justification, and it would lead to analysis and argument. Fortunately, our chemistry was such that none of these squabbles turned into grudges. That was that all the way to the end.

However, one major conflict that did not find a resolution between Dewang and me was over my active participation in bringing TiE to India.

Dewang continued to believe that TiE was in direct competition with NASSCOM. I tried to convince him that TiE was rather complementary to us—NASSCOM was focused on international clients, and TiE would focus on the Indian start-up ecosystem. I thought TiE could spark a culture of innovation-driven entrepreneurship in the country. But Dewang did not yield ground.

Most times, I like to take such large decisions with consensus, but for this one, I did go ahead in spite of his opposition. Today, TiE has twenty-two active chapters in India. Now that both TiE and NASSCOM are well entrenched in the Indian IT industry, I see tremendous opportunity and potential in the two industry bodies to collaborate and enable many enterprises to innovate and bring about financial, health, educational and digital inclusion of India's 1.4 billion people. In fact, these could eventually pave the path for successful companies from India to go global and deliver impact around the world.

Arbeit macht frei

On the gates of Auschwitz and Dachau are inscribed the words: 'Work sets you free'. As carriages packed with Jewish detainees trundled into the camps, I wonder how many of the doomed looked up and saw the true meaning of the words. Because the only escape from concentration camps was death from incessant work.

Dewang had constructed a similar prison for himself. He was at work for every minute he was awake. His jet-setting, frenzied lifestyle had upset his circadian rhythm. At one point, it looked like the only sleep he was catching was on flights. But he seemed to be revelling in it. It was almost like he was running away from his inner demons.

The day was 13 April 2001. Around lunchtime, I got a call from a government officer, which rattled my core.

Dewang was found dead in his hotel room.

He was barely thirty-nine, and I had spoken with him three or four days ago.

He was in Australia with a government delegation and had suffered a heart attack. The attack had proved fatal, and he had vomited blood all over the place. It took me a while to get over the shock. I called the then NASSCOM chairperson, Phiroz Vandrewala, to share the news that had already reached him.

I flew to Delhi the same night, although it would be a few days before Dewang's body reached there. A post-mortem report and other formalities were holding it back. Nobody knew how to handle the sudden situation. We went into a huddle—to think, to deal with the ramifications of this devastating loss.

Soon, it was all over the news. Condolence messages began pouring in from ministers and other VIPs. The suspicion of foul play was on everybody's minds. When important men die young, it is natural for journalists to consider conspiracy theories. Dewang enjoyed a cult-like following. But in recent times, his detractors had grown in numbers. He was deeply connected with politicians, and one can never really tell if anything dangerous had transpired. Many were also jealous of his celebrity status. Several competing countries could have had a motive in getting rid of Dewang, who was seen as the driver of Indian software's growth. The fact that he was so young caused people to disbelieve he had had a heart attack, and rumours of all sorts made the rounds for a while.

From the information I received, I was certain there was no wrongdoing. I spoke to his cousin who lived in Australia, and she completely dismissed the possibility of foul play. Several years later, I bumped into the then Mumbai Municipal commissioner, Ajoy Mehta. He had signed the post-mortem report in Australia. He, too, ruled out a conspiracy. Given Dewang's heart condition, high-stress levels and lifestyle at the time, a natural death did not look impossible.

NASSCOM was the only family Dewang really had. His body reached India on the third day. Some members of the team began to plan the funeral.

Come to think of it, the signs were all too evident for anyone close to him to see. His marriage had ended in a messy divorce in the mid-1990s. His parents had already died, so this left him with no immediate family, except for siblings who had grown distant. NASSCOM was his only family in earnest. So, he had drowned his personal grief and troubles in work.

To begin with, he always had poor health. He was diabetic and had an ailing heart. When I met him for the first time, he had already lost most of his hair and used to wear a wig. He was not yet thirty then. But health was the last thing on his mind. As work consumed him, he kept slipping up on essential medicines. Whenever he got off work, did he rest? No. He attended social commitments. We once witnessed him lose consciousness and froth at the mouth. But Dewang continued to rage on until, quite tragically and abruptly, work did set him free.

Closing time

In death, too, Dewang had stirred up a media storm. Every TV news channel had a non-stop live coverage of the events that day. The next day, newspapers covered Dewang widely.

I lit the funeral pyre.

Many relatives turned up, whose names I had never heard of from him. He was close to very few relatives, and none were in Delhi. I assumed some close relative would show up to take care of his personal belongings and inheritance on seeing the news coverage. Some far-flung relatives did show up, but many were clearly there for just the money and couldn't be trusted. For me, the scene was all too familiar, much like at my father's funeral, when several people showed up with absurd claims.

When nobody credible was found for two weeks, in the absence of a will, NASSCOM leaders entrusted me to consolidate Dewang's legacy and build a trust in his name. Since Dewang left no will, I met with his legal heirs, including his four fuis (his father's sisters, based in Ahmedabad, Baroda and Michigan), and requested them to contribute their shares to the Dewang Mehta Trust. They were all gracious in their generosity. Thus was born the Dewang Mehta Foundation Trust.

We began the process of selling off his belongings, including his house in Karol Bagh, Delhi. It was complicated. We appointed an agency to carry out an auction. It was held in the NASSCOM office. It took a long time, but finally we managed to sell off the property.

It took us over four years to get the foundation started. The challenge was to transfer the money from his bank account to the foundation, as he was not around anymore. But there was a process in place for this kind of a situation, and we followed it. Dewang's close associate at NASSCOM, Sangeeta Gupta, took the lead. Early NASSCOM EC member and banker P. Sriganesh steered the trust formation.

NASSCOM co-founder, FutureSoft founder and philanthropist, K.V. Ramani, started a school in Chennai in Dewang's name. Persistent Systems' Anand Deshpande named a company auditorium after him. Fun and Joy at Work founder Dr Raju Bhatia started the annual Dewang Mehta Awards for business management students. We also started a skills development centre in Umreth (near Baroda), Dewang's birthplace in Gujarat.

Dewang wanted to encourage innovation in India. Every year, the foundation runs a contest for the most innovative project in Gujarat across 100 engineering colleges. We donate the interest on the principal amount for this. We also instituted the annual Dewang Mehta Memorial Lecture, something that is delivered by an industry leader.

An ordinary man

Dewang Mehta was born in a middle-class family. But he chose to give up a comfortable job, took a considerable risk and joined NASSCOM for less pay. He was driven by his ambition to do something larger than himself, to impact the whole country, something that would last beyond him. He did that, and how.

Through NASSCOM and the software industry, Dewang changed the destiny of millions in India. He arrested the 500-plus years of the downward cycle of the Indian economy and provided an opportunity to put India on an upward cycle of economic growth.

He was twenty-nine years old when I recruited him. He breathed his last when he was thirty-nine. During his ten-year tenure, the software industry grew from $120 million to $6.2 billion. At the time of his demise, the industry was already employing 1.3 million people and had created over 6 million indirect jobs.

As time passes, successive generations are growing up unaware of Dewang and his contribution to their well-being in modern India. Public memory of him is failing. And I think I know why. He was an ordinary man, full of human frailties.

He was, at times, driven mad by his ambition and fame, like all of us can be. In the last few pages, I have taken special care to point out his many shortcomings. Because not one of them can take away from what Dewang really did for millions in India and for India herself.

Will India have it in its heart to remember him as he was? His stuff is greater than what legends are made of. To me, Dewang Mehta was about possibility. About an ordinary man doing extraordinary things.

11

From Krishna to Ram

Indians love mythological metaphors as much as their American clients love sporting ones. Dewang Mehta's death brought to life mythological allegories people would use to describe him.

Dewang was often likened to Krishna from the Mahabharata. In some versions of the epic, Krishna is the mastermind behind everything. He foresees where the kingdom is headed and is dismayed. He realizes a significant change is needed and triggers a situation that cascades into the dramatic war, the Mahabharata War. The Bhagavad Gita, a poem within the epic, has Krishna advising that 'war is dharma, and a warrior must not shirk it'.

Dewang embodied chaos. He was an anarchist, a destructor of the status quo. He was always working towards shaking up things. A contemporary Krishna, he pulled the strings of the industry and entrepreneurs who were seen as warriors, fighting it out in the marketplace.

In the 1990s, the industry needed a charismatic Dewang to disrupt the business environment.[1] But with the turn of the century, Dewang's aggressive approach had begun to lose relevance. The war was over, and India had won. It now needed a peacetime leader with a calmer vision.

We had to make the shift from the Leela Purushottam[2] Krishna to that of Maryada Purushottam[3] Ram.

Continuing to rage on would be a mistake. India's IT industry had matured to a point where it had to consolidate its global reputation and settle down to work on the next big opportunity. The industry was already earning $6 billion then and had created over a million jobs. This accomplishment had to be shored up.

Naturally, the next president of NASSCOM would have to have a crack at the more difficult task of growing from this much larger base while protecting what had been achieved by that time. Dewang's strategy of hype had run its course, and we needed a leader who believed in systems, processes, structure and conventional wisdom, like Lord Ram from the Ramayana. We needed someone to restore order and rewrite the rule book.

Clear and present danger

Such was Dewang's reality-distortion field and his name was so synonymous with that of NASSCOM that many people made the error of assuming his death was the death of NASSCOM. It was

---

1   Late Mr Pramod Mahajan, the IT minister of India at the time, understood the value NASSCOM was bringing in and specifically Dewang's contribution. He had started calling Dewang the real IT minister of India. Dewang had indeed left big shoes behind, and it was going to be a tall order to fill them.

2   Leela Purushottam loosely translates to 'the supreme man who indulges in divine play'. Lord Krishna is known to have numerous tricks up his sleeve. He is often depicted as the shrewd provocateur, who uses his divine plays to support good over evil.

3   Maryada Purushottam loosely translates into 'the supreme man who follows the rules, norms and conventions of the time'. According to Hindu mythology, Lord Rama is widely known as the perfect man.

widely accepted that Dewang's drive, intellect and patriotism were unique and irreplaceable. Little did they realize that NASSCOM was not looking for another Dewang. It was looking for a Ram.

A succession was being planned while Dewang was around. His sudden death left us with no time. It worsened the perception of NASSCOM's imminent doom. This rapidly cascaded into danger by itself. We had not even begun the search for our Ram when something disturbing occurred. I immediately interpreted the development as a deliberate attempt to destroy NASSCOM's position and influence in the industry.

In 2001, Prime Minister Atal Bihari Vajpayee[4] was travelling to Singapore to discuss trade deals. The Confederation of Indian Industry (CII) was helping him meet industrialists. As a part of the initiative, CII also announced an IT Summit in Singapore without even consulting us. We would have been happy to work with CII, but they were clearly trying to wrench away NASSCOM's mandate. The CII veiled it as an initiative in the interests of the country. We tried our best to explain why software, an intangible, was best understood by NASSCOM, but they did not pay any heed to us. Perhaps, the venerable CII had also made the error of assuming that NASSCOM's end was nigh.

Technically, if anyone from the industry wanted to attend this event in a personal capacity, independent of NASSCOM, they could. But nobody did. I wrote a letter to CII, expressing my unequivocal disapproval of their opportunistic tactic, as this happened immediately after Dewang's passing. Many NASSCOM leaders too called CII, asking it to back off.

---

4   I must mention Mr Vajpayee for coining the 'IT IT' war cry. It stood for 'Information Technology, India Tomorrow'. In fact, Mr Vajpayee's cabinet had Mr Pramod Mahajan as the Minister of Telecommunications between 2001 and 2003. He was one of those few politicians who understood the role the information technology revolution could play in uplifting India. He extended his support wherever he could, and he would routinely open doors and often accompanied us to vital national and international forums.

As if luck was on the side of the truth, Mr Vajpayee's visit got rescheduled to a later date. I asserted that we would be on our feet within a few months. However, the need to find our Ram, and soon, was now all the more urgent.

Desperately seeking Ram

Even as CII jostled to elbow us out, many other industry associations and individuals were rooting for our continuity. Messages from politicians, bureaucrats, beneficiaries and well-wishers poured in, all iterating that they stood by us in this difficult hour. F.C. Kohli, Narayana Murthy and Azim Premji called and encouraged us to not hesitate in seeking their help.

Everyone was concerned about the uncertainty in filling of the president's office. Mumbai's prominent politician and member of Parliament (MP) Murli Deora called me and insisted that I take up the job temporarily. He warned, 'Ye desh ke bhavishya ka sawaal hai.'[5] Taking up this responsibility was a noble duty. But I also owed Onward-Novell my time, and my hands were full. I politely declined. I assured him that we would make the right choice and he needn't worry.

Until then, NASSCOM had enjoyed the agility of a small organization, but at the expense of systems and processes. Though ad hoc, it was nimble, moved fast and kept costs low.

Nevertheless, once the industry rocketed exponentially, so did the opportunities and challenges that came with it. The business had not just become massive; its growth showed no signs of abating. There was no way NASSCOM could have sustained its work any further without a transformation, without rebuilding itself organizationally.

The coming-of-age challenges of start-ups are well understood. Disney, HP, Apple and Microsoft were all garage operations before they were corporatized and moved into larger offices. The moment for their reinvention was more or less planned out. In our case, Dewang's sudden death forced that moment to its crisis.

---

5   Translates to: 'The country's future is at stake.'

On the day after his funeral, an extraordinary meeting was called in NASSCOM's Delhi office. Most NASSCOM members, including the EC, past chairpersons and ordinary members, who were in Delhi for the funeral, attended. For the first time, past chairpersons had been called together with the current EC.

The agenda was obvious: We had to discuss the way forward for NASSCOM. The first priority was to fill the president's office with a person capable of managing us in a markedly different and mature industry. I chaired the selection committee for this along with a few former chairpersons and Phiroz Vandrewala (who was representing TCS at NASSCOM), the then chairperson. Phiroz rose to the situation and started coming to the NASSCOM office every alternate day. He assured stakeholders that he would provide a bridge leadership while the transition to a new president was completed.

The selection process was arduous and complicated. For over ten years, Dewang's personality had been imprinted into the organization's DNA. In his decade-long tenure, the industry had transitioned from a grinding wheel to a flywheel. We wanted the next president to be as competent, competitive and driven as Dewang. We also wanted a leader who had a different personality, so that we could build a systems-driven organization. The new leader still had to be ambitious, articulate and patriotic.

We realized that to find our new president we had to first redefine NASSCOM's vision for this stage of maturity. We got down to it in earnest, alongside the rigour of crafting the president's role and listing critical skills and attributes.

Organizational consulting firm Korn Ferry was hired. We briefed them that just like with Dewang, the hunt should not be restricted to the IT industry. The selection committee was unanimous that the IT side of the job could be taught. We were focused on finding a leader with the right personality for the role.

The word was out; we started receiving calls from individuals who wanted to be considered for the job. It made us proud to see numerous highly qualified and capable individuals expressing their interest. We continued our evaluations: we wanted only the best of the best.

Korn Ferry worked with us to shortlist ten domains where they could cast their net. This included academia, NGOs, the IT industry, corporates, politics, bureaucracy and the leadership within the diaspora. From each domain, we further made a shortlist of potential individuals. We eventually aggregated 100 potentials. At this stage, none of them knew that they were being considered.

We were aware that really successful people from corporate India might not be interested in joining a non-profit. But that was the challenge for NASSCOM in its pursuit of excellence. Korn Ferry then began speaking with these 100 candidates to ascertain their level of interest and availability. My colleagues and I stepped in several times to sell the NASSCOM vision. This process reduced the list to twenty people. Of these, another ten politely declined the role.

Wipro Chairperson Azim Premji is known to hire ace leaders. I remember that he offered to help. I thus took our final shortlist of ten candidates to him. He knew six or seven of them and immediately shared his feedback by pointing out who was 'disorganized' and who 'only talks and won't deliver', and who 'is good'. That helped us weed the list further and reduce it to the final three. Then started the selection committee's rigorous interviews and elimination processes.

At Onward-Novell, I had injected Novell Inc.'s robust hiring practices. I brought these to NASSCOM as well, to ensure that we did not make a mistake while identifying our Ram.

Kiran – the ray of hope

Our efforts to find a successor eventually worked out splendidly. We found our man: Kiran Karnik. He had an eclectic background. He is an alumnus of the prestigious Indian Institute of Management, Ahmedabad, and a man of great intellect. He had worked with the Indian Space Research Organization as well as the Discovery Channel.

Nevertheless, he had his share of naysayers. Some people thought he was too soft and wasn't charismatic or assertive enough. These people were falling into the trap of comparing him with Dewang.

The difference between Dewang and Kiran was stark. Also, the transition from one to the other was sudden because it could not be done any other way. Dewang could not stay away from the limelight. Kiran preferred to maintain a low profile and let his work do the talking. Dewang had a certain assertiveness and dynamism in his demeanour. Kiran was softer and more methodical. The circumstances under which Dewang had taken up office were quite different from Kiran's as well. Many people felt that Kiran was a compromise, but he was deliberately handpicked to lead us as we forged ahead.

I requested Kiran to meet F.C. Kohli, Narayana Murthy and Azim Premji before he took up office. After he received their blessings, we announced Kiran's appointment in September 2001. The news spread like wildfire. Once again, I got a call from Murli Deora, who wasn't happy with our choice. I assured him and said, 'Murli Bhai, I appreciate your concern. He is dramatically different from Dewang. And this is by choice. Let us talk again after six months. You'll see.'

Soon after, the tragedy of unprecedented proportions struck. On an unsuspecting morning, four passenger planes, mid-flight, turned into weapons killing thousands of innocent people. The 9/11 attacks in the US changed the world overnight. In the aftermath, everything was in jeopardy: from international business to the safety of immigrant workers.

Kiran was less than a week into the office when the shockwaves of the tragedy struck. As the new NASSCOM boss, it was now his prerogative to help the industry and the world understand what Indian software planned to do in this most uncertain hour.

It was difficult to predict anything. Billions of dollars and millions of dreams were at stake. But it does take a calamity to bring out the best in us. Kiran shone. He was soft-spoken, but firm. He remained calm under adversity. Even though it was a big challenge to bring people from various backgrounds (press, industry, policymakers, embassies and more) together, he used his prowess with articulation to save the day. He explained the complex nuances in simple yet eloquent language and persuaded various stakeholders. He said, 'While the on-site consulting business may suffer a few challenges, the offshoring business will flourish. The revenues may drop for a bit, but in the long run, India would retain the edge.'

Murli Bhai did call back and said, 'Achcha banda dhoonda hai.'[6]

Empowered with the president's position, Kiran had hit the ground running. NASSCOM's industry numbers were relatively accurate when compared to other Indian or international agencies. But it still had some distance to travel.

One of the first things Kiran did was to transform NASSCOM into a data-driven organization. He was further encouraged by Ashank, Srirangan, Murthy and others. Ashank, in fact, has been a long-time champion of data-driven thinking and decision-making.

At that time, we used data from the top twenty IT companies and extrapolated that for the industry. Everyone (from analysts to researchers to consultants to the government to the industry itself) used this data for analysis and projections, even though there were many gaps in it.

These numbers, which were once looked down upon with scepticism and doubt, were now considered sacrosanct. NASSCOM was clear that it 'owned' the Indian IT industry data. Because this was a cyclical process, Kiran wanted to strengthen it. He brought in Sunil Mehta, a business analyst with solid integrity. Sunil was extraordinary with numbers. Together, Kiran and Sunil made our data reliable enough for industry leaders, educationists and policymakers. While at NASSCOM, we always used data to drive the industry. The rigour in data collection and analysis underwent a massive change under the leadership of Kiran.

---

6   Translates to: 'You found a good guy.'

I remember I once suggested that NASSCOM would do well by highlighting how the R&D and engineering services of Indian companies were growing faster than the 'global capability centres' of foreign companies. When Sunil heard me, he said, 'Harish Bhai, data doesn't say this'. I corrected myself and reworked my message. The power of NASSCOM's data was all-pervasive!

NASSCOM thus became an important data and analytics organization. It began guiding industry strategy. It provided businesses with headlights to see where they were going. The NASSCOM brand also earned respect and trust with its very transparent reports, including the sought-after strategy report that had become sort of a Bible for the industry. Suddenly, NASSCOM was the data and information shop everyone turned to for authentic information on the Indian IT industry.

By everyone, I really mean everyone. The impact of our data was felt in the most unlikely quarters. People used it to plan everything, from the curriculum for software engineers to office facilities to residential complexes, malls and even airport capacities. Service providers like lawyers and chartered accountants also used our data to estimate their growth and plan for it. Analysts used the data to project industry growth, guiding investors in India and abroad. And, of course, the government used our data to estimate earnings from personal income taxes. In 2019, the industry contributed ₹890 billion to the exchequer, and this does not include the contributions by the industries that are indirectly benefited by a robust IT industry.[7] The RBI used it for planning forex, one of the most critical resources for India's growth, fuelled by foreign oil, capital equipment and, later, smartphones.

NASSCOM's data collection, curation and reporting processes had become robust. Yet, I remember picking up a TCS quarterly report

---

7   As per a research commissioned by Harish Mehta and published by Prof. Tulsi Jayakumar of S. P. Jain Institute of Management and Research, Mumbai, the IT industry's contribution to personal income tax was 19% in 2019.

and finding no mention of NASSCOM numbers. Coincidentally, at that time, TCS CEO N. Chandra was NASSCOM vice-chairperson. I asked him why was he not comparing TCS with NASSCOM's growth projections? He needed no convincing. Under his leadership, TCS started comparing its results with NASSCOM projections. Buoyed by this, suddenly, almost every listed technology company started using NASSCOM data as a benchmark. It lifted the organization's brand considerably.

The numbers we chase—we don't really pull these out from thin air. These are pragmatic and are backed by solid research reports. The first time we claimed that we would be a $1 billion industry, it was in a report by the World Bank. A few years later, a NASSCOM–McKinsey study commissioned in 1998 reported that we could be a $50 billion industry in the next seven years. We did hit the number, albeit two years late, with Y2K acting as a catalyst and 9/11 being the deterrent.

These reports and the guidance of numbers helps us lay out the responsibility of each stakeholder and build a roadmap for achieving these.

I think Kiran's stint at NASSCOM is testimony that adversity often brings out the best in people. When the world faced an economic crisis after the 9/11 attacks on the US in 2001, we thought we were going to suffer as badly. However, led by Kiran, we persisted and stayed on a course of rapid growth. Then, in 2008, when the financial world faced one of its largest shocks in the aftermath of the sub-prime crisis and the Lehman Brothers' bankruptcy, we, the IT services companies in India, were staring down the barrel of a gun. The bulk of the clients of IT companies consisted of financial services businesses from across the world and, overnight, the spending were going to get slashed. The National Stock Exchange's IT index fell by a whopping 58 per cent. However, as an industry, we bounced back. And yet again, Kiran was at the helm. True to his name, Kiran has been a ray of hope!

Committing to committee

A start-up is an exciting place to be in. There is confusion and uncertainty. Calls for action are shouted across the floor as though it were a buccaneer's quarterdeck. But what happens after the start-up survives the storm? The chaos is quickly replaced by order. Not just any order, but an order that disconnects an organization from the gut responses of an individual and plugs it into processes instead.

This is a dangerous transition to make and often needs a new set of leaders. Somehow, the organization has to behave like a grown-up, and continue without losing the youthful ideas and energy that made it successful in the first place. Kiran took charge of executing this transition and helped shape the new NASSCOM after 9/11.

At NASSCOM, in Kiran and his team, we now had the new set of leaders. It was time for me to step away, and let elected members drive the agenda of the industry and India. I began attending alternate EC meetings instead of all four in a year.

Two years into his term, in 2003, Kiran called me with a nagging concern: he was unable to see NASSCOM's future leaders emerging from the EC. Many on the executive committee were MNC members, who had a short tenure with their organizations. Some from large organizations were either the second or third in command. They were all highly competent individuals; however, their position restricted their effectiveness at NASSCOM. I was concerned and once again began attending all EC meetings. I got together with past chairpersons who were regularly attending meetings and formed a task force to look into this matter of finding future leadership.

The process-driven appointment of presidents was necessary, but it was most certainly not adequate. The message from Kiran's call was clear: we just couldn't wait for the next generation of leaders to come to us. If we were to remain relevant, we needed to reach out to them, understand their aspirations, and attract them to contribute towards NASSCOM's cause. And that of the industry and of the nation. Also, this wasn't a one-time activity. To make this sustainable, we needed a process, once again.

We also realized that there was no process to engage past chairpersons in any official capacity. These past chairpersons included prominent names like F.C. Kohli and the ubiquitous Narayana Murthy.[8] Yet, such stalwarts neither had any official responsibility nor the opportunity to engage with the organization.

The awareness of this wasted potential and the need to groom the next generation of leaders led to the forming of the past chairpersons into a council—the Chairpersons' Council (CC).[9]

The CC was entrusted with identifying future NASSCOM leaders, courting them and converting them into active members. The CC identified potential leaders for the next five years and encouraged them to contest for EC seats. The CC's role is thus more philosophical than operational. A key responsibility is to ensure that the values of NASSCOM are not compromised even to the slightest extent. An individual's zeal for growth must never take precedence over the larger goal of the industry's growth.

Every year, the CC assessed industry challenges over the next three years. It then identified the most appropriate EC member to take up those challenges as the chairperson a year later. The CC would nominate this member to the EC for being elected as a vice-chairperson. Anybody from the EC could challenge this nomination and contest an election against the CC's nominee. In practice, this happened on only one occasion in the course of almost twenty elections, and even then, the CC's nominee won the election. In time, people realized that the collective wisdom of the CC was the best judge of leadership and came

---

8   Because of my close association with NASSCOM, I have had the opportunity
     to spend time in private and in public with Murthy. Often, after our meetings
     where Murthy had to maintain a certain gravitas and posture, Ashank,
     Murthy and I would retire to dine at our regular table in a quiet corner of
     the Copper Chimney restaurant at Worli, Mumbai.
9   Seeded in 2003, it was initially called the Chairmen's Council.

to accept its nominations. The vice-chairperson would get elevated to the chairperson's office in the subsequent year. This again proved to be the best practice. We understood the importance of this process and had it incorporated into the NASSCOM constitution.

The problem with direct democracy is that it becomes a competition of popularity instead of merit. And since NASSCOM is a serious business association, we have to put our best foot forward every year. The CC nominations were the perfect middle ground solution, and it is working very well even now. This reminds me of a joke that I would often crack: if we were to go by simple majority, India's national bird would have been the crow and not the peacock.

In my discussions with my good friend K.V. Ramani, he underlined that at NASSCOM, it was never really about consensus or even democracy. It has always been about arriving at optimal decisions. At NASSCOM, we often disagree on various things, but each time we have disagreements, we air those internally and get into a debate. We never take those to a public forum. So, I have to agree with him on optimal decisions.

As we moved on, another weakness surfaced. The EC members, who held the votes, were constrained by their short tenure of two years. They thus lacked a long-term view of NASSCOM. After some years, we came to the conclusion that the CC's responsibilities should go beyond that of an advisory group. We drew up a list of a few responsibilities for the CC that, without being binding, could serve as a guideline for the EC. Among others, the list included the following: long-term direction of NASSCOM (including its mission and vision), starting of new organizations like the NASSCOM Foundation, corpus allocation for the Data Security Council of India (DSCI)[10], acquisition of hard assets, brand building, firming up the code of conduct,

---

10 DSCI was set up by NASSCOM as not-for-profit industry body that works towards making the cyberspace safe, secure and trusted by establishing best practices, standards and initiatives in cyber security and privacy outreach activities. More about DSCI is at www.dsci.in.

succession planning, selection of presidents and new initiatives to push NASSCOM's long-term agenda.

Later on, we decided to formalize the responsibilities. I spoke to the chairperson at the time, and he warmed up to the idea. A task force of EC members was selected to review the CC proposal.

When this proposal was presented to the task force over a conference call, it was met with immediate and vehement opposition. The EC task force thought the CC was trying to usurp its powers. Our enthusiasm and attachment to NASSCOM, our sense of ownership, was misunderstood.

The EC task force came back with its recommendations. It wanted only the last two chairpersons to attend the meetings. Further, it did not want any past chairperson to speak at the meetings and remain a mere 'active listener'. When I read this, I was shocked and realized that our intentions had been completely misconstrued.

I spoke to my colleagues, revoked the guideline document immediately, and wrote an apology mail to the chairperson at the time, burying the recommendations of the CC. We had failed to communicate our good intent, and it was causing angst. The whole matter had crumbled into an us-versus-them situation, and our energy was being dissipated on non-productive arguments. For the first time since NASSCOM's inception, we were polarized, and for the wrong reasons.

I comprehended how challenging it was to change NASSCOM at that stage of maturity. NASSCOM is a voluntary, peer-to-peer, non-profit organization, whose members are not bound to serve in any capacity. This implies that NASSCOM needn't be anyone's priority. Everyone had a successful career, and we were now forcibly reminded that we hadn't had formal mentoring of new EC members, resulting in misunderstandings. To woo the members, we should have followed the classical approach of selling to a group of diverse and successful CEOs to get consensus: educate every member before the meeting, listen to them and address their concerns. It is difficult to fix things that are not broken.

The industry today is pegged at $190 billion. The full-time team that manages the single voice of the industry is so diverse and yet so tiny that in terms of economic value added, each team member's contribution comes to more than $1.5 billion! The team is further supported by more than 180 professionals from across the industry in various voluntary roles: as members of the executive council, sectoral councils, regional councils, special groups and more. It's a challenge to immerse them in NASSCOM values.

For NASSCOM, a grown-up industry has meant many things. We had to keep all the member companies on the same page while devolving powers of office-bearers so that the systems become greater than any individual. Also, whole new sub-industries were opening up as newer opportunities emerged with time. To develop these, in 2013, Narayana Murthy[11] headed a task force that recommended the creation of many sectoral councils. What followed was a slew of committees focused on achieving these goals.

---

11 At the time, the key NASSCOM office-bearers had to meet to chart the course of action. Chandra of TCS was the chairperson. In his tenure, he wanted to kickstart three large initiatives to make an impact. One of those was restructuring NASSCOM to include newer, emerging focus areas that went beyond IT services. These were software, R&D, start-ups, e-commerce and others. Chandra knew that change is not easy, especially at an industry body like NASSCOM. He decided that the restructuring taskforce had to be headed by someone who everyone respected.

During one of our coffee meetings, it dawned on us that we should get Murthy to head the taskforce. However, in his polite manner, Chandra said he didn't know Murthy in a personal capacity. I was left surprised. How could Chandra not have Murthy a phone call away? I realized that Chandra was being his modest self. I, on the other hand, knew Murthy well and I offered to set up the meeting.

When I called Murthy, he was gracious and surprised that his number-one competitor was requesting for a meeting. We eventually travelled to Bangalore to meet Murthy. When we reached there, Murthy received us warmly and personally ensured that he made Chandra feel at home. He even invited Kris Gopalakrishnan, another co-founder at Infosys and the incoming president at CII.

By now, IT services, BPM services, engineering R&D (ER&D) services, GCCs, Internet services, SMEs, software products and many such were now demanding NASSCOM-level attention.[12] This meant that these sectors were at the cusp of explosive growth, and with the right focus, we could, hopefully, add a few billion dollars to the top-line.

During Shekhar's tenure as president from 2013 to 2018, the industry continued to grow and diversify. Getting the EC involved on every issue was becoming very cumbersome. A senior leadership team (SLT) comprising four people was set up. These included the outgoing chairperson and the current chairperson, vice-chairperson and president.

However, this new systemic NASSCOM had to rise above individual personalities and management styles. To ensure that NASSCOM didn't become a parking place for anyone, every committee member, taskforce, nominee, trustee and director appointed had a tenure attached. The president's tenure was fixed for a minimum of three years and a maximum of five years.[13]

The NASSCOM secretariat now enjoys huge influence over industry policies, industry initiatives and industry positioning.[14]

12　To address these specific demands, NASSCOM has since created sectoral councils, where leaders from these industry areas come together to work towards addressing issues specific to these industries.

13　The role of NASSCOM's president is a vital one. The president represents a sunrise industry that is all-pervasive. It is more than a job and the person often becomes indispensable, and could become larger than NASSCOM itself. We learnt the same during Dewang's tenure.
Apart from this, the world we live in will become exponentially complex, and we need an ongoing injection of new blood and fresh thinking. We thus created this planned obsolescence at the very top of NASSCOM.

14　By design, the secretariat at NASSCOM is as powerful as elected leaders. We wanted the NASSCOM team to have a sense of ownership towards NASSCOM and that could only happen if they were accorded the same respect, responsibility and power as the co-founders.
People who join NASSCOM from other industry associations often tell us that they feel they have a voice here as they can hold open and, if required, uncomfortable conversations with leaders from member companies. They

Power by virtue of NASSCOM affiliation should thus never become larger than industry interests. Hence, the devolution of power, strong processes, constant training, value systems and a constant rigorous evaluation of all of these for all senior positions becomes mandatory.

I am fairly confident that the principles and the processes created to safeguard these values will ensure that NASSCOM continues to serve the member organizations, and more importantly, the country.

Let me now take you to what I believe was one of the greatest tests NASSCOM went through when all the tenets that we inculcated were put to trial.

---

feel empowered and are respected as equals; unlike at other associations where they are considered merely a part of the administration staff. The sense of ownership was further strengthened as the NASSCOM secretariat has the right to disagree with even the most important decisions.

While the secretariat comprises professionals who have been hired by the body for specific roles, there is no distinction as employer or employee when it comes to day-to-day working.

12

The 'Finest Hour'

Houston, we've had a problem.

—Commander Jim Lovell, Apollo 13

It was supposed to be NASA's third lunar landing.

On 14 April 1970, almost fifty-six hours into their journey to the Moon, astronauts Jim Lovell, Fred Haise, and Jack Swigert heard a massive bang. There was an explosion on the service module. Both oxygen tanks were emptying rapidly. All three crew members of the Apollo 13 faced imminent death. The oxygen was also used to produce electricity, and consequently, power, computers and communications could fail before the three died. At the time of the accident, the men were 330,000 kilometres away from home, hurtling farther into space at an incredible 5,400 kilometres per hour. The spacemen were doomed to breathe their last in the solitude and cold darkness of the unforgiving infinity.

Yet, Jim's voice was calm when '… we've had a problem' crackled into headsets at the mission control. It took fifteen minutes for NASA's best minds to realize that their mission had just changed. They were not landing men on the Moon any more; they were going to bring them back. Alive.

Besides the lives of the astronauts, NASA's reputation and the future of space exploration hung by a thread. Nevertheless, the next few days were extraordinary. Apollo 13 carried on all the way to the Moon and used its orbit as a slingshot to fling itself back towards Earth. Dozens of engineers on the ground simulated the situation inside Apollo 13, tick by tick. They worked on improvising solutions with whatever was left in the explosion's aftermath. Complicated calculations were made and remade. Scenarios were painted, rejected and painted over and over again. With every passing second, possibilities were disappearing. President Richard Nixon cancelled all appointments and reached the Goddard Space Flight Centre. He had already called the families of the astronauts. Planetwide, millions watched the developments on TV. Channels scrapped regular programming to report the mission's fluid fate. Pope Paul VI led a prayer with 10,000 people. In India, 1,00,000 people prayed together. On 14 April, the US Senate asked businesses to halt work at 9 p.m. for employee prayers. The Soviets ceased communications on radio frequencies that the mission control was using for re-entry. Soviet battleships in the Pacific and Atlantic offered help to NASA recover the command module, *Odyssey*, after it splashed down. If at all. The world froze with unblinking eyes.

On 17 April 1970, there was a splashdown. All three astronauts had cheated death. They were back on Earth. As the world watched, what would have been NASA's most public failure got labelled by the media as its 'finest hour'.

Fast forward to 2009 and zoom in on India, the Satyam Computer Services scandal was raging on. The accuracy of the resemblance between the infamous situation with Satyam and the Apollo 13 saga always amazes me; between how NASSCOM helped save the day then and how NASA pulled off the impossible. In both cases, the unthinkable happened without warning. In both cases, a spotless reputation was at stake. In both cases, the work ethic of the organization snatched the situation from the jaws of fatal disaster and turned it into its brightest glory.

I compare a business scam minted of greed to a space adventure born of wonder. Is it absurd? It is not. The Satyam scandal was an accident, and it had put NASSCOM's decades of hard work in building brand India Inc. at grave risk. The future of Indian software was in peril. Many bright young people were on the brink of losing their careers, and Satyam's Fortune 100 clients were perhaps never going to return to India, causing a snag that would eventually rip apart the fabric of the Indian software industry.

The Indian economy itself was in peril.

What Apollo 13 was to the future of NASA and space exploration, the Satyam scandal was to NASSCOM and Indian software. I still shake my head in disbelief at the Satyam story. Clearly, the saga was NASSCOM's 'finest hour'.

Lift-off

NASSCOM consciously defines itself with modern values. Its constitution enshrines principles that have radically changed India's workplace ethic. Over the decades, software entrepreneurs have collectively helped NASSCOM protect their industry's image of integrity, meritocracy, quality service and timely delivery. These, in fact, were included in the attributes of brand India Inc.

Ironically, two decades of reputation building were almost squandered away by the dishonesty of a single company called Satyam. Ironic because 'satyam' is Sanskrit for 'truth'.

By the beginning of 2009, Satyam Computer Services had become the fourth-largest IT company in India, employing around 50,000 people. It had come out of nowhere and grabbed a large percentage of Fortune 500 companies as its clients. It was winning multiple awards everywhere. In 2009, it had done India proud by signing up with FIFA as its IT partner for two football world cups: South Africa in 2010 and Brazil in 2014. Satyam had also expressed plans to expand into other sports like basketball and Formula 1. It was suddenly beating every other IT company in India. Sadly, the Satyam saga proved the aphorism that 'if the story is too good to be true, it probably is.'

Satyam was founded in 1987 by the endearing Ramalinga Raju. The industry was abuzz with stories around Raju's gentle, unassuming and charismatic personality. He often turned up for lunch at the office cafeteria and ate with employees. He worked long hours and was involved directly in delivering services to many clients. In spite of declaring great results year-on-year, he didn't show much interest in joining NASSCOM.

By then, NASSCOM's chairpersons' council had taken on the responsibility of bringing in the next generation of leaders. Raju fulfilled every possible criterion. We considered reaching out to him. It was then that the first red flag was raised. A CEO of a major IT company pointed out that the results Satyam was declaring couldn't be tallied up with the kind of deals it was bagging. Some of us thought perhaps that the CEO was discouraging us because Satyam was a competitor. Yet, we did defer our conversation with Raju by one year.

When Raju kept up an astonishing growth from one quarter to the next, we decided to finally invite him to NASSCOM. I spoke with Raju, encouraging him to join the body. I explained to him about how he could contribute to the industry and also benefit from it. He saw value in what we had proposed and agreed to join immediately. As expected, he became an EC member and soon after became the chairperson in 2006.

There wasn't a more proactive chairperson than Raju. He was very ethical in his dealings, and did not use his position to promote Satyam or any personal interests. On one occasion, we realized we desperately needed to hire a lobby group to challenge certain US government regulations. Unlike in India, lobbying is a legitimate business in the US, run with as much transparency as any other business. The lobbying company asked for $1.5 million to represent us. NASSCOM approached the Indian government, and it offered to contribute half of it, but the remaining had to be collected from the industry.

We discussed many models. What if all members contributed in proportion to their turnover? What if the top 200 contributed equally? Finally, we decided that the top five companies should contribute equally, as they stood to benefit the most from the lobbying. These companies were, however, reluctant to pay.

Raju found a way forward. In the middle of an EC meeting, he took the lead and announced that Satyam would contribute $50,000 every quarter, which completed his quota to the fund. Not to be shown up by a new company like Satyam, the other four followed within a month and agreed to contribute as well.

Raju talked very positively about India, its IT industry, and NASSCOM's future. He would attend events at places like Harvard and Stanford and share his learnings with us. We saw in him a good-hearted person who left no stone unturned in his hospitality whenever he hosted us.

Shaila and I were among 30,000-plus people who attended Raju's son's wedding in Hyderabad. Yet, he had managed to keep the wedding simple and well-organized.

Raju would dedicate 10 per cent of his time to the Emergency Management Research Institute, or EMRI. This was part of his company's corporate social responsibility (CSR) strategy. EMRI's mission was to provide free medical emergency services to people across the state of Andhra Pradesh. EMRI's ambulances would reach the emergency spot within half an hour of a call. Its employees were so aligned to their mission, they wouldn't accept a single rupee as a tip. EMRI had become famous, and other states had started engaging its services. It had become synonymous with its helpline number: 108.

Raju knew the ultimate benefactors of this service were the insurance companies. Reduced fatalities led to reduced claims. This simple insight helped Raju rope in life insurance companies, who paid EMRI expenses because of business reasons, not altruistic ones.

By 2008, EMRI had gone beyond Andhra Pradesh and was operating in eight other states. It drove more than 1,600 ambulances and responded to an average of about 10,000 emergency calls daily. Raju's clean water project was yet another marvel. The whole industry was enamoured by his philanthropic and entrepreneurial zeal. At the time, he appeared to be the ideal brand ambassador for the industry.

'Houston, …'

It was 7 January 2009. I was in front of the TV, and the news channels were playing only one piece of news on loop. Raju had just confessed to an accounting fraud of unimaginable scale. He had put it all down in a letter to the board.

Cognitive dissonance. I believe that is what they call it: to experience a barrage of facts that just do not align with what you have known to be true. Everyone in the IT industry must have suffered it simultaneously as the TV, unceasingly, reported one detail after another, each more astounding than the other.

Raju had confessed to inflating cash and bank balances, had shown non-existent interest income, and had understated liabilities. On that day, Satyam's stocks plummeted 82 per cent on the Bombay Stock Exchange. Shareholders lost thousands of crores of rupees.

Raju explained in the letter that, personally, he had taken no money out of the company. The only reason he had been inflating numbers since 2001 was to convince customers and investors that Satyam was growing at a breakneck speed.

In the period of the scam, Satyam's competitors were also growing at a brisk pace. Raju believed that if he had to outpace them, he would have to achieve even more ambitious targets. In his letter, he confessed that he had inflated revenues by ₹5.88 billion in the last quarter and had booked no extra costs against it. This meant a blatant bloating of profits by that staggering amount.

Satyam was supplying fake documents to its auditors, PricewaterhouseCoopers (PwC). They, too, were hauled in for scrutiny. Satyam had forged documents, claiming the money was in the bank. These banks later revealed that the cash was non-existent. Not only auditors but there were also several other layers of checks and balances that Satyam had successfully fooled for years. The whole episode made everyone wonder who Raju really was. Was he a businessman? Was he a philanthropist? Was he a crook?

The questions were many. Some are still unanswered. Was PwC an accomplice or a victim? Regardless, investigators named them in their 'first information report' (FIR). PwC came under serious flak from the auditing community, not just in India but across the world.

Apart from auditing companies, Satyam had successfully fooled government bodies like SEBI, the Ministry of Corporate Affairs (MCA), its banks, and all its independent directors. Moreover, Satyam was listed in the US, which meant they had to comply with disclosure norms there as well, and they did so without letting them get a whiff of the goings on for several years. The scam had proved to be of truly colossal proportions, and it had cast a long shadow on the otherwise squeaky-clean image of the Indian software industry.

To this day, the single biggest mystery is the reason for Raju's confession. There was no reason at all for him to have come clean when he did. What prompted him? Some believe he did it because that was the only way to save Satyam. If an external source had discovered his fraud, the company would not have survived.

How many people were complicit in the crime? It is anybody's guess. Raju had insisted he was solely responsible. Did that save the ecosystem that ran Satyam? Even in his confession letter, he shared recommendations on how to run the company in the aftermath of the scam. Then there are those who believe that Raju was cornered by investors and chose to confess before they spilt the beans.

I had been to Raju's office and met many people on his team. Apparently, nobody in the company had access to the complete balance sheet. He had separate teams in different buildings, managing his financial manipulations.

The CEO who had warned us at NASSCOM was spot on with this intuitive scepticism of Raju. I thought I was good at reading people. But Raju had fooled me.

Two days after he had mailed his confession to the board, Raju was locked up in Chanchalguda Central Jail, Hyderabad. While he awaited investigation and court hearings, the world had already put brand India Inc. on trial.

NASSCOM had gone into crisis mode. Something had to be done. Immediately.

Mission control

The NASSCOM president at the time, Som Mittal, had been faxed the confession letter early in the morning. Given the respect he had for Raju, Som initially thought it was a prank. He called the SEBI chairperson to check and was shocked to learn that it was real.

This was the first known fraud at this scale in the IT industry, perhaps the world over. More importantly, it was a confession. That ruled out any possibility of a misunderstanding or Raju's innocence. If it hadn't been a confession, there would still be hope that maybe there was more to it.

What would now happen to Satyam's hundreds of customers and thousands of employees? How would any international client ever trust an Indian IT company after this? It was not just a company-level fraud. It threatened to wipe out all the good work that NASSCOM had done since its inception. The scam was damaging the whole industry, and it could take a long time to recover from it.

Som had to decide if he was going to get NASSCOM involved in this directly. However, he faced a chicken and egg situation. He had to get a buy-in from the government to save Satyam and, at the same time, get NASSCOM to agree to intervene as an industry representative.

He went around meeting people on the same day.

The general mood in government offices was that they should not get involved and just let the law take its course. Some even said, 'Why should we care? It's a matter between Satyam and its shareholders. Bhaad mein jaaye saare.'[1]

Many advised Som that NASSCOM should not get involved. A scandal is dangerous, and any kind of association can be misconstrued as collusion. This was also why politicians stayed away in the beginning.

But Som would have none of it. He understood the impact this could have on the industry. He was convinced that if he didn't have a personal agenda, nobody could point the finger at him or NASSCOM. He spoke to the CC and the EC, besides other advisors, and resolved that it was imperative that NASSCOM step in.

Even though, as a policy, NASSCOM does not intervene in internal company matters, we realized that this was larger than just a corporate governance issue. During the debate, it emerged that if Satyam went down, it would probably take the entire India Inc. brand—that we had worked so hard to create for so long—down with it.

We almost did not intervene, but the collective wisdom of the leaders of the IT industry made sure that we got involved in saving Satyam.

Som further recognized that even though financial statements had been manipulated, there was still real value in Satyam's business. It had real clients and thousands of honest employees who would be left jobless if no affirmative action was taken.

It was essential to move fast. After plotting a game plan, Som consulted with the industry leaders, including the companies that competed with Satyam. He then met officers in the MCA, the Department of Economic Affairs, the Department for Promotion of Industry and Internal Trade, the PMO, and the Planning Commission. He didn't even have appointments scheduled for most of these, but

1   Translates to: 'Let them all go to hell.'

when they learnt he wanted to discuss the Satyam debacle, they simply met him.

Som took great pains to impress upon the government the need for Satyam's survival. He explained that it was India Inc. we had to protect. If Satyam sank, its Fortune 100 clients, for whom they were running mission-critical applications, would sink with it. Their operations would come to a halt, putting millions of transactions at risk, upsetting an entire ecosystem of automation and forever tarnishing the India Inc. brand.

The media was brandishing it as the 'Satyam scam'. I felt it was inaccurate. It was clear that one man was the perpetrator. Hundreds of thousands of other people associated with Satyam were innocent. It should have been called the 'Raju scam', if at all. In such cases, typically, the first thing the authorities do is put a lock on the gate of the company. Som advised them against it and instead, worked with them towards saving the company—an unprecedented initiative in the history of India's government-industry relations. It was easier said than done. How was anyone going to save a listed company that had been cooking the books?

The government was obviously ambivalent. So, Som decided to go to ground zero to be closer to the situation and work in concert with government officers, so that they could make informed, collective decisions. Within a few hours, Som was on a flight to Hyderabad.

He reached Hyderabad around midnight and straightaway met Satyam's senior management. He saw that everyone was in absolute shock, just like us. The whole team was in disarray, clueless about what had hit them. Som collected all the information he could till four in the morning.

Hours later, when Som returned to Satyam headquarters, he found the entrance was overrun with camera crews, and TV production trucks were all over the place. If the media recognized him, the news flash would read: 'NASSCOM president spotted at Satyam HQ'. This was clearly not desirable.

So, Som sneaked in from the back of the building. He had to scale a wall!

Once inside, he started gathering more information. He checked how much cash was actually available and how it compared with salaries that would eventually be due. He unearthed new liabilities. For instance, insurance premiums of employees working overseas were unpaid. He made notes about the kind of customers Satyam had and how he could minimize the impact on their relationship. It was a big, unmanageable mess.

The morning after, Som headed back to Delhi and debriefed everyone. They heard him out. Then, they quizzed him. Upon Som's recommendation, the government decided to sack the board immediately and cancel the board meeting that was due the very next day. It was decided that a new interim board would be appointed to determine the way forward.

The next step was to hunt for the right individuals to form the new board. Som shared his recommendations. Someone in the government asked Som to join, too, but as a true adherent of NASSCOM's values, Som declined politely. His contribution as a neutral agent would be much more valuable. He could enable processes from the outside, instead of becoming a direct stakeholder. Contrary to the usual perception of the government machinery, the government moved at great speed, and a board of three people was put in place. Kiran Karnik, NASSCOM's previous president, was appointed as the chairperson of this new board.

Business schools teach us that competing companies are enemies and that business itself is war. When a giant like Satyam falls, it is natural for competitors to swiftly poach key employees and clients. To ensure Satyam's survival, it was vital that there be no poaching. Not until the government had fixed the company. The bureaucrats needed a few months to pull everything together, especially to make changes at SEBI so as to enable their plans.

To keep Satyam alive till the government got its act together, Som turned to the NASSCOM community with a non-poaching plea. Over a conference call, he explained the concerns to the executive council, chairpersons' council, and senior members of NASSCOM. This phone call was extremely crucial because it brought together the potential beneficiaries of Satyam's collapse. Each of us faced this dilemma: do we put our personal interests ahead of the industry's good? Many of us had been around since NASSCOM's inception and understood the importance of seeing the bigger picture. Apart from one or two people, most agreed to cooperate in this challenging time. Some of us were tempted to utilize this moment to ramp up our own businesses, but in the end, NASSCOM's values prevailed. One member asked, 'This is a golden opportunity for me to grow by acquiring Satyam's customers. Why should I agree?' The group counselled him, and he fell in line. We had a unanimous agreement that none of us would go after any of Satyam's clients or poach their senior employees for two months.

Onward was also in the engineering services business at the time, and we competed directly with Satyam. I knew several of its senior employees. We discussed the situation, but, given the scenario, neither anyone from my team agreed nor anyone from Satyam ever mentioned the idea of them coming onboard Onward.

The mess at Satyam took a while to sort out. But NASSCOM's rescue plan had ensured that the company continued to run, independent of Raju, without skipping a beat. Satyam employees worked as diligently as they would have under normal circumstances as if no scam had happened. Almost all of them continued with Satyam throughout the bad times.

Som reached out to Satyam's clients, assuring them that the company would not be dissolved and their projects would be delivered as committed. He reassured them about the steps NASSCOM and the government were taking. They responded with faith because of NASSCOM's credibility and neutrality.

Som and NASSCOM ensured that this act of industry solidarity made headlines. We stood with Satyam's employees through the crisis and believed they were completely innocent. They were not debarred from NASSCOM membership. To resurrect the image of the industry, some companies got their quarterly results re-audited before declaring them. Som himself met several senior editors to make sure this news got adequate coverage alongside the negative one that Raju and Satyam were attracting.

Splashdown

Eventually, Satyam's full board was in place. It comprised reputed professionals from the government and industry. A few months later, things had settled down. Now was the time to find a buyer for Satyam. An auction was held, and it was won by Tech Mahindra. Satyam eventually was merged into Tech Mahindra and lived on. Almost no damage was done in terms of lost clients or employees. Even within India, the scandal almost dented the prospects of placing entrepreneurs on the same pedestal as a farmer or a soldier—two professions that are probably considered the most noble for an agrarian society like ours. However, I believe swift action by NASSCOM saved the day!

The scandal at Satyam was a systemic one. Every fail-safe that you expect a large corporate to have did not deliver. Starting with the self-regulation of a large company that touched so many lives. Then, from the board that consists of independent directors, to the external world-class auditors, to senior executives at Satyam, to even the corporate governance policies—everything just failed.

Going forward, we must scrutinize the role of these guardians that are entrusted with keeping businesses on the right track. Incidents like this can shatter all the hard work of so many people over the last, so many decades.

In a paper published in the *International Journal of Business and Social Research*,[2] Prof. Madan Bhasin described the fraud in powerful words. He said,

---

2   Located   at   https://thejournalofbusiness.org/index.php/site/article/ view/948.

The accounting fraud committed by the founders of Satyam in 2009 is a testament to the fact that 'the science of conduct is swayed in large by human greed, ambition, and hunger for power, money, fame and glory'. Scandals have proved that 'there is an urgent need for good conduct based on strong corporate governance, ethics and accounting and auditing standards'.

Satyam was the heartbeat of Hyderabad, a city that has come to be called Cyberabad because of its IT industry ecosystem. Over 10 per cent of the city's IT professionals worked for Satyam. There was a whole community of rich, young people, of whom almost a third were women. Most local businesses seemed to depend on Satyam directly or indirectly. If Satyam had gone down, it would have taken the city with it.

It's probably the only instance in the world where a company hit by a scandal of such magnitude survived it. NASSCOM had a pivotal role to play. Remarkable resilience was shown by Satyam's employees, too. In spite of the storm, they kept the work flowing with the same sincerity and dedication as earlier. This allowed Satyam's servicing teams to put up a brave face in front of its clients with the assurance that they weren't folding yet.

NASSCOM's handling of Raju's scandal is a phenomenal case study. Nowhere in the world has any industry shown this level of maturity. Even a sensitive brand like FIFA (the global regulatory body for football as a sport), which is likely to steer clear of any controversy, went ahead with Satyam's partnership. The Indian government, which most people blame for its inaction and slow bureaucracy, acted swiftly and efficiently. It was a triumph of the collective, proactive action taken by the industry to protect its image. It greatly enhanced Indian IT's stature within the country and overseas. Brand India Inc. had survived the crisis.

The Satyam incident happened more than two decades after NASSCOM was founded. Nevertheless, it made real its values like 'no personal agenda', 'India first' and 'collaborate to compete' (coopetition). The scandal had demonstrated that these were not hollow phrases, but real principles that the members of NASSCOM live by.

Jim Lovell once called Apollo 13 NASA's most 'successful failure'. Well, you could say that of Satyam and NASSCOM too.

Pitching NASSCOM

Som had shone during adversity and helped navigate one of the biggest challenges we had faced as an institution. His handling of the Satyam fiasco boosted his reputation and stature manifold. Just when we were back to feeling safe under the wings of a leader like Som, his term as the president of NASSCOM came to an end. Like his predecessors, Som was going to leave behind large shoes that had to be filled.

So, towards the end of 2013, NASSCOM was back to the complex problem of identifying a leader who could keep the entire industry and all the myriad stakeholders united as one cohesive whole. We instituted a committee to identify Som's successor. This was led by TCS's S. Ramadorai as the chairperson, and I was the convener. When we started to invite interest, we were informed that Shekhar, the secretary at DoE,[3] was retiring soon. Shekhar had an impeccable reputation and had done a brilliant job managing the aftermath of the 2G scam. He was known to draft balanced policies that took into account every scenario and yet kept India first. To add to that, he could articulate his thinking very well. Everyone in the selection committee held him in high esteem as a righteous individual who had always put aside his personal biases and affiliations to put the country first.

However, we at NASSCOM, had a completely different DNA and working style from that of the bureaucracy in the government. There were doubts if Shekhar would be able to manoeuvre his way within a not-for-profit organization like NASSCOM. Further, in his previous

---

3   The same Shekhar that was brought in by Chandrababu Naidu to transform Hyderabad.

avatar, the celebrity CEOs of the Indian IT industry 'reported' to him, and now, he would have to work closely with them on the same side of the table.

Eventually, we got him on board, and he did exemplary work at NASSCOM, especially around the net neutrality debate with the government and other stakeholders. The selection committee at NASSCOM was vindicated for its foresight to get a senior secretary as the president. To me, this in itself is testimony to how we as a group adapted quickly and went out of the way to look at what was suitable for the industry and the country as a whole.

I can confidently say that if not for NASSCOM, and numerous other decisions we took and actions we made, the India that we live in today would have looked very different. It's time that I try and define what NASSCOM really is.

13

An Association. A Catalyst. A Movement

Here is a fun question for you. Can you guess how many times I used the word NASSCOM in this book?

While I leave you guessing, it is time to describe what NASSCOM actually is.

Depending on whom you ask and the situation we are trying to tackle, we could be an India Inc. brand builder, a think tank, a lobbyist group, an interventionist or more.

None of these is wrong. And yet, none of these is right. No one is at fault for not being able to articulate who we are. NASSCOM operates in an area where technologies continuously change, and it plays different roles at different times and hence, the different understanding.

If I could pick one term to describe NASSCOM, I'd say we are a trusted catalyst for the IT industry and other stakeholders. We are and will remain independent. We will ensure that there is no vested interest in any outcomes, except the growth of the industry. We thus constantly intervene on myriad issues—from policy to guidelines to skilling, and more. Yet, we stay at arm's length when it comes to ownership and creating new institutions.

Over the years, the key responsibility of NASSCOM has been to build an industry narrative with a focus on global relations, skill-building, collaboration, trust and inclusion. We worked to grow the technology talent in India and position the ecosystem as the nation's key differentiator.

A large part of NASSCOM's work has been to strengthen advocacy with the government. We also work on driving policy changes that could help create new markets for our member companies.

A couple of incidents come to mind that exemplify this harmonious relationship that NASSCOM helps maintain between the government, politicians, policymakers, the ever-evolving industry, member companies and other stakeholders.

Once, we approached Dr Manmohan Singh, the finance minister in the P.V. Narasimha Rao government, to reduce import duty on import of software tools via media to zero.[1] It was at 25 per cent at the time[2], and the government earned a paltry ₹140 million a year from this. To us, these imports were critical, as these were software tools and data files needed to deliver the projects. This import duty was adding a lag to the timelines and impacting our efficiency as these could often get stuck with customs for weeks. The projects would get delayed, and this was undoing all the good work we did on brand India Inc.

---

1 The offshore clients would send us test data and the software tools required to render services. The government would treat this as import of software and thus levy import duty. More than the duty, the bigger challenge was the time it took to get approvals from various departments to get the data and tools in the country. Each delay snowballed and rendered us helpless to deliver on time.

2 Compared to media, the software tools and computers required to develop software for exports could be imported duty-free. However, the importer was expected to export software and earn 200 per cent of the cost of the imported computer within five years.

The finance minister said, 'Aap floppy pe jo software export karte hain, uski value kabhi $5 toh kabhi $50 hazaar toh kabhi $5 lakh bhi hoti hai! Wahin doosri taraf, aisi hi floppy par aap software ya data import karte hain—iski value bhi $5 se lekar $5 hazaar tak kuch bhi hoti hai. Hamare officers ko yeh samajhne me waise hi dikkat hoti hai. Aur ab aap ko, upar se, in pe zero duty chahiye!

'Iska matlab aap ki industry export–import karegi aur humein pata bhi nahi chalega. Sir ji, aise toh aap ki industry sab se badi havala[3] industry ban jayegi! Isliye yeh zero per cent import duty ka prastaav hum bilkul approve nahi karenge.'[4]

He further said that the government could absorb the ₹140 million in question, but not tolerate havala transactions.

We were unwavering and made our argument. We said, 'Sir, while there's always a rotten apple that may try to game the system, your support would encourage the ones that are honest and hardworking to grow the industry and create jobs. This would, in turn, earn net forex that is the need of the hour for the country.'

Our stand was that honest entrepreneurs should not be held responsible or penalized because some crooks who took advantage of a weak judiciary & weaker enforcement and thus went scot-free.

He bought the argument.

---

3   Havala is an alternative remittance channel that exists outside of traditional banking systems. The informal method of transferring money without it physically moving is further defined by Interpol as 'money transfer without money movement'.

4   Translates to, 'What you export on a floppy disk, its value at different times is $5, $50,000 or even $500,000. On the other hand, on a similar floppy disk, you import software or data and the value of that is also indeterminant. Our officers are anyway too inept to understand all this. And, on top of things, you want zero duty?

As regulators, we would never understand what you are importing or exporting. This way your industry would become the biggest havala industry in the country! We would never approve this proposal of zero per cent duty.'

This further augmented our capability to deliver solutions to clients overseas, and is one of the early examples of how the association and policymakers worked together to take India ahead.

More recently, in the mid-2000s, Mr Narendra Modi, the then chief minister of Gujarat, called us for dinner at his home in Gandhinagar, where he was dressed in the traditional Gujarati attire of a simple kurta and dhoti. He was concerned about Gujarat lagging in the software business. We explained to him that Gujarat had a bright future in the IT industry. We also pointed him to India's overall demographic advantage in the young workforce. The Western countries have an ageing population, and thus they do not have the requisite technology talent. China would have limited availability of young talent due to their one-child policy.[5] India could therefore leverage on this and make immense progress.

We spent some fifteen minutes taking him through all the numbers, charts and statistics, but as a group, we were not sure if he understood.

He put our doubts to rest the very next day when at an event in Ahmedabad that had 300-plus people in attendance, he said, 'Bharat naujawan hai.' This three-word articulation was as powerful, eloquent and eye-opening as our entire presentation. He further quipped, 'Mujhe lagta tha desh ki chinta keval hum politicians ko hoti hai, yahan to ye NASSCOM walon ko bhi desh ki utni hi chinta hai.'[6]

This is precisely what NASSCOM is. An industry body that works for the upliftment of the nation. In partnership with every stakeholder, including the member companies.

The tough problems that we often encounter at NASSCOM can only be solved when people with varied opinions freely brainstorm with each other with comfort. Problem-solving is an iterative process, and if you create a safe and trusted environment, creative juices flow

5   The policy has since been relaxed.
6   Translated into English, it roughly means, 'I was under the impression that it was only politicians who worried about the country. But here we have people from NASSCOM equally concerned about the country!'

better and can solve even the toughest problems. We can tap into the tacit and collective wisdom of participants. To enable this, we have made our annual retreats an integral part of NASSCOM.

I believe these in-person, face-to-face meetups are critical to building a sense of camaraderie within the diverse and eclectic bunch that we at NASSCOM are. When we go to these retreats, we leave our corporate and NASSCOM designations behind. These are exercises that help us forge friendships at a deeper level, where we can laugh at each other.

Thanks to this cross-pollination of ideas and diverse skills of competing companies, out-of-the-box thinking happens and even what seems impossible can be made possible. There are countless examples of this. The representation of NASSCOM on international forums, that too in a single voice, is testimony to that. The entire Satyam saga could only be managed because all of us came together and pitched in. Even how we arrived at the very definition of NASSCOM could happen because of collective brainstorming. Let me talk about it now.

So, who is 'us'?

Now that we know *what* is NASSCOM, you must be wondering *who* is NASSCOM?

Again, there are no easy answers, but simply put we are an industry association where members use their voting rights to guide its actions.

When we started, we were a representative for a group of software services companies based in India. We then invited and included companies owned by Indian-origin founders and teams that wanted to conduct business in India and abroad. We then expanded to include Indian back-office operations for MNCs that leveraged the unique talent and opportunity that India represented. Next, we added companies engaged in BPM, E&RD, R&D, apart from GCCs, start-ups and more.

With time, the scope of 'who is NASSCOM' kept widening, and each 'addition' was debated for months. Most of these debates were easy to settle. The opportunity, both for business and social impact, was there for everyone to see, and we just had to ensure that we kept our focus on making it easier for entrepreneurs to flourish.

After seeing our impact, other service industries like travel, tourism, retail and more wanted to be a part of NASSCOM. It was tough to say no to them. After all, these industries were also championing job creation for Indians. However, we realized that non-technical services were not an area of strength for us. We thus politely declined to represent them. We also learned to say no to such subsequent requests.

The tricky debates were the ones in the early 1990s, which involved deciding on the re-entry of global majors that wanted to come back to India. It may come as a surprise to younger readers that companies like IBM first entered the country in the 1960s. Texas Instruments set up their largest development centre, outside the US, in Bangalore way back in 1985. However, the business environment forced most of these global businesses, tech and non tech, to quit in less than a decade. The ones that stayed back had to dilute their equity to 40 per cent or less.

We, at NASSCOM, knew that if we wanted to make an impact on a global scale and get India its rightful place on the world map, we had to win the trust of large global companies. To most of these companies, the capabilities that NASSCOM and member companies built in India was the encouragement they needed to set up shop in India. However, they wanted 100 per cent ownership in the back-office operations that they were keen to set up. These companies were worried about data integrity, operational control and third-party interference.

On the other hand, policymakers and stakeholders were wary. History books have ingrained deep suspicion in our thinking that seemingly harmless business operations like the East India Company can eventually take control of our destinies. The regulators had a more rational and immediate fear about keeping tabs on these companies and preventing them from engaging in possibly anti-national, clandestine activities.

For NASSCOM, this posed challenges on two fronts. To start with, it would have required working with the government to create special policies for these global setups. Second, as the 'Indian' industry, we speculated that they would compete directly with us and hamper our market share. Some of us were wondering if they would poach our talent with more lucrative offers.

Both seemed like short-term repercussions of allowing bigger competitors into the country. Some of us believed that if we could encourage them to come to India, it would augur well for the entire ecosystem. Further, it would position India as a country with a favourable business environment, and that would help brand India Inc. immensely. Which, in turn, would help the businesses of NASSCOM members.

We had heated debates that raged on for months. Do we allow these global companies to enter India on their terms? Do we invite them to become members at NASSCOM?

We took more than eighteen months to capture perspectives and opinions from all stakeholders. Each time a new dimension was added to the discussion, we would get back to the drawing board. It started to seem like a never-ending discussion.

This was when some of us became the anchors required to keep the discussion focused. The anchors would channelize the free-flowing creative mavens who would spark interesting ideas. We ensured that people could speak freely without any fear or inhibition and yet not get distracted from the key objective.[7]

---

7   This allowed for new opportunities and ideas to dawn on us. In fact, this closely mimics how Silicon Valley operates. Over many decades, they have perfected a process of bringing in new technology and disrupting the market. A cursory look at how they grew will reveal how they evolved. Some sixty years ago, when orchards in California started to be called Silicon Valley, they were using silicon-based chips to make semiconductors. It took them about ten years from then on to evolve to PCBs that eventually became the motherboard. In another decade, industrial computers had arrived. Fast forward another ten years, and they had the primitive operating systems like the DOS and others. From there, in another decade and half, the Internet happened. Post that we have seen rapid transformation to smart phones and now to cloud computing and AI.

It was during one such set of discussions that a line of reference emerged. It was: 'Whoever develops the human capital in India is us, a part of NASSCOM.'

This sealed the matter and has since become a guiding principle for us.

Once that was settled, we went ahead and prepared a report showcasing the impact on India's fortunes if the government allowed 100 per cent foreign ownership for back-office operations. This was around the same time when Dr Singh was still the finance minister. One of his secretaries responded to the proposal and asked us, 'Aap kiske dalaal ho?'[8] Another officer of his team said, 'East India Company ki tarah kya tum bhi desh ko bechne chale ho?'[9] We were upset, but not surprised at the short-sightedness of the bureaucrats.

However, logic prevailed, and Dr Singh agreed to implement the proposal.

What was almost stopped in its infancy has today matured into 1,400-plus GCCs and ER&D services players from out of India. Together, they contribute approximately $34 billion (or approximately 2 per cent) to India's GDP and employ more than a million people. They are further poised to grow to $100 billion of revenue by 2030.[10]

More than just the tangible outcomes, these back offices gave us something that we would have otherwise taken a lot of time and money to achieve—learning from the competition. When these global players set up operations in India, they brought with them world-class

---

8   Translates to: 'Whose pimp are you?'
9   Translates to: 'Are you trying to be another version of the East India Company that is trying to sell out the nation under the garb of business?' Even though it has been more than seventy years since India's independence, we continue to remember and fear the Trojan horse approach of the British to establish their rule over India.
10   While the credit must go to individual companies, entrepreneurs and millions of engineers, I believe NASSCOM has been playing the critical role of building the ecosystem, enabling policy, creating market access, anchoring knowledge in the shape of research insights, and acting as a conduit of knowledge at regional and national levels.

benchmarks in infrastructure, operational practices, quality and more. These MNCs innovated on every aspect of the business. The Indian companies thus had no other option but to learn, adapt, replicate and innovate.

As they say, competition is the best guru.

These companies started life as glorified staffing set ups and evolved into technology and innovation hubs. They have built their own models of outsourcing and co-development engagements with service providers, both locally and globally. Some are run directly by MNCs. Several of these service providers have a global presence and have gone on to become multinational businesses themselves. Some GCCs have evolved into full-life-cycle service providers within their own parent companies and have started to compete with other service providers. Some have even become so vital to their parent companies that they are charting the future course of action for them.

The ER&D industry is now one of the fastest-growing segments within the overall IT ecosystem.[11] The growth and significance of ER&D is accelerating across vertical domains, geographies and applications.

We didn't just add to India's GDP; we successfully created an environment for companies like IBM that had left India to return. As a second-order effect came along companies that had never considered India as a destination. This, to me, is yet another testimony to how the very definition of NASSCOM enabled us to create an impact beyond what we could have imagined when we started all those years ago. We must continue to encourage and invite these global players to set up shop here in India.

Keeping the sharks away

They say that with great power comes great responsibility. I do realize that NASSCOM, as an industry body, is fairly powerful and

---

11   As of March 2020.

commands a venerable stature. While this attracts great people who want to contribute to the nation, it also invites a few sharks.

One of our jobs is to keep these sharks away.

Behind closed doors at NASSCOM, we often hear of incidents of people wanting to offer bribes to our secretariat officers in exchange for confidential information. These requests are promptly turned down, and any further conversation of similar nature is discouraged.

One time, a VP of marketing from a member company asked us how much it would cost them to get their founder made the next chairperson. The proposal was laughed at, and a stern warning was issued.

Further, to attend the highly sought-after NASSCOM events, we get participation requests from businesses like real estate, law firms, and other service providers to our member companies. We consider their aggressiveness a nuisance and try to filter each request. We only allow the most relevant ones to participate. Further, the norm is that no one should use the podium at NASSCOM to speak about the organization they represent. We still get a few overzealous speakers, but we try and avoid the commercialization of these sessions.

I recently attended a NASSCOM conference, and realized that the quality of the audience is better than ever. The maturity of questions and the depth in the answers left me inspired. This is the very role these conferences and events must play. Each such event is a symbiotic opportunity to learn from peers and experts alike. Peers must come together to brainstorm on common issues they are confounded by. Experts must share what they know. We must create an environment like a university where the focus is steadfastly on learning and sharing as much as possible.

NASSCOM initiatives and forums must maintain their sanctity and remain free of blatant commercialization.

The NASSCOM impact

Over the last few months, I have read eight to ten different memoirs or autobiographies from eminent personalities about where India has

reached in her seventy-plus years of existence. The authors include
bureaucrats, RBI governors, erstwhile ministers and people from the
Planning Commission (now known as Niti Aayog). I was shocked
and disappointed to read that none of them even mentioned the
word NASSCOM, let alone offer a compliment for contributing so
wholesomely to the country. They seemed to have missed the fact that
the IT industry earned the forex that acted as the oxygen required
for a gasping economy. They are not alone. Even in the papers
published in celebrated and venerable journals by institutions like the
Johns Hopkins University Press, the writers missed the role played by
NASSCOM in India's uprising.

While some blame is on them to have ignored the impact made by
the IT industry, we at NASSCOM should take greater responsibility.
I think we became too low-key and failed to communicate in clear
terms the impact and contribution that we've made to the fortunes of
the country.

Many informed and well-meaning people give credit to the
economic reforms of 1991[12] to have changed India. I have a slightly
different take. The reforms were indeed major enablers and provided
the fertile soil for industries to build their foundation. But, it was
NASSCOM that planted the saplings, nurtured them and eventually
produced roses. And alongside the new India also grew.

For starters, the IT sector contributes directly to the country's
economic well-being. It is expected to contribute $191 billion to India's
GDP in 2021.[13] This, in simpler terms, means that out of every ₹100
that India earns, about eight is contributed by the IT industry. Further,
a bulk of it—almost $100 billion—comes in the form of net foreign

12 Under the government of Mr P.V. Narsimha Rao, Minister of Finance
Manmohan Singh brought about sweeping changes and transformed India
from a controlled economy into a liberalized one. The intent was to introduce
free-market economic reforms and invite private and foreign investments.
13 Over the last ten years, the industry would have earned net foreign exchange
of $600 billion cumulatively.

income. For $100 billion, you could import the latest smartphone for one-third of India's population!

One of our member companies, TCS, is now the biggest IT services company globally in terms of its market cap and employs people of more than 145 nationalities. In December 2020, the market cap of just the top four IT companies listed on Indian stock exchanges was almost ₹20 lakh crore. The wealth thus generated has been shared by the promotors, shareholders and public at large.

Second, the IT sector has contributed to shaping the social fabric of India. The growth fuelled by IT has percolated beyond the eleven metros and mini-metros to tier-2, -3 and -4 towns. Cities like Hyderabad, Pune, Bengaluru and Gurgaon were literally created and grew exponentially only because the wheels of the economy were made to spin fast by the IT industry. It created the 'Great Indian Middle Class', where life is built on the tenets of hard work, self-discipline, thrift, frugality, honesty, aspiration and ambition. The middle class takes immense pride in our past and yet, has the aspiration of becoming the best in the world.

This middle class is growing fast and spending faster. These are first-time homeowners and are upgrading to cars from their two-wheelers. They spend on experiences, lifestyle and travel within India and abroad. This boom is creating secondary and tertiary jobs. A consumption age is being ushered in. This, in turn, is enabling the banking, financial services and insurance (BFSI) sector to push bank accounts, insurance products, loans, credit cards and more.

The country is sprinting and taking over the world. Leaders like Satya Nadella and Sundar Pichai are quintessentially middle-class Indians who worked hard and now are at the helm of companies with a market cap of a trillion dollars.

Third, we helped increase gender parity in society, both at the workplace and home. Computers, like nature, do not discriminate, and everyone is equal as long as you give the correct answer. Almost one-third of the IT workforce is made up of women, and each of them has come up on merit, talent and hard work. Nearly 50 per cent of new recruits today are women. In fact, we are witnessing more women taking up the baton of entrepreneurship.

To me, this is the most heartening impact made by NASSCOM and our work. The future will not be sustainable if we fail to encourage and empower women. With time, as women start taking a more participative role in the running of the country, we will see the second-order effects of the same. A better gender representation is good for society and the economy. In my experience, women who hold leadership positions (in both tech and non-tech organizations) ensure that we gain more as they eliminate bias from thinking and decision-making.

Fourth, the IT industry is known for following a high standard of ethics. As a listed company, Infosys set a new global benchmark in corporate governance standards. The openness and transparency in quarterly and annual results opened the floodgates of India's FDI (foreign direct investment). Indian corporates followed, and brand India Inc. started shining.

Fifth, for Indians at large, the contribution made by the IT industry with large IT projects has been life-changing—from the public call offices (PCOs) and the Indian railways' reservation system in the 1990s to the more recent Passport Seva Kendras, the GST system to the payments revolution with UPI (a global first), to the MCA21 (designed to fully automate enforcement and compliance of the legal requirements under the Companies Act, 1956) and the biometric identity system of Aadhar for more than a billion Indians. Credit must go to the RBI for pushing for banking automation and to SEBI for being the driving force for the computerization of the stock exchanges.

Indian IT companies are even contributing to the local economies of countries across the globe by helping them transform their businesses. We have more than 1,000 development centres in eighty-plus countries and employ hundreds of thousands of people worldwide.

India stands tall as one of the largest digital hubs in the world. The heartening thing is that this revolution has just begun. India can learn from automation experiences from around the world. We can leapfrog over their learning curves in finding solutions for India. The revolution will find further traction as and when the government builds capacity to absorb technology, has a sense of urgency to reimagine processes and puts in place the procurement standards that are fair to service providers.

Even the rarest of the rare events like COVID-19 couldn't put the brakes on our progress or lessen the impact that NASSCOM has had. Rather, our response to the pandemic has been nothing short of remarkable. We remained resilient even though we are perceptually a developing country. Led by Keshav Murugesh (the NASSCOM chairperson at the time) and Debjani Ghosh (the NASSCOM president since April 2018), the team at NASSCOM, the entire IT industry, MeitY, the government (led by Mr Ravi Shankar Prasad,[14] the Minister of Electronics, Information Technology and Communications in the Government of India) had to work non-stop for over seven days to get IT included in the list of 'essential services' that were allowed to continue operations. After all, the industry was managing applications that were integral to the core business of thousands of global corporations.[15] Their work allowed the country to function, and ensured that we

---

14   Mr Prasad has been a very vocal supporter of NASSCOM since he assumed office. We often consider him one of us when we interact with him. We need many more such advocates for NASSCOM within the government.

15   This was particularly challenging as, in India, policies made by the Centre need to get interpreted at the state and then district level before they are implemented.

The team had to make the seemingly impossible effort of standardizing the SOPs and guidelines for more than 300 districts, at a time when every minute was critical. In states like Maharashtra, they even worked closely with the state police to help IT/ITeS companies in the mind-boggling logistical task of moving millions of pieces of office equipment to employees' residences so that the work could continue.

delivered uninterrupted service to our customers across the country and the globe.

The Indian prime minister, Narendra Modi, told us, 'When the chips were down, your code kept things running.' It's yet another feather in our cap.

There is more that I can talk about the IT industry and NASSCOM, but I think I'll leave you with what the late Dr Sumantra Ghoshal[16] told us at the NASSCOM Leadership Forum in Mumbai. Talking about the impact of the IT industry on the fortunes of the country, he said, 'The thousand years of [the] economic downfall of India was arrested by [the] revolution brought about by the IT industry.'

Finally, Prime Minister Modi described NASSCOM best in his keynote address at the celebration of twenty-five years of NASSCOM at Delhi, when he said that we were a movement and not just an association.

Movement we are. Movement we shall remain.

Fuelling the movement here onwards

At the risk of sounding like a doomsayer, there are murmurs among analysts from across the world about India's IT industry losing its sheen. One of the most prominent independent technology journalists and thinkers even questioned if NASSCOM was becoming boring.[17]

To find a solution for this, we need to reinvent the very way we have organized ourselves. NASSCOM could learn from a popular software development methodology of Agile—a decentralized, cross-functional, outcome-oriented and collaborative method. We must be aligned to deliver impact and not get siloed in departments.

---

16 Dr Sumantra Ghoshal (1948–2004) was a scholar, educator and management thinker. He was a professor at the London Business School and founding Dean of the Indian School of Business in Hyderabad.

17 Phil Fersht on https://www.horsesforsources.com/nasscom_2019_boring_022319. Retrieved on 28 June 2021.

In fact, going forward, we would be championed by two important groups—one, the new-age industry leaders, who will eventually play the roles that the stalwarts are playing today; and two, the start-up leaders. It is heartening that the young and dynamic leaders from IT companies and BPOs are already playing an active part in this group. The power of this group would be amplified manifold when we can attract the leaders from the start-up world as well. Entrepreneurs like Sridhar Vembu of Zoho (a bootstrapped, home-grown unicorn that is giving global giants like Google and Salesforce a run for their money) need to feel connected to NASSCOM and the mission that we are on. His team is already leading the way into the future with their initiatives like work-from-anywhere (especially from tier-4 towns and villages).

They will drive agendas like innovation, lead us to new industries, conjure up new strategies for NASSCOM and ensure the body stays relevant. On the other hand, the leaders who have been at NASSCOM for a while now, the Chairpersons' Council (CC),[18] has to ensure that the NASSCOM ethos does not remain limited to mere phrases.

As NASSCOM grows older by the year, we add one more stalwart to the ever-expanding CC. True, the largeness of the group adds a lot of weight to the thought leadership at the table. But it poses a challenge, as well. With time, some former chairpersons may not actively remain involved with the running of NASSCOM. Some may take on more active roles. The power structures may thus become inharmonious.

So, to perpetuate the NASSCOM ethos and maintain the NASSCOM integrity, we need to relook the roles and power centres. We may need to add a few clauses in the NASSCOM constitution to

---

18 CC now has a total 31 members (twenty-seven former chairpersons, three former presidents and the current president) and is a powerhouse of capabilities. Each member is immersed in the NASSCOM ethos and is active in their pursuit of their respective passions. These range from education to healthcare to supporting start-ups with patient capital and, in my case, writing this book!

ensure we respect the consensus created by the collective wisdom of the CC.

Nevertheless, I am sure a collaborative structure composed of the experienced and the new will emerge and will respect NASSCOM's values: to put India first, speak in a single industry voice, work with consensus, collaborate and compete, focus on growth, have robust conflict-resolution processes, have conscience-keepers as anchors, spot a weak signal in spite of the noise and share a sense of ownership.

If these two groups work in close cohesion, I am sure the movement from here will evolve into its best avatar and, as Alan Kay said, invent the future.

Particularly, the CC has an increasingly crucial role to play. As a group, we collectively have a diverse experience and rich understanding of what works and what doesn't in the Indian context. A recent survey done amongst CC members revealed that they crave administrative reforms in the government. They want to contribute proactively at the policy level to build a healthy digital society. It is also clear that most members would like to contribute beyond the realm of IT services and at an India level. The members wish to use technology solutions to solve the country's complex social problems, inject a scientific mindset and help create millions of entrepreneurs in India.

If we leverage the CC's vivid understanding well, it could have a multiplier impact on the fortunes of the country. We can collaborate with other stakeholders (like the government, academia and other industry associations), and add to the mechanisms to accelerate India's digitalization. Even though the CC can take numerous paths from here onwards, I can reveal that the group has started to think deeply about how we could be involved in ushering in this change at the country level.

Recently representatives from the fledgling nutraceuticals industry came to meet Rajiv Vaishnav and me. They face the same challenges we faced when we started—new business, multiple players, distrust, negligible awareness in the market and more. They met almost every industry body in the country and chose to take inspiration from the NASSCOM model. They even went ahead and hired one of our colleagues from NASSCOM to institutionalize their association. History repeats itself!

Honestly, I was pleased. To me, it has come as a validation of the work that each of us has put in to make NASSCOM what it is today. If our work can help seed more movements, other industry associations and create new Dewangs, I believe we have done our job.

I am often asked where and how this movement will end. The easy answer is, never. The future is unpredictable, and we need to encourage ongoing interventions. True, we may create a Steve Jobs, an Elon Musk along the way, but the movement will not stop till millions of entrepreneurs rise and transform India from a developing nation to a developed one. And along the way, uplift the life quality of an average Indian to one of the top five in the world.

14

Transformation 2.0

Sone Ki Chidiya

The other day, I was with some students from an engineering
college in Mumbai. In the open house, one of the students asked,
'what would it take for India to be a Sone Ki Chidiya all over again?'

Her question got me thinking.

In the past, India had prospered on the back of our expertise in
trade, artistry, and business acumen. That time is long gone now.
However, I know that today we may not be the richest nation in the
world anymore and may not have the most abundant natural resources,
we definitely are second to none when it comes to intellectual capital.

One thing is clear to me. To regain our rightful place, we would
have to have each citizen works towards the singular goal of being
the Sone ki Chidiya. Technology would probably have to become the
bedrock on which we would establish the might. More than attaining

financial freedom and sovereignty, we must become a country where every citizen will have the means and the skills to be productive.

At NASSCOM, we've made early advances in the direction. At one of our events, we came up with a document where we postulated that in the next twenty-five years, we shall evolve into a Smart Nation— one that uses its intellectual capital, technology know-how, and talent for innovation to build an empowered, clean, healthy, sustainable, and digitalized country. We shall achieve a 100 per cent literacy rate, enabled by digital solutions. Each household will be healthy, and technology will help overcome the constraints of insufficient doctors and inadequate healthcare infrastructure. Decision-making will be backed by data, and citizens, businesses and governments will have seamless access to this data to create pre-emptive policies. That, in turn, will move the flywheel and eventually make India one of the best places in the world to live, work and do business in.

However, technology alone though may not be able to bring the riches back to us. In a world that is more connected than ever, we would need to go beyond our predefined roles and work hand in hand. Even the government and policymakers will need intellectual muscle that goes beyond what is trapped in the silos of various industries. Closer partnerships will have to be forged among various stakeholders. We are lucky to have a steering system in form of various government bodies[1] that has driven and given direction to the nation. In the future, these bodies will have to work even more closely with citizens and industry bodies such as NASSCOM.

I further suggest that the government partners with citizens and considers setting up cross-domain, multidisciplinary think tanks that corral the best minds from social sciences, mathematics, economics, engineering, and every other speciality needed. These think tanks should ideally have no predetermined outcomes, be free of ideology,

---

1   These include the Supreme Court, RBI, SEBI, Central Vigilance Commission (CVC) and Central Bureau of Investigation (CBI).

be driven by evidence-based research and must keep a billion Indians at the focal point.

India has always known the one-way guru-chela relationship. The time has come to replace that with an ongoing, two-way one. Maybe even many-to-many. Rather than a top-down policy and regulation-first approach, both industry and the government must keep an open mind on the policy framework. The outcome of the policies must give people choices. After all, people are inherently smart and can decide what is right or wrong for their future. The need for the government is to step back and not act like a Big Brother.

If we zoom out of the role of the government and take a note at other aspects, we'd find that the problems in India will continue to be markedly different from the rest of the world for some years to come.

For one, political parties in India seem to be on a never-ending mission to annihilate each other. I find it appalling that our democracy is at best incomplete, and full of divisive politics and immature behaviour. This ties the hands of policymakers, slows down the implementation of projects and thus the speed of development.

To add to this political conundrum, India is still vastly poor. It is also younger. To improve the lives of all our citizens, the country will need a string of revolutions across numerous domains: from healthcare to education to employment to entrepreneurship and beyond. I believe technology can spark these revolutions with its ability to spawn dozens of exponentially growing industries within each domain.

To grow these industries, I believe we need to not just ape the West, where they automate things and make people redundant. The new India needs to be built by using technology to create more jobs and make people more productive.

Consider healthcare. India has an acute shortage of doctors and doctors per capita is relatively low compared to the developed counterparts. Scaling up the healthcare education infrastructure is important. But it is a slow process. While that happens, technology can come to the rescue immediately by increasing the capability of the current force of medical professionals. A doctor can become many times more productive with technologies like AI, nanobots and telemedicine. In fact, digital healthcare could be in the 2020s what traditional IT services have been in the past. If we extend our services beyond our borders, we could become the global healthcare hub, and nothing stops us from becoming the 'hospital of the world'.

Similar thinking can be applied to solve even the most perplexing challenges in almost every discipline.

We could, and must, evolve into a country rooted in our traditional values and yet use a scientific mindset to reclaim our historical place as a global economic superpower. I am confident that if we apply collective knowledge and insights, we will create our egalitarian utopia where thousands of entrepreneurs lift India and its millions of people out of poverty and tragedies.

Advantage India

As I talk about the future of India, a few things may sound like hyperbole, but hyperbole and grand plans are what we need to stay relevant in the future that we are embarking on inventing.

Technology not only changes itself rapidly, but also disrupts other industries and rewrites their rules. Information technology tends to attack at the very fundamentals. The shifts in banking, finance, retail, travel, hospitality, and communications are just the beginning.

At an individual level, the evolution of technology meddles with societal intangibles, like personal liberties, morality, and cultural transformation. Multiply this with the dramatic mushrooming in the number of technology domains, each needing an industry-wide collective strategy as well as governmental policy framework support.

Take the example of online voting. The technology to get a billion Indians to press a simple button and shift the country's power structure has been available for a while now. What seems to be lacking is trust, robustness, integrity, and security. The very bedrock of democracy is at stake, and we would need to consider the philosophical and real-world implications of making such a button, that lacks these essential virtues, mightier than the pen. Or the sword.

These newer, emerging areas bring their own set of problems. Who decides on the ethical and moral dilemmas that the designers of automated vehicles face? Who moderates the freedom of speech offered by the largely anonymous Internet? Where do we draw the boundaries of personal information and state surveillance?

How are the government, the entrepreneurs, and the people to ever keep up with all this? How are they to form common opinions and insights that guide the engineer's hand? How do we conduct this waltz at the speed of thought itself? Who's responsible? What role would NASSCOM play while various stakeholders navigate these crests and troughs?

I'll save you a guess and give you the answer.

The responsibility has to be shared by each stakeholder in the ecosystem. However, entrepreneurs will have to take the lead and be the harbinger of change. Support must come from the government in the shape of policy, regulation, and judiciary. We are on the cusp of a revolution, if not over it already. After all, our service offering to the world is no longer based on legacy systems, and we are tackling hard problems by exploring fields like deep tech. Indian entrepreneurs are fearless and boast of disruptive business models. Skilled talent is increasingly available, and teams are being backed by patient capital. India's demographic advantage,[2] and our natural gift of thriving in mathematics, logic and ambiguity will further add fire to India's race to the top.

It is heartening to note that the government and the policymakers seem to have recognized this potential. Recently the minister of commerce in the current government challenged us to deliver an

---

2   India is slated to add more than 90 million to our workforce by 2030. China, on the other hand, is looking at a contraction by 51 million.

industry top-line of $500 billion, almost 30 per cent more than what we have planned for. He extended his support and asked us what we would need from the government to get to the number.

With the current base of $190 billion, each additional percentage point adds a seemingly unsurmountable peak to the already lofty goal we have.

Rather than scampering for cover, this target is an exciting challenge to us at NASSCOM.

As we sprint to catch up with the future and conquer these stiff slopes, three things that will enable us are skill development, innovation and, more recently, as the aftermath of COVID-19, digital transformation.

Skill development has been a key battle at NASSCOM. Going forward, it will be even more critical as this would be the key differentiator in establishing India as the talent engine of the world[3]. We survived the challenges of not having enough project managers by 'importing' them. We had to live with the scarcity of beta testers required to deliver on robust quality assurance. With each curve in the industry's evolution, we have had to acquire the skills needed to ride that bend—from Java to proprietary technologies like Oracle and SAP to open-source technologies like Python and more. Going forward, we need to be a lot more proactive with talent.

India and the IT industry have largely benefited because we could catch the innovation waves just ahead of time. We used this lead to add to the skills of our manpower, and, as soon as the potential customers

---

3   In 'The Chinese Dragon by Rajiv Bajaj: Must read for those building global products from India' in nextbigwhat.com on 22-07-2020, Rajiv Bajaj, the MD of Bajaj Auto, has put forth his perspective on how Indian bike companies beat the Chinese counterparts, not just in Indian market but even in Africa. He talks about how Bajaj Auto and TVS identified, nurtured, and grew talent from the grassroots. He talks about the importance of investing in R&D and for the long-term, if we are to remain competitive. While he may sound critical of the IT industry in the article, I believe we need to take lessons from automobile industry and make similar structural changes in how we look at talent.

were ready to release the requests for proposals (RFPs) and line up service providers for their requirements, the Indian IT industry was ready to deliver.

The talent–skills–education–training–delivery flywheel is mission-critical for any industry's success. At NASSCOM, we understood the importance of institutionalized technology education soon enough, and we worked towards augmenting it. We were instrumental in continuously upgrading two of India's most successful education programmes: the MCA and the IIIT. For the IIITs, we worked closely with the governments (both central and state), the industry and academia. The central government gave financial grants to seed these. The state government gave infrastructure for the campuses, and the industry funded the ongoing operations. We also recommended a governance structure that was eventually accepted and implemented by the government. Today, the twenty-three IIITs offer more than 3,400 seats per year. More than 1,730 colleges offer the MCA programme. The battle is only uphill from here, with the business world now needing a mix of the left and the right brain to succeed.

To bridge the gap between education and employability, in 2020, the FutureSkills Prime[4] initiative was launched by NASSCOM in partnership with MeitY. In less than a year since the launch, it had more than 1,00,000 active users monthly, and the ambition is to take it to every student in the country. I believe it would help foster the talent of tomorrow and establish India as a talent engine of the world. The FutureSkills Prime initiative has been a landmark success and has recently been featured in UNESCO's report on vocational education. I am sure you will hear more about it in times to come.

Human creativity, emotions, empathy, and intelligence will emerge as the new pillars of growth, and we must support them. Innovation in the emerging disciplines of AI, IoT, cloud and cybersecurity will ensure that we continue to maintain our advantage. These are also the

---

4   The initiative has been under development since 2017, when the team first presented the concept plan to the NASSCOM EC.

disciplines where we can grow manifold. We must stake large bets on supporting entrepreneurs working on these.

COVID-19 has thrown open opportunities that were previously unheard of. India is best positioned to take advantage of increased digitization and remote hub-and-spoke operations. This digitization was ushered in faster and better than what all the lobbying groups across the globe could have done, even if they got together as one. New areas where digital transformation was earlier unthinkable have now opened up. Businesses across the world are open to offshoring and globalizing their operations. Work from home (WFH) has entered the lexicon of most companies. There's an incredible opportunity to build capability fast and deliver to these businesses that are primed for change.

If these changes are made in how we operate, I don't see a reason why the Sone Ki Chidiya wouldn't take to the skies again.

A million technopreneurs[5]

We need to work on deep-seated cultural issues before we truly become the land of abundance.

For starters, we need to stop treating businessmen who are struggling (or have failed) as criminals, especially in the IT industry. The IT system is based on taking chances anyway, and failures are not just expected, but mandatory.

In India, failure has a stigma attached to it, and it is reflected in every walk of life. Every time Team India loses a cricket match, personal, vicious abuses are hurled at the spouses and children of the players.

---

5   I am mindful of the use of the word technopreneurs and not entrepreneurs. A technopreneur leverages technology to create impact at a scale that reaches beyond a handful. I must also qualify that no idea, no start-up, no entrepreneur is too small. Each idea has the potential to change the world for the better. If you are sitting on an idea, no matter how small or outlandish you believe it is, you must act on it and turn it into reality.

The world celebrates success with accolades and trophies, but failure often has no friends. We could change this by encouraging more conversations about how failure is a necessary ingredient for success. We probably need to educate parents so that the next generation is primed to handle failure while chasing their lofty goals.

Reasons for failure can be many: unpredictable government actions, poor market conditions, ideas that are ahead of their time or plain bad entrepreneurial decisions. These are often outside the control of the entrepreneur.

For big, risky projects, it is imperative that we fail quickly at the hardest problems. In developed countries like the US and companies like Google, they celebrate failure and have built a culture of rewarding failure. They regularly work on large projects (called moon shots) that have the potential to change the trajectory of not just the company but the entire world. These projects, by their very nature, are risky, and the cost of failure rises exponentially with time. So, it's imperative that the fail points are discovered early on. To encourage this fail-early thinking, they offer rewards to find ways to kill these projects. These companies thus thrive on failure. If we could replicate this in India, imagine what it would do to the country's fortunes and risk-taking ability.

This fail-early approach also removes the fear of backlash or ridicule and creates an environment where all ideas are welcome. I'd go on record to say that innovation breeds on failure. Someone told me, 'Enthusiastic scepticism is a partner of boundless optimism and not an enemy. It unlocks the potential in every idea.' The idea has remained with me since.

Despite the widespread stigma associated with failure, around the early 2000s, NASSCOM realized the importance of start-ups and resolved to nurture them. It took time, but the initiative started crystalizing by 2010 when we noticed the next wave of start-ups tapping into the Internet and domestic markets.

It was then that the 10,000 Start-Ups initiative was conceived. Spearheaded by Rajan Anandan, the then MD of Google India, it sought to catalyse the start-up ecosystem in India. The ambition was to enable technopreneurs and incubate, fund and support 10,000 technology start-ups over the next ten years.

Such initiatives, too, had their share of naysayers, who asked why NASSCOM was getting into it. They wondered if NASSCOM had the bandwidth to manage these added expectations of tens of thousands of members. We explained to them that the well-being of the services industry was non-negotiable, but this could not be ignored. It is further aligned with our vision for making India a product nation[6].

Engaging with start-ups, however, has been challenging. They would attend our events but were wary of signing up as members. Without them becoming members, we would find it difficult to guide them or address their issues in a meaningful way. Further, some of these start-ups have been discovered to be not so clean on ethics or governance. The media tends to hype the success of these companies and the key issues get buried. We need to be more cognizant of the ecosystem we operate in.

Apart from this, another issue is the monopolization of a particular domain by big investors. By pumping in mindless amounts of capital, these investors stifle innovation and choke up the entire ecosystem. In the recent past, I have observed numerous such stories, and they have left me disappointed, to say the least.

Further, our experience at NASSCOM has taught us that the government needs to hear a distilled, single view from the industry.

When I look at the start-up world today, I don't find enough young people, start-ups, companies or even unicorns willing to think beyond

---

6   While India has excelled in the services business, we still lag in the product game. The reasons are aplenty, and the starting point is that the temperament and talent required to deliver a product is entirely different from that required to work on a service. The business models are fundamentally different. The investments required are different. The risk-reward ratio is stacked against us. Teams and companies focused on products and services are different even on the cultural level. I'd go as far as saying that we don't have the hunger to excel at the product game.

their immediate ventures. They must learn to conjure dreams that are much grander. They must come together, suppress their competitive instincts, and find a common voice for their industry. Only then will they be able to work with the government to build a healthy ecosystem that no single company can make by itself, however big it may be. True, historically, a few pockets of excellence[7] have been built by companies, governments, and the individual efforts of their leaders, but we shall need more of these if we are to take the leap from a developing country to become a developed one.

I understand it may not be easy for an industry to have consensus over most issues[8]. But that's what needs to be focused on, and that's what NASSCOM achieved to a great extent with the software services industry. This is why insider phrases like 'no personal agenda' and 'brand India focus' are not merely empty words. They are values and a framework that can be replicated across industries. We did it once with the IT industry but need to keep doing it again and again with many other industries if India has to secure her future.

Only when such a collective grand vision of the future is created can you find that single inspired voice. The government can then be co-opted to help create the policies for it. After all, it is not the government's job to be tracking the latest challenges faced by an industry. Its job rather is to process the information presented to it and then form the best policy in the country's interest. And one that considers long-term impact, provides a level playing field, ensures fair play and allows younger companies to take birth.

---

7   J.R.D. Tata built Jamshedpur, Jharkhand. Sharad Pawar built Baramati in Maharashtra. Cities like Chandigarh and Gandhinagar were built largely by the efforts of political leaders in power at the time.

8   A senior IAS Officer from Maharashtra told me, 'Start-ups and MSMEs are like the royal clans of the yesteryears. They are constantly at battle among each other and can't seem to unite to take on the impending war. Our start-ups are ponies of Chinese and American money and are fighting for turf in India.' I have to say that he's not wrong.

I must state that it would be unfortunate if my recommendation of presenting a single voice is construed as something that stifles dialogue. There's a thin line that separates single voice and single view. A single voice is a unified perspective that a group of companies presents to stakeholders. It is often arrived at by dialogue and debates and by incorporating different viewpoints from participants. Plus, these viewpoints could change frequently, especially for start-ups, as the industry is evolving rapidly.

From the vantage point of my conversations with these young entrepreneurs, I know that they have different expectations. They want immediate action and often lack the patience to get a successful partnership in motion. They are more likely to tweet about their frustration with the government and are happy to get a few retweets. Shekhar pointed out something similar and said, 'They need to understand the difference between being heard and being listened to.' The government becomes aware of their problem, but, for definitive action, there needs to be a communication strategy and process.

I would like to see NASSCOM, TiE and others move onward to a larger project for creating a million technopreneurs. At least 50 per cent of these must come from under-represented cohorts like women, rural innovators, social enterprises and intrapreneurs[9] within large businesses. Further, we must encourage technopreneurs to build innovation-driven enterprises. They have to serve domains as diverse as pharma, manufacturing, banking and more. To foster these, special care must be taken to focus on start-ups that will define the future.

These start-ups must create an inclusive society where growth reaches the ones that have been denied so far. I have a wish list of how

---

9   Intrapreneurs will increasingly play a vital role in the ecosystem as this group will lead their respective employers into newer territories and service lines that are currently non-existent. Also known as entrepreneurs in residence (EIR), these professionals operate like a start-up within the parent organization and create immense value for themselves, the shareholders, and the entire ecosystem. This change in mindset from being mere jobseekers to job-creators is what is needed to solve India's problems.

these start-ups must contribute. At least 10 per cent of these should work on deep tech. At least 25 per cent should have women in the founder's role, and special incentives must be made available to start-ups where more than 50 per cent of the team is made up of women. At least 10 per cent of these start-ups must have differently-abled persons in their leadership teams.

We need such diverse representation to usher in the future and deliver to the bottom of the pyramid.

Partnering with pre-emptive, collaborative policymaking

The COVID-19 crisis could only be tackled because technology enabled us to do collaborative research, share information in real-time and assess impacts immediately. In human history, this is the fastest we've been able to develop a vaccine. Further, we distributed manufacturing across the globe and deployed vaccines from these hubs. This could happen because of global, cooperative trade practices supported by robust information systems. In India, the digital-first method of the vaccine rollout wouldn't have been possible if not for the technology infrastructure built previously. I want to hazard a guess that if COVID-19 had struck us fifty years ago, probably a large chunk of the human race would have been wiped out. Technology has proved its mettle as an enabler of change, a companion to policymakers and a life-saving tool in the hands of people at large.

Further, from school-going children becoming instant experts on technology to seniors adapting to video-communication tools, no stratum has been left untouched by the impact and utility of technology. The rate of technology adoption has made even the hockey-stick curve look flat.

This is a golden opportunity to introduce unapologetically brash technology reforms and create full-throttle monumental shifts in the fortunes of the country. This is the right time to introduce large initiatives around technology infrastructure and push indigenous tech innovations.

The government should be pre-emptive and use the policy carrot to encourage entrepreneurs and stakeholders to build a society guided by scientific thinking. In fact, technology enforces ethical behaviour, which is probably the solution to India's troubles.

We should encourage a two-pronged approach where, on the one hand, we work on strengthening existing technology infrastructure and, on the other, bolster our R&D investment, fundamental research and applied research capabilities. This would make our nation all the more atma nirbhar (self-reliant) in areas such as cyber security, which are critical to the development and sovereignty of our country. In fact, the government must identify a few areas where technology could be used as a tool to solve large problems confronting our nation and support techno-entrepreneurs as they go about creating solutions that deliver impact at scale.

Going forward, I believe pre-emptive, consultative policymaking will become the most important driver for the technology landscape that is growing more complex by the day and is increasingly teeming with global players. It is imperative to provide a level playing field to homegrown, small businesses. Every micro, small and medium enterprise (MSME) should be encouraged to adopt technology and become R&D-driven.

To support the government and policymaking, the industry needs to do its bit as well. Imagine the scenario where an industry refuses to participate and resists pre-emptive policymaking, and yet continues to put in the hard work to take a new technology product to the market. What if, all of a sudden, the government catches up and enforces policies against this new technology? The blanket ban on cryptocurrencies is an example of such a nightmare[10]. Overnight, entrepreneurs, who

---

10   In 2018, the RBI had banned Indian banks from facilitating cryptocurrency transactions, thereby sending the nascent industry in a spiral. While this ban

were technology bright sparks, were regarded as criminals. These
blanket bans that are often imposed without consulting the industry
also increase distrust, thereby creating a downward spiral that leads to
inevitable doom.

In India, policy always seems to be a step behind innovation. Once
an industry grows to a certain size, the policy automatically follows.
Many of us in the software services business worked hard to find a
delicate balance of working with each other and the government.
On the one hand, we kept them away from micromanaging us, and
on the other, we worked closely and sought support from umbrella
services. Back then, we had labour arbitrage as a weapon, and that was
sufficient to take on competition. Quite contrarily, today, companies
even within an industry don't talk to each other. How are they to invite
the government and work with it on pre-emptive and consultative
policymaking then?

Then there is the matter of IP protection. While innovation needs
a free hand, it also needs IP protection to flourish. The protection can
be offered by an independent judiciary that is efficient with the swift
delivery of justice. Again, the judiciary will know what to do if they act
on a single voice rather than fragmented opinions.

The pace of change today mandates the need to bring in a
government willing to invest for a very long term, even if there are
no evident returns for the next ten to fifteen years. Often, many new
technologies cannot promise swift commercialization. The private
sector thus is often compelled to drop a frontier technology that could
be the key to a powerful future. With government support, the industry,
educational institutes, and R&D groups can acquire the formidable
chops required for thriving in the future.

---

was lifted by the Supreme Court in 2020, there have been mixed signals from
the regulators and policymakers since. At the time of writing of this book,
even though multiple crypto start-ups have achieved unicorn status, there is
no formalised regulatory framework that guides the actions of the industry
or safeguards the interests of investors.

I'd go on to say that the hangover from a planned economy mindset needs to change. The rusted bureaucracy needs to be polished and sharpened. The government needs to find ways to build capacity and capability internally. Work must be done to understand the current and future skill gaps of officers. Further, interventions to 'build, buy and borrow' talent must be developed, just as we do in the private sector. Forward-looking bureaucrats and officers must be encouraged and promoted. The government must also inject lateral skills by borrowing from private enterprises, NGOs, and other disciplines. I know it's idealistic, but there is also merit in encouraging various departments within the government to collaborate. The entire conversation needs to move away from 'rule framing' to 'exception monitoring'. If you continue to engage in 'rule framing', it will remain a negotiation, and the nation will be damaged, perhaps irrevocably.

The technology world has started to grow to envelope governmental boundaries at various levels of Centre, state, city and even the gram panchayat levels. The government straddles the role of a regulator, policymaker, builder of ecosystems and, eventually, consumer of IT products, solutions, and services. The government must thus evolve its decision-making processes by using analytics and AI for deeper visibility and insights.

Further, while laws and regulations are local, many technologies are now global, and the geographical borders are more permeable than ever. From the migration of birds to rivers on their way to the ocean to the change in the pattern of winds, no natural phenomenon is bound by these fences. The recent focus on atma nirbharta needs to take inspiration from nature and allow free flow across the borders.

My take on atma nirbharta may sound different from the populist one.

While, in principle, atma nirbharta is good, we can't be self-reliant in a vacuum. We must aim for paraspar nirbharta (mutual dependence). Due to the complex and intertwined nature of technology, we can never be atma nirbhar in making every component of a product. And we shouldn't. We must find our strengths and focus on those. For the rest, we should partner, collaborate, and create joint partnerships with other countries. The COVID-19 vaccine rollout across the globe is an excellent example of both atma nirbhar and paraspar nirbharta.

We must not be swayed by the idea of self-reliance to the extent that we stifle innovation and free-market principles. Our policy framework thus must encourage working with countries that are our major sources and markets. We must find a calibrated joint solution.

The countries that have the best collaboration and partnerships[11] are thus truly atma nirbhar, and we must strive for that.

The other dimension is that technology policymaking often goes beyond the considerations of specialized, siloed domains. Increasingly, high-technology policymaking is informed and advised by topics of morality and ethics. Self-driving cars, for instance, need to learn or inherit 'values' that will help them make split-second decisions. For example, as an accident unfolds, millisecond by millisecond, a self-driving car may have to make a choice between hurting young children playing on the sidewalk or elderly crossing the road. Should the vehicle then consider the economic impact of these losses or be guided by human compassion? Who encodes these decisions? The programmers? Or the government that represents the voice of the people? Such are the dilemmas of pre-emptive policymaking.

Take the case for privacy and data-protection laws. Europe has already announced its position by issuing its General Data Protection Regulation (GDPR) and it was implemented in 2018. In the same year, I was approached by a young entrepreneur who lost a project in Germany simply because India's stand on GDPR was still not clear.

---

11   An opportunity here is with our neighbour, China. I am not a political expert, but, over the last four decades, China has emerged as a powerful nation on the back of political intent and advances in trade. I believe it will continue to grow, both as an economic superpower and as a global trade hub. As China begins to assert itself on global forums, we must watch it closely. I'd go so far as to say that China and India must forge a strong partnership and become paraspar nirbhar.

In one of my conversations with Yatish Rajawat[12], he pointed to some really thought-provoking ideas. He said,

> The next few decades will be about three Ds—data, design, and digital. None of these has sovereign borders. The fate of businesses and nations will be determined by the aggregation and consolidation of data. It will be crucial to design the right policies and business environment to enable businesses to succeed. The competitive edge of nations will be decided by the trifecta of how entrepreneurs build data resources, how they create a digital infrastructure that relies on more than just the ad-supported business models, and finally, how they harness human capital to generate value. Catalysts like NASSCOM and others will have to look beyond national boundaries and seek to build a pan-Asian healthy, vibrant ecosystem for data and infrastructure, as national borders are no longer enough to encapsulate the aspirations of Asian nations.

I couldn't agree more. There are tens of other such domains that India's policymakers haven't even started exploring.

As I write this, a company that runs a popular food delivery app has announced that it hopes to replace its delivery executives with drones. There are obvious policy implications here. Hundreds of thousands of delivery personnel would lose their jobs, and the cameras on these drones could cause serious privacy violations.

In another aspect, let us consider the Internet. On one hand, it is the best school ever created, and, on the other, it is probably a vehicle of weaponized disinformation. I believe there is no institution in the world trustworthy enough that the Internet can't turn into a lie! Consider the case of deep fakes. They are crippling the entire judicial system that used to rely on cameras and videos!

---

12 Yatish is a public-policy specialist, celebrated journalist, and a researcher. Over his career, he has worked with the *Economic Times, the Times of India, Dainik Bhaskar, DNA* and more.

The young and the restless

Blame it on my age, credit it to my experience or call it the ways of the world, I get to spend a lot of time with the young. They approach me to seek inputs on their ideas and often for support for their startups. I am often amazed at their clarity of thought and burning desire to succeed in these youngsters. These young ones are truly the restless as well. These are exactly the people we need to take on the innovation challenge, to take bold steps and push the pedal.

To take wings, we as a nation need to bring about a change in mindset. Our forefathers lived and died in times of scarcity and passed on a shortage-based mindset, which still guides actions for most of us. We thus have a very limited risk-taking capability. For such a society, the service business is a lucrative bet as it offers predictable profitability and healthy margins year-on-year. This cranks a reliable engine that creates jobs, adds to net forex for the country and contributes to the society.

The peculiarity of our culture is that we are not innovators per se, but we adjust quickly to whatever is thrown at us.

Instead of challenging the situation we are in, we adapt. We blindly follow preachers, gurus and often dogmatic traditions. Recently, a yoga guru encouraged his followers to give up the research-led methods to safeguard against COVID-19. While there is merit in our ancient practices, we must not dismiss scientific methods built on the principles of inviting questions, submitting to scrutiny, and accepting evidence-based assertions. We as a society seem to be okay with a poor healthcare system. We like to buy the cheapest alternatives and not the ones with the best quality. The education system is focused largely on rote learning and not exploration.

It is reassuring that the young and restless are already a new breed and are questioning the age-old dogmas. I find them bubbling with energy and enthusiasm. Many of them have travelled the world and are yet proud of their Indian roots. A great change is in the works.

They are bringing global best practices to the country and innovating to solve for India-specific problems. They realize that India herself offers a captive consumer base of more than a billion people.

I am hopeful that we will make strides in the product game now. In the near future, I am not sure if we'll see a Microsoft or a Google spring from India, but we will for sure have tech-driven manufacturers and software as a service (SaaS) product companies emerge as global giants. These would be products developed for Indian consumers that will mature with iterative cycles of development, deployment, and feedback. They would then be taken to people and companies across the world.

The government needs to play a more proactive role to support these young and restless. The role has to be that of an anchor. The government can do so by allocating more resources and mandating that the bureaucracy encourage the private sector to flourish and take risks. Right now, it's the opposite. We penalize those who take bold steps and, to add to their misery, we look at them with suspicion.

Further, innovation and initiatives will fall short, and impact would be dwarfed if wealth is not created for everyone—from innovators to those at the bottom of the pyramid. From my conversations with the youth, I believe they already understand this.

Next, what I called the vile nexus of lala, neta, baba, jhola, babu, gundas, judge, and others must be broken. These groups have ganged up to form power centres and work for their short-term gains, often at the cost of the nation. This is probably the toughest problem to have confronted us as a nation. This nexus is like a rogue vehicle on the road, which runs over millions of poor, innocent people. These further gives birth to antisocial elements and stymies the development of the nation. The true unleashing of India cannot happen without untangling this nexus. I am hopeful that the young technopreneurs will lead the way and bring together all the stakeholders to break the nexus and defeat this parasite that is eating us from within. Of course, we need all the stakeholders to play a role in this battle, especially the citizens. We, as individuals, need to quit our armchair activism, and must speak up and participate in resolving at least the local level issues. Even the simple act of exercising the fundamental right to vote[13] would be a great start.

Finally, even though we have come a long way from where we were, I believe a lot of work still needs to be done in the areas of policing, legal framework, cybercrime, digitization of various government processes, creating centres of excellence (CoEs) in various states and more. I believe that the new superheroes from the Indian technology industry would come as an unintended second-order impact of work in these areas. The young need to look at these spaces as a large opportunity. Where else in the world would you get to work on problems that touch the lives of more than a billion people?

The business environment in India is like a dark night with a few stars dotting the sky. The stars are far apart and often don't 'talk' to each other. NASSCOM tried and succeeded to an extent in binding the IT stars into a constellation that has become the pride of India. I am sure more NASSCOMs will take birth and create more constellations. The need of the hour, however, is to have more stars, even fireflies, dotting the sky.

It's surprising how I find most of my inspiration from nature. On a recent trip to Bhandardara near Mumbai, I spotted some fireflies[14]. Each firefly is like a spark that illuminates itself for a tiny bit and gets lost again to the darkness.

However, some species of fireflies are known to mimic each other, and you'd often spot them illuminating in groups. When these groups

---

13 I read somewhere that 'a vote is the most powerful, non-violent method of change in a democracy'. We must exercise our fundamental right to bring about change. However, any election at any level sees less than 60 per cent participation on an average.

14 As I talk of fireflies, I am reminded of the 2014 book, *Redesigning the Aeroplane While Flying*, by former Planning Commission member, Arun Maira. In it, he describes some possible scenarios for Indian enterprise, one of which is titled 'Fireflies'.

light up, they leave you marvelling at the power, beauty, and impact of nature.

I think the problems of India are deep, dark, and vast. What we need and what I can see is that very soon, thousands of technology start-ups, academics, entrepreneurs, intrapreneurs, NGOs, government officers, farmers, artists, millions of skilled people, and you, the reader, will become the bright sparks, the fireflies they were destined to be...

...Then, together, they will rise and light up the sky.

In the next few years, there's no doubt that the world will drastically change. A substantial part of this change will be propelled by technology, allied innovation, and real-life application in every walk of life. The possibilities are truly endless.

I hope you agree that we'd be right at the top. Even though it is inspired by the Sone ki Chidiya from the past, the future is, and definitely in, India!

Epilogue

Many young people ask me about the secret of success. Yes, education at the highest possible level is vital. Yes, self-help books are important. Yes, continuously adapting and growing is imperative. Yes, time must be invested in learning the skills needed for future technologies. The questions the young ask make me suspect they are in on the plot. I cannot do better with my advice.

What I can do is talk about living beyond just making a decent living; about the journey from self-gratification to self-actualization. Why it is necessary to go beyond acquiring skills, to allow diverse interests to acquire you instead, to shape you into a multi-dimensional personality. Why a well-rounded view of the world is essential.

I am nostalgic about my formative years in a rooted Jain family where intellect and the spirit were equally valued. Our wonder years shape us with such specificity that we cannot change their influence easily. I, for one, wouldn't want to change anything about it.

Talking of change, it has been a key driving force in my life. At each point in my life, I have had to change tracks, often when I was not prepared. As a young boy, for my education, I changed my location from Sion-Koliwada to Xavier's at Fort. Then to Pune for my engineering and eventually to the US for my master's.

I changed the discipline of my studies from electrical engineering to computer science. After I graduated, when I couldn't find a job in computer science (in which I had done my master's), I became an application software engineer and then pivoted to working as a commercial database manager. While these could be upsetting for a young person at the start of their career, I maintained a positive attitude and was confident that challenges are temporary.

When I moved back to India, I was hoping to change my life once again. It did change, but not in the manner that I had imagined.

Ba and Kaka

Warren Buffet often talks about the idea of the Ovarian Lottery, and I think I got myself a great hand when I found myself born in the home of Revaben and Shantilal Mehta.

Growing up, my mother's religiosity was responsible for my early beliefs about living in a world I had yet to discover. While I try to imbibe these values in their purest forms, I remain steadfast in not being dogmatic. I remain what I call a work in progress or WIP. Nevertheless, a lifetime of experiences, spanning planetwide cultures, have not eroded the verities of those childhood lessons. Allow me to talk about the lessons one more time.

Anekaantvaad: There are as many truths as there are sentient beings. Personal experiences such as failures, successes, understanding and conditioning spawn personal truths. Who is to tell what is wrong? And what is right? In the absence of an absolute or universal truth, what is to guide how you live a life? My personal truth has been to favour actions that empower the larger good of humanity and everything else that cohabits the world. Anekaantvaad helped me coalesce a multiplicity of truths that others around me have. It helped me find harmony in the midst of people with conflicting ideas. It bestowed leadership upon me. I could align many to achieve some things that are now bigger than all of us.

Aparigraha: When we let go of attachments, insecurities, and the desire to control, we begin to work towards the greater cause of humanity. This is where self-actualization happens. Thanks to Kaka's influence, as an agnostic, I don't dwell on the existence of god. This childhood lesson further removes the need to do so.

Later, I came to understand Sweekar. We must have the courage to change the things we can and the humility to accept those we cannot. There is wisdom in accepting the immobility of a rock face and finding a way around it, rather than destroying oneself while lamenting the obstacle.

Ba's lessons in Jainism were tempered by Kaka's atheism.

He taught me to ask meaningful questions. He helped me pull back the focus from the minutiae of everyday living and take in the whole circus. I have vivid childhood memories of accompanying him to his evenings with friends and acquaintances, including J. Krishnamurti. Earlier in the book, I have written about Krishnamurti asking me directly if I thought I were made of atoms and what consciousness was. These experiences made me lose interest in religion and its dogmatic boundaries. I began leaning on basic human values. Today, we need a super-religion, like a super-app encoded with an aggregation of several human values, which can be launched whenever we falter.

Perhaps I got by without this super-religion super-app because of Shaila. She was the keeper of *my* conscience. She encouraged me to work selflessly for society first. True, she wanted me to excel in whatever I did, but she never complained about whatever we had. Or whatever we did not. She could find contentment in every situation. She could express the rare virtue of being ambitious for wealth creation without being selfish about it. She was a partner in every sense of the word, even when it was about going through the mundane motions of daily living. She shouldered many parenting responsibilities alone while

I laboured over my passion. She brought up three wonderful kids, each strong, distinct and independent. Any parent would be proud to have them.

While weighing individual success, I tend to tip the balance in favour of selfless contribution to the country and humanity. Many believe that I do this to a fault. They ask: 'Oh, what's in it for me?', 'But why should I help my competitors?', 'What if I am left behind?', 'What about my family?', 'Why should I invest my prime years to benefit others?', 'Why can't I contribute after I have made money?'

These are primal questions. Anyone still struggling to find a purpose in life needn't look far. They must consider nature, which gives, nourishes, and replenishes without asking, 'What is in it for me?' Once you move beyond the self, your true nature will unlock itself.

To the question 'Why can't I contribute after I have made money?', my answer is to make big dreams real, more than the money, the ecosystem needs out-of-the-box thinking. Creative ideas often happen when you are young and are ready to change the world. My experience makes me hazard that this is when even impossible problems become solvable. By the time you have made your money, this window is usually shut.

When you collaborate to grow the pie, you let your creative energies flow to solve ecosystem issues. Not only does your share of the pie grow, the size allows many others to take slices for themselves. You increase the possibilities for yourself and everyone. You can compound growth when you collaborate, cooperate and compete. Gandhiji famously advocated becoming a trustee, a custodian for unlocking prosperity for all, without the shackles of ownership and attachment.

Shaila

The other great hand that life dealt me was my union with Shaila. She was all that I could ask for in a companion. She was by my side at each key juncture in life. By her conduct throughout her life, she taught me the tenets of staying calm in crises, and proceeding with optimism and acceptance. When the times were good, she would remind me to stay in the moment and appreciate the wondrous life we had together. And when the times were hard, she remained steadfast and transformed herself into a pillar of support that I could seek support from and stay on course.

In 2008, however, the cancer that Shaila had successfully defeated decades ago was back with a vengeance. This time around, the doctors gave her less than a 5 per cent chance of survival. It was unnerving, but somehow, I had the confidence that with Shaila's optimism and calmness, she would make it.

While undergoing treatment, she remained stoic and gave me the strength, when ideally, it should have been the other way around. And I wasn't wrong. She battled hard and recovered fully. I am proud of her never-say-die attitude and her calmness.

We seemed to have navigated the crisis and put the worst behind us. But barely three years passed before the disease struck her again.

In 2012, she had a major remission, and cancer had metastasized. We were recommended hormone therapy as it had proven to be a viable option. However, it didn't work. By 2013, we had to put her on chemotherapy, which failed, too. All through the tumult of emotions and the painful ordeal, Shaila stayed calm. She seemed content that her children were able and self-reliant, and her family had prospered. She was ready and willing to leave the world, as all her wishes had been fulfilled. She accepted her fate and surrendered herself to the forces of nature.

I felt abandoned. My constant companion, my support system, the mother of my children, was no longer with us. I was speechless, unable to express my void.

I knew that life and death are inseparable. I had to continue to live, if not for myself, for my children and their families. I learnt the lesson that relationships are forever, but the time we have together is not. This was the darkest hour for me as a person, and I had to work hard to find a renewed purpose and meaning in life. I leaned on nature for inspiration and continued on the road that leads onward.

The nature of nature

My affinity for plucking lessons from nature has served me well throughout life. I take great courage and inspiration from the never-say-die attitude of nature. If there is an obstacle, the river finds a way around it. If the ground is hard, by sheer persistence, seeds germinate and give birth to new life. Nature has designed various species to be able to adapt to their conditions, both adverse and favourable. And nature does not stop. It continues to evolve, and it continues to push species to evolve as well.

Tenets from nature gave me the arsenal required to solve complex real-life problems that are often made up of incomplete information. It taught me to keep at it and yet detach myself from the outcome. I have had frequent and unexpected challenges thrown at me, and they've often caught me off-guard. However, hidden within each challenge came opportunities. I had to work hard, rely on my instincts and act. Maybe nature was trying to make me tougher by trying to break me and making me stronger at the same time.

When I was at Brooklyn Poly, in my first exams there, I scored a 90+ and yet got a grade of B+. I knew that the class was full of smart people, including scholars from Bell Labs and people who had secured the Fulbright Scholarship. However, I did not know that the professor used a system of relative grading. That means you were not only competing against a test paper but also against others in the class. I had to up my game and study harder to get better grades. Which I eventually did and earned a few As.

When I returned to India from the US, I knew that the country was in a state of emergency, but I was again caught unaware that Kaka's business was going down without a chance of revival. I had to find my own feet and not only to make my career, but also to support the family.

As a partner at Hinditron, while the business was mostly good, we made numerous mistakes and lost substantial money. Some because we made errors in judgements and some because the environment wasn't conducive for the work we did. And then, one fine day, just like that, I had to quit Hinditron and create a new business overnight.

Starting Onward posed some more challenges that I was unaware of. India was engulfed in riots as the aftermath of the Mandal Commission's recommendations. As the chairperson of the newly formed NASSCOM, I faced the wrath of some really powerful businessmen who had vested interests at MAIT and were abusing their powers accorded by MAIT. With Onward, I had another set of challenges. My erstwhile partners had shot off not-so-kind letters about me to business associates. However, thanks to the team at Onward (led by G.S. Kelkar and Nandu Pradhan), we could take birth, and we took off. We started as a garage operation and yet managed a fifty-fifty JV with the world's second-largest software company, Novell. This was on the back of the trust I had earned with them in my previous avatar.

While all was good at Onward-Novell, there was yet another unseen setback in the works. In the typically American kill-the-competition-in-war manner, the strongly competitive Microsoft started to pose an existential threat to Novell. To tackle that, Novell decided to pivot to open-source. But how long could a company compete with continuous investment in innovation against a free product marketed heavily with an unlimited budget? I did not see how the JV could make any money in India with a subscription business—the cost of servicing the business was going to be more than the revenue it generated. If we were to do it today, in the 2020s, maybe yes. But back then, it was impossible. So, I exited Onward-Novell in 2006 and delivered handsome returns for my shareholders. I also retained enough for myself and the next generation to live comfortably. When the news of the exit broke, numerous well-wishers advised me to retire and enjoy the good things life has to offer. I must say I was tempted. I took some time off to think about where I wanted to go from there onwards.

But then I realized that retirement is a word that does not exist in my dictionary.

So, in the next phase, I worked to re-strategize Onward's business to mechanical and chemical engineering applications. I was confident that these would follow the growth trajectory of the IT business. However, I faced an unforeseen challenge yet again. Chief engineers and R&D teams wanted to hold tightly on to their turfs and did not want to outsource.

At NASSCOM, we took a risk by hiring Dewang when he was all of twenty-nine. I believe I led him to his calling by convincing him to join the organization, where he could channel his patriotism and help grow India's IT industry. I worked closely with him to nurture him and mentor him. Dewang was leading us to a new era when his untimely death took him away. We were not prepared for the hiccup. While it was a big loss for the IT industry, we did recover and smartly moved on to the next phase with Kiran and subsequent leaders.

When I brought TiE to Mumbai, I handpicked Rajiv Vaishnav[1] to lead it. Just like Dewang, Rajiv was not a conventional choice. He did not have a background in IT or entrepreneurship, but his work with the Indo-American Chamber of Commerce gave him the experience and understanding of the US culture, which was imperative for the role. However, within the first two years, we had to face the dot-com bust of 2000.

I even co-founded India's first corporatized venture fund with Infinity Venture Fund. It delivered on the promised impact, but had we not faced the dot-com bust, we could have done a lot more with it. I was pained to see so many dreams shattered.

I've been caught off-guard more times than I was prepared for. Just like nature, I've kept at it, adapted to the new realities and navigated the change. I genuinely believe that I am a mere participant in the evolutionary process, and I consider myself lucky to have discharged

---

1   Rajiv is now a venture capitalist, and continues to support founders and start-ups.

my duties as a family man, created a business like Onward and got the opportunity to volunteer at NASSCOM, TiE and other organizations.

Big 1 or Big 5

I am often asked, why is it that Onward is not part of the Big 5? Let me attempt to put a response on record.

With the advantage of hindsight, I can say that we at Onward took numerous moon shots, but many risks did not pay off. We were among the leaders in the Accounting Ledger Processing Machine (ALPM) space, with more than 20,000 copies installed. In late 90s, we had envisioned developing a bank branch automation product and then the core banking software. We made substantial investments in the product, but we missed the bus[2].

In the early days of Hinditron, when we were in the on-site consulting business, I did not appreciate the 3 A.M. calls that we would get from our clients in the US. Thus, at Onward, we did not want to be in that business. However, it was this very on-site consulting business that helped many IT companies in India grow by leaps and bounds. This business spewed the cash required to invest in long-term bets like the offshore delivery capabilities. At that time, it felt like the right thing to do.

Of course, Onward managed the Novell partnership extremely well, and we expanded our garage operation into a sizable software group. The partnership, Onward-Novell, at a point had a 95 per cent market share with NetWare. It gave handsome returns to shareholders.

---

2   We believed that the core banking automation costs would be prohibitively expensive, even when appropriated over high volume, lower value transactions. To give you a context, on our product, the average cost of running a transaction would have been about ₹30, even if the ticket size of the transaction was just ₹50. It was like levying a 60% transaction cost!
So, we did the right thing to move our focus on the branch automation product, and we invested substantially in it. However, the product did not work as expected and we eventually missed the bus.

When the Y2K hit us, the NASSCOM members capitalized on the opportunity provided by the Y2K challenge and grew astronomically. We at Onward however thought it was a short-term opportunity and decided to stay away from it. Onward-Novell JV was anyway going well. However, if I had known that Y2K-related services would allow us a foot in the door with the Fortune 500 companies and allow for long-term contracts in the future, we would have invested in it, even though we did not have the capabilities at the time

Fast Forward three decades, Onward today, is a niche Digital & Engineering Services company with a strong team of 2400+ amazingly talented and dedicated Engineers and Technology Consultants that are spread across our 13+ offices in 6 countries. I serve as the Executive Chairperson and I am honoured to work alongside our talented leaders and team members, current and past. Each member at Onward has always gone beyond expectations and gotten us to where we are today—at the launch pad for a much bigger and brighter future.

Finally, to me, the larger metric of success is my family, and the relationships I have nurtured and developed over my life. And with those, I am probably the Biggest 1.

Where does Harish Mehta go from here on?

My work is far from done.

At Onward, I am the executive chairman of the board and a mentor to the team. Onward is lucky to have a young and dynamic leadership team led by Jigar, my son. I routinely throw them in the deep end of the pool and watch from the sidelines. It may sound extreme, but they are not wrong. I continue to take inspiration from nature, and I believe that the leaders of tomorrow are just like caterpillars growing in the protective environment of the cocoon. Both leaders and caterpillars need to go through the pain of shedding their skin to emerge and show their true colours. The leaders have no cocoon in which they can work on their metamorphosis; they must actively learn while they are in the thick of things in the real world. How can I not let them splash around in the deep end?

As an industry professional, I play active roles at industry bodies like NASSCOM and TiE. My role, though, is more consultative and is that of a storyteller and guide to the leadership. I am also more of a self-appointed conscience-keeper. Nobody has assigned me this role, and I'm definitely not the only one performing it. Many current and former team members and chairpersons have also continued to perform this role. Sangeeta Gupta deserves a mention here. She is an institution in herself. As part of the NASSCOM secretariat, she has been the backbone to almost every NASSCOM president and chairperson, and has provided continuity to the organization for more than thirty years now.

I am further trying to bring more organizations together, and get them to collaborate and move in a unified direction. Along with other stakeholders, I work on inculcating a scientific mindset within these organizations. This is required if we have to make an impact on the grassroots and add to the per capita income of those at the bottom of the pyramid. To me, the adoption of a scientific temperament is an imperative if India has to become a leader in the twenty-first century and beyond.

I continue to support young entrepreneurs as an angel investor. I have an active portfolio of more than 35 start-ups. Apart from helping with capital, I am available to them for guidance and opening doors. I am also on the investment committee at the Indian Angel Network (IAN) Fund.

As a technologist, I have sharpened my focus on deep tech and industry 4.0, especially in the manufacturing–engineering business. My interest has recently pivoted to digital engineering.

As a curious mind, I like to follow trends. I am a regular reader of age-old, trusted publications like *Fortune*, *Wall Street Journal* and *Economic Times*. More recently, I have started to read new-age digital 'news' outlets like The Ken, The Morning Context, ET Prime,

TechCrunch, Hackernoon and more. I continue to spend time with books and typically read two or three books every month.

I love watching cricket, including the innovative format of the IPL, particularly the replays. I recently saw an amazing web series on the life of Harshad Mehta on an OTT ('over the top') platform. I binge-watch documentaries on Netflix and Curiosity Stream. I also like to walk for about thirty to sixty minutes each day. At times, I practise some yoga.

I am a chess enthusiast and take every opportunity I get to advocate the game. I was the chairperson of the advisory committee for the World Youth Chess Championship held in 2019 in Mumbai, where we saw the participation of more than 700 young players from 100-plus countries. Even though the game originated in India, it is celebrated and played across the globe. I believe chess has the potential to develop the cognitive abilities of young children at literally no cost. Chess is particularly useful to deliver impact when compared with modern teaching pedagogies. At home, all three of my children have played chess at competitive levels. They are so good that I try to refrain from playing against them.

You can't keep me away from 'toys'. I love gadgets and emerging tech—augmented reality (AR), virtual reality (VR), robotics and more.

As I near the end of the book, I am grateful that even though I have had personal and familial health issues over the years, I have a great family and active social life that I've built atop the pillars of trust, mutual respect and accessibility.

Shaila left us in 2014. Someone said that when a wise person leaves us, the loss is similar to that of burning a library. It's been eight years now, but not a day passes when I don't miss seeking inputs from the library that Shaila took away with her.

My eldest daughter, Prachi, and her husband, Bhavik, are settled in Mumbai. Prachi is a serial entrepreneur and is passionate about children. Her last two ventures about rethinking the playschool business and inculcating chess among young children are the fireflies we need.

Her latest venture is her son, Arjun. Bhavik is a unique combination of the analytical left-brain intelligence and the right-brain creative firehose. By day, he is a business leader with a shipping major, and after office hours, he is the life of the party. He is often the most enthusiastic person in the room.

My son, Jigar, is a passionate, ambitious and focused techno-entrepreneur. If there's a task to be done, come hell or high water, he will get it done. He's been working at Onward since 2005 and has risen through the ranks over the years. I take immense pride to report that he was elected the MD of Onward Technologies by the company's board in 2016. Since then, under his leadership, Onward is, well, marching onward![3] His wife, Natasha, is the CEO of our household. She has the unique quality of taking a firm stand for things she believes in. Natasha, is also the CEO of this book. Even though publishing is new to her, she took to it like a duck takes to water, and worked day and night for over three years to make this book happen.

Heral, my youngest, is the genius of the family. There are hardly any pictures of her from her younger days where she's not holding a trophy or an award. She is a Managing Director at Rothschild and Co., in the AutoTech sector based out of London. Her work takes her far and wide. I'd say she's taken after my globetrotting father in that respect.

As a father, I couldn't be prouder of my family and their achievements.

I think I resonate strongly with the word 'Onward'. It is part of my DNA. I am not the brooding type to mull over the past. I am always looking onward. Had I not been so, Chirant's untimely demise would have destroyed me emotionally. His wonderful smile still flashes in front of my eyes, and I remember him with love and fondness. Yet, I cannot afford the luxury of being stuck in the nostalgic past.

---

3   Onward recently raised a round of funding from a private equity (PE) investor to strengthen its presence in USA and Europe.

I must now take my leave, for my new bosses, my grandchildren, Alysha, Rhea and Arjun, demand my attention. I love to see them blossom, and I am left wondering about nature's power to create, update and continue to march Onward.

Afterword

by Sitanshu Yashaschandra

As I read this fascinating and truthful account of the momentous initiative and success of NASSCOM, it reminded me of a comment by Immanuel Kant, the seminal thinker of the Western Age of Enlightenment. Kant has said, in his crisp and cryptic style, that 'Content' without 'Form' is blind and 'Form' without 'Content' is empty. In the context of this book, the Kantian caution assumes a new meaning. It draws our attention to a possible emptiness and a possible blindness that technology without humanistic and literary connectivity and humanity and literature without a link to technological and mathematical prowess, could generate. Not the emptiness of self-centered 'scientific' knowledge nor the blindness of undisciplined 'artistic' sentimentality (both rampant today in India and elsewhere, as huge economic-political frauds on the one hand and the thriving drug trafficking on the other demonstrate) should be our future. How to move towards a fullness of comforts and a foresightedness of

259

a thoughtful society – that is the challenge before us. The Maverick
Effect enables us all to focus thoughtfully on it and face it skillfully.

Harish Mehta's terminology and context are of course different
from mine. But I am able to translate him, from his language of
technology and management to mine of literature and humanities,
when he says, 'Nevertheless I am certain a collaborative structure
composed of the experienced and the new will emerge and will respect
NASSCOM's values: to put India first, speak with a single industry
voice, work with consensus, collaborate and compete, focus on growth,
have robust conflict management processes, have conscience-keepers
as anchors, spot a weak signal in spite of the noise and share a sense
of ownership.' Trust his, NASSCOM's values, especially of having
conscience-keepers and spotting weak signals would go beyond IT
industry and cover the fullness of India's multi-layered and hugely
diverse multitudes.

The century of Hiroshima and Nagasaki, of Tiananmen Square
but also of Gandhi and Mandela is just over and may recur more
ferociously, with Hitler—or compassionately with Gandhi. He has so
pointedly referred to Auschwitz and Dachau and the double-edged
inscription on their gates: 'Arbeit macht frei / Work sets you free.' The
slogan is correct, but the gates are, as Harish suggests, wrong. I think
this book makes us look at the different gates that are available to us,
to select the right one and to move deeper into the vast possibilities of
the 21st and 22nd centuries. Hope Harish's sagacious expertise would
help us citizens of India chose not only the right inscription but also
the right gate and pathway to our future.

How, then, to move towards a humane society (a 'Sane Society' as
Erich Fromm has said) with the help of skills of science, engineering
and commerce, is our *Yaksha Prashna* today. Two key words from the
title of this book show a pathway to it. They are, 'Movement' and
'Maverick.'

The word 'MOVE'-ment could be so printed only by a 'Maverick'!
Origin of the adjective 'Maverick' is of course known to Harish Mehta.

Horses and cattle owned by a Master were branded by red hot branding irons of their owner. That produced, albeit imposed an identity on the animals. But there remained, in distant wilderness, bison and horses that were 'Wild', that is Free. Science and technology, literature and arts, have been branded extensively in our times. There are so many Raj-Kavi-s today belonging to more than one master owner. There are hardly any Kavi-raj or simply Kavi. The word, 'MOVEment', with first four letters in capital, could be branded in our times as a 'four letter' word and declared to be obscene! I see an authentic purity in that word formation of yours.(Harish's).

What is a 'MOVEment'? As this book so simply yet ably traces its origin in the work of a courageous, gifted and cooperative small group, the emphasis on 'MOVE' brings out the dynamism of contemporary Indian scientific and technological culture. 'Move' (a verb) here does not signify a command, an order for the non-IT to move aside and make room for IT. It is, as this book tells, an invitation [to] join a joinery. But it also evokes a skillful strategy, a 'move' (a noun) in that sense, without which the 'IT Revolution' as Harish calls it, would not have taken place in India of today. The Green Revolution of farming in Punjab and elsewhere, the While Revolution of milk cooperatives in Gujarat and elsewhere was joined by the IT revolution in Mumbai and elsewhere. Each pioneer deserves our glad gratitude and sincere congratulations.

Revolutions often misfire. The French and the Russian ones each had a great beginning and an ambiguous, if not dubious, phase that followed it. Harish and his colleagues must be wondering about it all, I am sure. We all do. That is what has brought the two of us together here!

Poetry is not pontification, I believe firmly. So let me end this afterword to a phenomenal book by a reference to a shloka in *Ishopanishad*. Our insightful ancestors told us in *Isha Upanishad*, that human beings could cross the stretch of Mrutyu or Death by means of Avidya or our knowledges of the world that surrounds us, often times a dangerous word. IT is one of them, a brilliant and epoch-making one. But the *Upanishad* added, we should partake the taste of true 'non-death', a-mrutam, i.e., of being fully alive in compassionate knowledge and knowing compassion, by means of Vidya, or Knowledge that goes beyond skills, chemistry and algorithms, a Knowledge that is comprehensively compassionate.

Sitanshu Yashaschandra
Poet, playwright, translator and academic

Appendix

NASSCOM chairpersons over the years

From	To	Name	Member Company
2021	present	Rekha Menon	Accenture India
2020	2021	U B Pravin Rao	Infosys
2019	2020	Keshav Murugesh	WNS Global Services
2018	2019	Rishad Premji	Wipro Ltd
2017	2018	Raman Roy	Quatrro Global Services Pvt. Ltd.
2016	2017	C P Gurnani	TechMahindra
2015	2016	Dr B V R Mohan Reddy	Cyient Limited
2014	2015	R Chandrasekaran	Cognizant India
2013	2014	Krishnakumar Natarajan	MindTree Ltd.
2012	2013	N Chandrasekaran	TCS

2011	2012	R S Pawar	NIIT Group
2010	2011	Harsh Manglik	Accenture India
2009	2010	Pramod Bhasin	Genpact
2008	2009	Dr Ganesh Natarajan	Zensar
2007	2008	Lakshmi Narayanan	Cognizant India
2005	2006	S. Ramadorai	TCS
2004	2005	Jerry Rao	Mphasis Ltd
2003	2004	Som Mittal	HP Globalsoft Ltd
2002	2003	Late Mr Arun Kumar	Hughes
2000	2002	Phiroz Vandrevala	TCS
1999	2000	Atul Nishar	Hexaware
1998	1999	Raj Jain	R S Software India Ltd
1997	1998	Saurabh Srivastava	Xansa
1996	1997	K.V. Ramani	Future Software Ltd.
1995	1996	Ashank Desai	Mastek Ltd.
1994	1995	Late Mr F.C. Kohli	TCS
1992	1994	N R Narayana Murthy	Infosys
1990	1992	Harish Mehta	Onward Technologies

NASSCOM presidents over the years

2018	present	Debjani Ghosh
2014	2018	R Chandrasekhar
2008	2013	Som Mittal
2001	2007	Kiran Karnik
1991	2000	Late Mr Dewang Mehta

Acknowledgments

'So who knows truly whence it has arisen?
Whence all creation had its origin,
he, whether he fashioned it or whether he did not,
he, who surveys it all from highest heaven,
he knows - or maybe even he does not know.'

– Rig Veda

While a person's life, a start-up or any endeavour may look like an outcome of the work of an individual, I believe no one can truly claim to have fashioned things singlehandedly. I'd go as far as to say that nothing is original, apart from nature. My life, and this book for that matter, is no different. I have been a beneficiary of the support and kindness of numerous people over the years. The next few pages would talk about them and the people who made this book happen. It is probably impossible for me to recount the contributions of every person that has had an impact on me. More so, numerous people have stayed away from the limelight and yet were around to support me. The list thus may never be complete.

From the onset, I knew that it was a herculean task to tell the NASSCOM story. The project of this magnitude would have required numerous interviews with industry insiders, extensive research going back at least three decades and sharp fact-checks. However, the herculean task had to be done, and it was about time the NASSCOM story was told. The association deserves its rightful place in history for arresting the downward economic spiral that India was in.

I thus had to build a team to help me. The core team came together in Kireet Khurana, Parijat Sarkar and my daughter-in-law, Natasha. Kireet was the creative bedrock that we built the book on top of. Parijat had an omnipresent role to play—from writing to editing to research and to even keep the team going with his humour.

Over the last three years, the team would've read more than 25 books, conducted hundreds of interviews and must have written no less than seven drafts of each key part. The book itself went through multiple iterations, and at different times we were helped by Sachin Garg (who did the heavy lifting with the research, interviews and crafting the first draft), Zaki Ansari (who made the narrative more lucid and palatable), Saurabh Garg (who patiently worked on numerous iterations) and Prof. Tulsi of SP Jain Institute of Management and Research (who supported us with original research to fortify the arguments in the book). The team helped me create a succinct and compelling narrative, and that too, without taking away anything from the effort that various mavericks put into building NASSCOM.

Another team helped take the book to market. It comprised of my agent Kanishka Gupta and the team at HarperCollins India led by Sachin Sharma. We were further assisted by Elisha Saigal, Ami Desai, Himanshu Parmekar, Mikhail Pinto, S. Swaminathan, Pradyuman Maheshwari and Sunil Lulla.

Natasha, my daughter-in-law, championed the project and managed this army of creative mavericks. I am proud of the shape the book has finally taken, and I hope you, the reader, would approve of it too.

Many incidents reported in the book go back more than 30 years. It is a long time, and human memory is fallible. Thus, to ensure the veracity, the team met industry leaders like Adi Cooper, Ashank Desai, Debjani Ghosh, Late Mr F.C. Kohli, K Pandyan, Keshav Murugesh, K.V. Ramani, Narayana Murthy, Rajiv Vaishnav, Sangeeta Gupta, Saurabh Srivastava, Shashi Bhagnari, Swami Ganesh, former Presidents at NASSCOM and many more. Most of these interactions happened during the pre-COVID times, and in each meeting, these leaders opened up their archives, rummaged through their notes and sifted through their memories to help us with the book.

For the book, I would've liked to speak with my friends, Late Mr Vijay Mukhi and Late Mr Dewang Mehta. Both of them would've been key contributors as they were not only closely involved with NASSCOM but also had strong opinions. Just like the two of them, there are many more that could've helped me enrich this book, but they are no longer among us. I am further disappointed that they are not around to see this book come to life.

I have to acknowledge the contributions of NASSCOM's past chairpersons and past presidents. Apart from these, current and past members of the EC, members of various sectoral councils, special interest groups, the NASSCOM secretariat, office bearers, volunteers and the team at NASSCOM continue to work to take NASSCOM from strength to strength. These people are the real mavericks that literally built the IT industry and brought the juggernaut to life. The list is incomplete without acknowledging many other well-wishers who directly and indirectly contributed to NASSCOM and the Indian IT industry.

Apart from NASSCOM, I am a member of many other industry associations and clubs. These include TiE, the erstwhile Bombay Computer Club, Internet Users Club and TPATI (Trust to Promote Advanced Technology in India) and others. At these forums, I get to meet people with divergent ideas. I am continuously challenged intellectually, and I often pick up newer insights. I am grateful that I get to feed off the energy of people bubbling with ideas, each trying to bring about a change in the world in their own way. Meeting these people often reminds me of the time when I was starting Onward Technologies way back in 1991.

I am lucky to have the gift of compartmentalization, and it has served me well. Over the years, while I was running a full-fledged business in Onward, I was able to divert some attention and energy to work on NASSCOM, and more recently, on this book. This could only happen because of the steadfast support and ongoing endorsement from the team at Onward.

We at Onward have only been able to do well and scale because of people that showed their support early on. These are Capt. Bewoor, Nandu Pradhan, MVSS Narayanchalu, GS Kelkar and many more. Many people have invested their entire lives and careers with us. These are Yogesh, George, Suhas, Lorna and many more.

Onward is another child of mine and is coming of age fast. My son, Jigar, is leading the charge as we take on larger, much more complex challenges. Emerging leaders like Pratish Mehta (also my nephew), Vignesh Padmanabhan, Sujata Singh, V Shankar and others are taking over the baton as Onward races ahead. Manohar, Santosh and others run my office and deserve a special mention. Even the shareholders and board members at Onward have showcased immense faith and confidence in me, my son Jigar and other leaders at Onward.

More support for this book came from my children Heral, Jigar & Natasha, Prachi & Bhavik, and my grandchildren, Alysha, Rhea and Arjun. They allowed me to take time off and immerse myself in the project. When I needed a breather, they kept challenging my biases and kept me on my toes. As I see them grow up and blossom each day, I am inspired to be a better father and a grandfather.

Like I have said earlier, it was dealt a lucky hand when I was born in the home of Reva Ben and Shantilal Mehta and had siblings in Ranjan & Harshad Bhai, Nila & Sharad Bhai, Rita & Amit Bhai and Hiten & Rupa Bhabhi. The contrasting personalities of my parents, constant encouragement from my siblings and support from the extended family allowed me to broaden my thinking and build the foundational pillars of values, beliefs and actions. These pillars allowed me to take tough decisions with equanimity and prepared me to face uncertainty and adversity.

Shaila has been my superApp and the omnipresent force behind all my actions. She inspired me constantly to do more than what I had imagined myself to be capable of. Not a single day passes by when I don't miss her counsel, her unwavering support and her optimism towards life. Shaila's parents and her family, including Rita Bhabhi & Arun, Manu Bhai, Late Nalini Ben, accepted me as one of their own and have stood like a rock with me since.

For me, nature has been a constant inspiration, and one of the most important lessons I took was the need and importance of pause and reset. I am fortunate that I have had a long, fulfilling and, most importantly, well-rounded life where I worked hard and found avenues to unwind after a hard day at the office. I've found comfort in the company of numerous friends, poets and communities that have enriched my life at various places and times. These are my avenues to unwind and recharge. Here is an incomplete list.

I am starting with my classmates from COEP. I still have thick friendships with them, including with the ones that went to the US and formed the H&J group. The 'Sapta Sur' group that was started by twelve families to share our passion for music, till date is among my closest family friends and confidantes. The 'Dil Se' group keeps me young with our shared passion for travel. An unintended advantage of working in a global business like technology is that you foster friendship with people across the globe. I have numerous friends sprinkled worldwide, specifically in Silicon Valley, Provo-Utah, Boston, Connecticut and closer home in Mumbai and Pune. But then the experiences gathered with all your friends and well-wishers over the years are tough to contain in a few lines. More so, this book merely talks about the part of my life that overlaps with that of NASSCOM. If you know me well, please don't be surprised to see a large part of my life, especially the last twenty years or so, underreported.

Before I close, I have to say that I am grateful to a host of unsung heroes that made a difference to the fortunes of our great nation. These include millions of Indians that chose IT as their career of choice. The academia that taught, groomed and mentored these people have my gratitude. The Techno-Entrepreneurs of Indian IT deserve a mention for leading by example and driving the industry forward. Credit and thank you must go to the investors, both global and Indian, for spotting the opportunity and trusting entrepreneurs with capital and connections. After all, cash flow is the lubricant that keeps the corporate engine cranking.

These entrepreneurs and investors were supported by the machinery of the Government of India that worked tirelessly without any expectation of the limelight. These include politicians at both the state and central governments, hundreds of bureaucrats that removed the clogs and eventually the institutions like MietY, DOT, SEPC and others. I also want to acknowledge people on various social media platforms. They have been demanding for a long time that I write the book and tell the NASSCOM story. I hope this book serves the purpose.

I must thank the civil servants that were placed away from our homeland as ambassadors and diplomatic staff. These were further enabled by the generosity of governments of the countries that these were placed in. These governments made the policy environment conducive, enabled for free movement of talent across borders and had the foresight to see a world that was more connected than ever. Even the customers from around the globe helped us propel forward by partnering with us over the years. I hope this book will open their eyes to the uniqueness of the Indian IT industry. Our journalist friends in various media houses, both in India and abroad, were kind to have helped carry our message to more people. Again, these journalists continue to work tirelessly without any expectation of a reward.

As I end this note, it is my desire that we as a society start to celebrate the unsung heroes and not just the winners. My life, NASSCOM as an institution and this book are a testimony to the force that these unsung heroes are!

Here's hoping you, dear reader, will rise as a hero!

Harish S. Mehta
Jan 2022, Mumbai

PS: As the cost of sounding repetitive, the list of people that have contributed to my life, to NASSCOM and to this book will never be complete. I'd use the companion website to continue to add to this list. Please visit us at www.themaverickeffectbook.com.

About the Author

Harish Mehta is the founder and the executive chairperson of the Onward Group, having led two avatars of the business – Onward Novell Software (1991-2005) and Onward Technologies (2005 onwards). The 50:50 JV between Onward Group and Novell, Inc. at the time was the first of its kind in the country. Onward Technologies is a publicly listed company that employs 2400+ people and is focused on engineering and software services.

NASSCOM, the industry body that represents India's IT and BPO industry, was seeded and took birth in Harish's office in Mumbai in 1988. NASSCOM created a trusted environment where competing companies could collaborate towards a larger objective of building India as a trusted destination for the software services business.

At NASSCOM, currently, Harish is the convenor of the Chairperson's Council. His leadership saw the team seeded several initiatives that helped propel the NASSCOM vision further. These include working towards building a robust brand India Inc., laying the foundation of the STPI scheme (which further enabled the creation of software parks and export processing zones), extending income-tax benefits for the industry, framing of stringent copyright laws to control software piracy, the opening of communication links and creation of India's first cyber-lab.

Apart from his work at Onward and NASSCOM, Harish is passionate about injecting a scientific mindset in India and encouraging innovation-driven entrepreneurship. He is relentlessly pursuing his vision to make India a technologically smart nation. He believes that innovation-driven entrepreneurs will act as change agents for the upliftment of society.

He is an active angel investor, mentor, and advisor. He brought TIE (Silicon Valley-based not-for-profit organization) to India in 1999 and was the first president of TiE Mumbai. He is a founding member of the Infinity Venture fund, set up in 2002 as India's first corporate VC fund. He is also an investment committee member at the Indian Angel Network.

His other pursuits include active volunteering at Onward Foundation and Dewang Mehta Foundation.

Harish holds a Bachelor's degree in Electrical Engineering from the College of Engineering, Pune and a Master's in Electrical Engineering (Computer Science) from Brooklyn Polytechnic Institute, NYU, USA.